THE BEAUTY
OF CHRIST

THE BEAUTY
OF CHRIST

A Introduction to the Theology of Hans Urs von Balthasar

Edited by Bede McGregor, O.P.
and Thomas Norris

T&T CLARK
EDINBURGH

T&T CLARK LTD
59 GEORGE STREET
EDINBURGH EH2 2LQ
SCOTLAND

Copyright © T&T Clark Ltd,1994

First published 1994

ISBN 0 567 09697 1

2002684

British Library Cataloguing-in-Publication Data
A catalogue record for this book is available from the British Library

Typeset by Trinity Typesetting, Edinburgh
Printed and bound in Great Britain by Bookcraft, Avon

CONTENTS

v

NOTES ON CONTRIBUTORS

Deirdre Carabine:
>was formerly Newman Scholar at University College, Dublin and is now Professor of Philosophy at the Uganda Martyrs University in Kampala.

Peter Henrici, S.J:
>was formerly Professor of Modern Philosophy at the Gregorian University, Rome, and Dean of the Faculty of Philosophy in the same University, and is now auxiliary Bishop of Chur, Switzerland.

Breandán Leahy:
>is Lecturer in Systematic Theology at Clonliffe College and Mater Dei Institute of Education, Dublin.

Bede McGregor, O.P:
>is Professor of Missiology at St Patrick's College, Maynooth.

Thomas Norris:
>is Lecturer in Dogmatic Theology at St Patrick's College, Maynooth.

Gerard O'Hanlon, S.J:
>is Professor of Systematic Theology at the Milltown Institute of Philosophy and Theology, Dublin.

John O'Donnell, S.J:
>is Professor of Dogmatic Theology at the Pontifical Gregorian University, Rome.

Noel Dermot O'Donoghue, O.D.C:
>was formerly Professor of Philosophy at St Patrick's College, Maynooth and subsequently Lecturer in Systematic Theology at New College, Edinburgh.

John Riches:
is Professor of Biblical Studies at the University of Glasgow.

Johann Roten, S.M:
is director of the International Marian Research Institute at the University of Dayton, Ohio, U.S.A.

John Saward:
was formerly Professor of Dogmatic Theology at Ushaw College, Durham and is now Professor of Systematic Theology at St Charles Borromeo Seminary, Philadelphia, U.S.A.

John Thompson:
was formerly Moderator of the Presbyterian Church in Ireland and is Professor of Dogmatic Theology at Union Theological College, Belfast.

ACKNOWLEDGMENTS

Many people helped to make this work possible. Our sincere thanks go first to the contributors who came from far and near; to his Eminence Cardinal Cahal B. Daly for writing the Foreword; to Monsignor Miceál Ledwith, President of Maynooth college and friend of Fr Hans Urs von Balthasar who encouraged and gave substantial support for the conference on which the book is based; to the Bishops and kind friends without whose sponsorship it would not have taken place; to the colleagues who advised and collaborated with us, especially Fr Tom O'Houghlin; to a dedicated group of seminarians from St Patrick's College, one of whom, the Reverend Ciarán Woods, died tragically only two months before ordination – *solas na glóire ar a anum dhílis* (this is Gaelic for 'May the light of glory be on his noble soul'); to Hanspeter Heinz, Professor of Pastoral Theology at the University of Augsburg; to Mr Stratford Caldecott for his practical and patient counsel. To these and the many other friends, too numerous to mention, we express our heartfelt thanks.

Bede McGregor O.P.
and Thomas Norris
St Patrick's College
Maynooth

FOREWORD

The Imitation of Christ is notoriously scornful about the university theologians and theology, the philosophers and philosophy of the author's time, the late fourteenth and early fifteenth century. Thomas à Kempis impatiently says of what he calls the teaching of 'the schools':

> What does it profit you to dispute deeply about the Trinity, if you be wanting in humility, and so be displeasing to the Trinity? In truth, sublime words make not a saint and a just man; but it is a virtuous life that makes one dear to God. I would rather feel compunction, than know how to define it. If you should know the whole Bible outwardly, and the sayings of all the philosophers, what would it all profit you without charity and the grace of God ... (*Book I, Chapter I*). Truly, a humble rustic that serves God is better than a proud philosopher who ponders the courses of the stars and neglects himself ... Cease from overweening desire of knowledge; because many distractions are found there, and much delusion. Learned men are very willing to seem wise, and to be called so. Many are the things which it is of little or no profit to the soul to know.
>
> The more you know, and the better, so much the heavier will your judgment therefore be, unless your life also be more holy. Be not lifted up by any skill or learning you have; but rather fear for the knowledge that is given you (*Book I, Chapter II*).
>
> What signifies making a great dispute about hidden and obscure things which we shall not be reproved in the judgment for having been ignorant of? And what matter is it to us of *genera* and *species*? He to whom the Eternal Word speaks is delivered from a multitude of opinions ... I am often times wearied with the many things I read and hear; in You alone, my God, is all I wish or long for. Let all teachers hold their

peace, and all created things keep silence in your presence; do
You alone speak to me.

The humble knowledge of oneself is a surer way to God
than he who researches after science ...

Because many take more pains to be learned than to
lead good lives, therefore they often go astray and bear no
fruit at all, or but little. Oh, if people would be as diligent
in the rooting out of vices and the grafting in of virtues as
they are in mooting questions, there would not be so many
evils and scandals among the people, nor such laxity in
monasteries! Truly, when the day of judgment comes, it
will not be asked of us, what we have read, but what we
have done; not what fine discourses we have made, but
how like religious we have lived. Tell me where now are all
those doctors and masters with whom you were well
acquainted while they were yet alive, and in the glory of
their learning? Others now hold their preferments and I
do not know whether they ever think of them ... Oh, how
quickly the glory of the world passes away! Oh, that their
life had been in keeping with their learning! Then would
they have studied and lectured to good purpose ... He is
truly most learned who does the will of God and forsakes
his own will (*Book I, Chapter III*).

The author's apparent dismissal of theology has been called anti-
intellectualism. This, together with his expressions of contempt for
the world and disparagement of the self, have lead to a virtual
banishment, if not banning, of the *Imitation of Christ*, once pre-
scribed and standard spiritual reading, from the libraries of seminarians, and of persons in religious formation and students of theology.
In the post-Council period, this book has been held to be one of the
most characteristic expressions of all that the Second Vatican
Council reacted against: the flight from the world, the disparagement of the intellect, the belittling of nature, the demeaning of the
human, the refusal of dialogue with the world.

I think that the *Imitation* has been dismissed too facilely and that
it is due for a re-evaluation. The scholastic theology against which
the *Imitation* was reacting had indeed become barren and arid, a
substitution for the living Word of God, rather than an exploration
of it. Thomas à Kempis is dismissing, not theology but a debased

way of theologising. He could be seen as pleading for a different way of doing theology, where theology becomes attentive listening to the Word of God, rather than an intellectual construction, modelled on the philosophical speculation current in the culture of the time. He was in fact calling, not for a rejection of theology, but for what we might more rightly describe as 're-sourcing' of theology in Scripture and the early Fathers. His reaction to the academic theology of the schools, was, I suggest, not entirely different from the renewal which prepared the Second Vatican Council and which pervades its documents.

The *Imitation* is a passionate repetition, over and over again, of Augustine's words, in reference to the Bible, *Tolle lege* (Take up and read). Towards the end of his life, Thomas à Kempis remarked: 'I have sought for rest everywhere but I have found it nowhere except in a little corner with a little book.' The author loves and lauds the holy Fathers for their turning of theology from words into daily living. His whole attitude is succinctly expressed in the sentence:

'God wills us to become perfectly subject to himself and by the love that burns in us to transcend all reason.'
(*Book I, Chapter XIV*)

This long excursus on the *Imitation* has, I believe, relevance to the theology of Hans Urs von Balthasar. Theology in every age, and in our own time no less than in the fifteenth century, can become accommodated too completely to the surrounding intellectual culture. Fr Michael Paul Gallagher remarked somewhere that religion can easily become acculturated 'within the superficial horizons of the dominant culture, as if kidnapped by merely liberal assumptions'. Prophetic voices are needed to call theology back to the 'experience of the Holy', 'the encounter with the Living God', from which all theology must flow and to which it must return, if it is to be worthy of its name as discourse about God. Thomas à Kempis was such a prophetic voice in his time. Hans Urs von Balthasar's was such a voice in our time, as is the voice of his admirer and friend, Pope John Paul II.

THEOLOGY AND PRAYER

Theology is both relativised by prayer and perfected by prayer. A

British philosopher, J. N. Findlay, in an article designed to demonstrate logically that God did not exist, because the very definition of God is intrinsically self-contradictory, ('Can God's existence be disproved?', in *Mind* (1948), reprinted in *New Essays in Philosophical Theology*, eds. Flew and MacIntyre, SCM, London 1955) began by offering a working definition of the word God: it means, he suggested, 'the adequate object of religious attitudes'. The definition is a useful one. Among the most basic of religious attitudes are adoration and prayer. Theology is discourse about God; and it can scarcely be true to its name unless it evokes a felt need to adore and to pray. Otherwise, the discourse, however learned, will not have been about God.

This has been a deep conviction of the Church from the beginning. The gospel of St John was regarded as the theologian's gospel, because it was the contemplative gospel; and St John was held up as a model for theologians, and was called 'John the theologian', 'John the divine'. The theologian was from early tradition expected to be a person of prayer. There was held to be a close connection between theology and contemplation: the original meaning of 'speculative theology' was contemplative theology. The early Fathers, especially the Greek Fathers, associated theology closely with doxology. The liturgy especially was felt to be theology finding its natural expression in worship. Nearer to our own time, Yves Congar said:

> I believe strongly ... in the strengthening and regulating of the faith and of life and of conduct by the practice of the liturgy. The liturgy has opened for me the best doors for the perception of the mysteries and for access to the peace which is the free gift of the Spirit of God.

Hans Urs von Bathasar said that among the greatest needs of the Church in our time was for 'theology on its knees'. The greatest theologians have been men and women of prayer, and the most profound theology leads to contemplative prayer. St Teresa of Avila put much of theology and much of contemplation into a short but profound sentence when she said: 'Do not try to hold God within yourself but hold yourself within God.' St Teresa exhorted her Carmelite nuns to offer their lives in prayer, in vigils, fasts and self-sacrifice, for 'theologians and defenders of the faith'. St Clare of Assisi left as a legacy to her Poor Clare sisters the mission to pray for priests and theologians as teachers of the faith. Theologians will never know how much their intellectual labours have owed to the prayer and penitence of contemplatives, those women and men in whom theology becomes most fully itself by growing into prayer and love.

Hans Urs von Balthasar never ceased to give testimony to what he had learned from the contemplative, Adrienne von Speyr. He insisted that what the Church needs most in our time is saints. Pope John Paul, who admires Balthasar so greatly, shares these convictions with him. In his encyclical *Redemptoris Missio*, on the Church's missionary mandate, he declares that the true missionary is a contemplative in action, and the truest missionary is the saint. He speaks of the 'ardour for holiness' required for authentic missionaries. We can say the same about theologians.

And so we come back in the end to *The Imitation of Christ*, and to the words:

> What a wonderful thing it is to be wholly set on fire by You and die to myself, for You are a fire always burning and never failing, a love purifying hearts and enlightening the understanding ... (4: 16).
>
> Let all teachers hold their peace and all created things keep silent in your presence; do You alone speak to me (4: 17). All reason and natural investigation ought to follow faith and not precede or infringe upon it (4: 18).
>
> God wills us to become perfectly subject to Himself and by the love that burns within us to transcend all reason ... (1: 14).

Cardinal Cahal B. Daly
3 May 1993

INTRODUCTION

The name of Hans Urs von Balthasar is beginning to be known in the English-speaking world generally. His relatively late arrival is surprising if one remembers the enormously broad range of his interests and the breadth of his achievements. These interests cover subjects pastoral, ecumenical, apostolic (he is, with Adrienne von Speyr, the founder of secular institutes that continue to flourish), literary (he is the translator of Paul Claudel into German), philosophical and, of course, theological. As for his achievements, they are such that a man of Fr Karl Rahner's stature describes them as 'really breathtaking'.[1] His bibliography contains over one thousand items.[2] And yet his 'most important works, at least in his own eyes, are not his writings, but his foundations,'[3] for he was a theologian only to be a pastor. Thus in spite of his prodigious literary output, he is primarily a pastor of souls, convinced of the splendour of Christ as the magnetic centre of history, and ready to squander every human effort so that the desired encounter between the Redeemer and the human being happen with maximum speed and lasting fruitfulness. Like John Henry Newman in the last century, who composed almost fifty volumes yet never as anything other than a drawing out of the treasures of divine revelation in order to communicate them afresh at a time when he saw 'love was cold',[4] von Balthasar had a clear goal – to transmit 'the infinite treasure of Christ' (*Ephesians* 3: 8) and to re-issue, as it were, 'a Christendom which still carried its thoughts into the limitless space of the nations and still trusted in the world's salvation'.[5] The amazing range of his

---

[1]   Karl Rahner, 'Hans Urs von Balthasar', in *Civitas*, 20 (1964/65), 602.
[2]   Cornelia Capol, *Hans Urs von Balthasar: Bibliographie 1925–1990*, Einsiedeln 1990.
[3]   Peter Henrici, 'Hans Urs von Balthasar: A Sketch of His Life', *Communio* 3 (1989), 306.
[4]   John Henry Newman, *Oxford University Sermons*, London 1900, 197.
[5]   John Riches (ed.), *The Analogy of Beauty: The Theology of Hans Urs von Balthasar*, Edinburgh 1986, p. 195: henceforth cited *Analogy*.

work, as well as its striking originality, have ultimately a simple unifying goal: 'to render the Christian message in its unsurpassable greatness (*id quo maius cogitari nequit*), because it is God's human word for the world, God's most humble service eminently fulfilling every human striving, God's deepest love in the splendour of His dying so that all might live beyond themselves for Him'.[6] Focusing that goal further he explains that, since 'the apostle of Christ is one who lets himself be killed for Christ' (Kierkegaard), all Christians must aim at 'the greatest possible radiance in the world by virtue of the closest possible following of Christ'.[7] Only such a 'virginity'[8] of the faith does justice to the gospel of Christ, gives glory to God, and enables believers to be the salt of the earth and the light of the world.

Knowledge of the sources and originality of perspective

The writings of Balthasar are striking as much for their originality as for their magnitude. His friend and mentor, Henri de Lubac,[9] recognised him as 'the most cultured person of his time,' one with an encyclopedic knowledge of the whole of western culture. 'If there is a Christian culture,' concluded the learned Frenchman, 'then here it is!'[10] His renaissance - like knowledge of the cultural and theological anthology of the West blends with an originality of theological viewpoint that is equally staggering. 'God does not come primarily as a teacher for us ("true"), as a useful "redeemer" for us ("good") but for HIMSELF, to display and to radiate the splendour of his eternal triune love in that "disinterestedness" which true love has in common with true beauty. For the glory of God the world was created; through it and for its sake the world is also redeemed.'[11] This conviction leads him to compose a 'theological aesthetic, the only one that has ever been written, a work that makes the bold claim of

---

[6]   Ibid., 195–96.

[7]   Ibid., 201.

[8]   St Augustine, *Serm.* 93, 4; 231, 7.

[9]   Hans Urs von Balthasar, *The Theology of Henri de Lubac*, San Francisco, 1991.

[10]   Henri de Lubac, 'A Witness to Christ in the Church', *Communio* 3 (1975), 230.

[11]   *Analogy*, 213.

pointing out to theology its unique centre and definitive centre'.[12] If Balthasar is to be seen as a genuinely great theologian – and that is a rare species – it will be in virtue of his appropriation of the treasures of the tradition and his recasting of them under the encompassing cipher - category of glory - beauty. It will be because he has unpacked the riches of revelation for our times, reasserted their content and offered them with a freshness of explanation that is attractive and inspirational. It will be because he has shown that the Christ, who from all eternity exists as 'the light of glory in the wellspring of the Blessed Trinity' (Gaelic expression), is the light for the third millennium. Of course time and the judgment of the Church will tell, as in the case of all the others who have become masters in 'the Israel of God' (Galatians 6:16).

Where to situate Balthasar as a theologian

The prospective reader of this volume may wish to situate the theology of Balthasar in relation to the preponderant currents in Catholic theology this century. On the occasion of a visit to the USA in 1977 for a symposium on his thought at the Catholic University of Washington, he addressed this very topic, giving a brief sketch of three outstanding currents all of which 'desire to be fully Catholic and to help the Christian in the world to witness more effectively'. Besides, 'each system has its own characteristic approach and its specific motivation that leads into Christian practice'.[13] The first is the 'transcendental trends' whose best known representatives are Fr Karl Rahner and Fr Bernard Lonergan. This method begins with the dynamic subjectivity of the person which it understands as a longing for communion with God so that each person could be defined as potential hearer of the Word of Revelation and so of the self-disclosure of Being. In this scenario, anthropology becomes incipient Christology, while Christianity has both solid rational justification in a scientific world and can give an account of its divine hope to dechristianised men and women.

A second major trend is one where 'some of the deepest sources of early patristic tradition have sprung forth anew' and which 'will

[12] Karl Rahner, ibid., 602.
[13] 'Current Trends in Catholic Theology and the Responsibility of the Christian', *Communio* 1 (1978), 78.

flow into the future'. A good instance of this approach is to be seen in the works of de Lubac whose *Catholicism: Social Aspects of Dogma* 'points to the essentially trinitarian character of the Catholic Church, which can only be achieved by genuine personalisation of all its members and which derives from our participation in the interior community of the triune God'.[14] This vibrant Patristic method has antecedents in the last century in the persons of Möhler and Newman who are heirs to the theological styles typical of the Fathers.

The third current is the one in which Balthasar locates himself. Although there is no convenient label 'one could speak of men overwhelmed by the Word of God in the way the beloved is overwhelmed by the declaration of the lover, "I love you because you are you"; or as one is overwhelmed by a great work of art – of Bach or Mozart, of Poussin or Dante – by something that is unmistakably unique and bears the imprint of grace'. This trend stands out in theologians like Heinrich Schlier who is fascinated by the evidence of the New Testament's catholicity, like Heinz Schürmann who delights in showing the catholic richness as well as the ethical implications of the biblical texts, and like Louis Bouyer who 'refuses to approach the historical Christ through any other media than the Word of God spoken to Israel'.[15]

An international conference

In May 1992 an international conference on Balthasar with the title, 'Christ, Beauty and the Third Millennium', took place in Maynooth. Organised principally by members of the Faculty of Theology of the Pontifical University, the conference had a well defined goal: to present an in-depth introduction to the theology of this modern Father of the Church. To this end the organisers chose the salient themes of his theology, arranging them in logical sequence and engaging recognised experts in the field. Their hope was that participants, who came in large numbers, might relish such an exposition of Balthasar's intentions, methods and themes over the days of the conference.

[14]   Ibid., 83.
[15]   Ibid., 80, 81.

There was, however, a second hope. In 1948, Balthasar had written an article on the separation between theology and spirituality during the past millennium, and on this separation's devastating impact on the life of the Church. 'In the whole history of Catholic theology there is hardly anything that is less noticed, yet more deserving of notice, than the fact that, since the great period of scholasticism, there have been few theologians who are saints. We mean here by theologian one whose office and vocation is to expound revelation in its fullness, and therefore whose work centres on dogmatic theology.' How very different was the millennium before the great schoolmen when 'we are struck by the fact that the great saints ... were, mostly, great theologians'! This schism between theology and spirituality has been, according to Balthasar, a more serious bloodletting for the Church than the Great Eastern Schism in the eleventh century or the Reformation in the sixteenth century. The result has been 'on the one hand, the bones without the flesh, "traditional theology"; on the other, the flesh without bones, that very pious literature that serves up a compound of asceticism, mysticism, spirituality and rhetoric'.[16]

This explains a central concern in all he wrote, namely, the refinding of the lost unity and the mutual nourishment between theology and spirituality, dogma and life. 'For the object with which we are concerned is man's participation in God which, from God's perspective, is actualised as "revelation" (culminating in Christ's Godmanhood) and which from man's perspective, is actualised as "faith" (culminating in participation in Christ's Godmanhood). This double and reciprocal *ekstasis*– God's "venturing forth" to man and man's to God – constitutes the very content of dogmatics.'[17]

This consideration urged the organisers to plan the occasion in order to link light and life, logos and ethos. Since God is in the detail, all the practical arrangements for the conference should promote the bonding of theology and life. Accordingly, all the needs of participants from arrival until departure were carefully considered in advance of the event in order to reflect the welcome God has extended to us all in Christ (*Romans* 15: 7). It was essential that all taking part should not only feel themselves in a family but actually

[16] Balthasar, *The Word Made Flesh*, p. 193.
[17] *The Glory of the Lord*, I, 125–26.

be in a family, a living communion of believers gathered into unity in order to live and think and celebrate that koinonia brought on earth by Christ who prayed and suffered so that all might be one (*John* 17: 21f). Thus the welcoming of guests, the minute attention to menus, the decoration of the lecture hall, the signposting of all the venues and many other tasks were undertaken with attention to detail. The results were tangible. People quickly felt at home, and speakers and listeners met and discussed in an atmosphere of life. And when the conference formally ended, there were some who lingered as if reluctant to leave that atmosphere.

The chapters before you

The chapters you are about to read are largely the fruit of that occasion. Professor Peter Henrici S.J. (now an auxiliary Bishop of Chur in Switzerland) introduces the man and his work,[18] but 'from the standpoint of his cultural and theological formation'. He emphasises that Balthasar's work 'includes much more than just the Trilogy, indeed, much more than the entire written work, vast though it is'. In the next chapter Fr Breandán Leahy of Clonliffe College and Mater Dei Institute, Dublin, describes Balthasar's idea of theological aesthetics, its discovery, content and significance. (A rather more critical appreciation of the aesthetics is provided in an Appendix by Fr Noel O'Donoghue.)

Professor John Riches of Glasgow next considers Balthasar's biblical theology as this is expressed in the sixth and seventh volumes of *The Glory of the Lord*. He shows that 'the New Testament is not the last chapter in the Old: it marks the beginning of the new world that springs from the divine kenosis of the Son. And the fullness which is imparted is not "given by measure": it is the inexhaustible glory of the divine self-giving which is only properly reflected in the multiplicity of the New Testament witness and of subsequent biblical theologies'.

Since Balthasar undertook extensive studies in the Fathers of the Church and since the treasures he discovered there permeate the whole of this theology, it was imperative to present this theme. Dr Deirdre Carabine, formerly a Newman scholar in University College, Dublin, shows that 'the documents of the Fathers can be

---

[18] See also P. Henrici, S. J., 'Hans Urs von Balthasar: A Sketch of his Life', *Communio* 3 (1989), pp. 306–50.

thought of as the Church's intimate youthful diary'. From them Balthasar understood that 'many problems which the contemporary age regards as without precedent had already been raised by writers in the past'. Still, 'his own thought is very much a response to the theological problems of today,' but with the 'vision and the vibrancy of his approach to theology'.

Fr Gerard O'Hanlon S.J. follows with 'a brief outline of theological dramatics in Balthasar' and then tries 'to bring this outline into dialogue with the attempt to create a social theology within our Irish context'. This chapter shows that since it is the deed that is decisive,[19] God's revelation consists in the struggle of his incoming love with human freedom in order to bring us into the realm of trinitarian freedom.

For Balthasar God's revelation is first received by Mary who gives 'God's infinity dwindled to infancy welcome' (Hopkins). The truth is that 'in Mary, Zion passes over into the Church; …in her, the head passes over into the body,' so that 'the Marian experience existed prior to the apostolic experience, and it thus wholly conditions it, for Mary as Mother of the Head is also Mother of the Body'.[20] The fact of Mary, however, sheds striking light on the mystery of the human being. Fr Johann Roten, director of the International Marian Research Institute in Dayton, Ohio, expounds Balthasar's anthropology in the light of his Marian thinking, for 'that which is Christian is anthropologically significant … or it is nothing at all'.[21]

Like Professor Riches, Professor John Saward is one of the team that produced the splendid translations of the *Aesthetics*. He writes on the spirit of childhood in Balthasar whose last work was on his desk a few days before he died, bearing the title, 'Unless You Become Like This Child'. Professor Saward sets out to show that 'in von Balthasar the child's heart shapes and orders the mind. In the *Theological Aesthetic* it is the young, uncluttered eyes which see the splendid form of revelation. In the *Theo-Drama* a child is caught up into the drama of Christ's self-giving love. In the *Theologic* a little one lets himself be led by the Holy Spirit into all the truth of the Father's Word made flesh.' Fr John O'Donnell S.J. of the Gregorian University rounds off the trilogy with a succinct summary of revelation as truth and logic.

[19] *Analogy*, 216–17.
[20] *The Glory of the Lord*, I, 338, 362.
[21] *The Glory of the Lord*, VII, 83.

Balthasar's love for the Word which, as we have seen, over-whelmed him, was a special feature of his encounter with Karl Barth. In 1951 he published his lectures on Barth which display 'the fundamental reconcilability of Catholic and Protestant theology at the point where each is most consistently itself'.[22] The eminent Presbyterian theologian, John Thompson of Belfast, outlines the history and the content of this seminal dialogue between the two Basle theologians.

Fr Bede McGregor O.P. then highlights Balthasar's 'gospel of Christian prayer' and underlines its uniqueness when compared with non-Christian forms. The characteristics of Christian prayer include its 'trinitarian and Christocentric nature, the Marian para-digm of praying, the communion of saints, mission, the giftness of prayer and its interpersonal nature in knowledge and love'. The interface here between Karl Rahner and Balthasar is most informa-tive, indeed exciting. Fr McGregor shows how Balthasar's theology both inspires and underpins a theology of mission, especially in view of the emphasis he places on the particularity of God's love as revealed in the Crucified and as communicated by the Holy Spirit.

Fr Thomas Norris of Maynooth makes the attempt to outline the unity of Balthasar's work. He describes this unity as symphonic, and outlines the movements that compose the symphony. Balthasar once wrote a volume bearing the title, *Truth is Symphonic*.

The Church's prophetical office of proclaiming and communi-cating the Mystery of Christ to all nations is intimately related to the vitality and variety of her theological schools. Since theology follows from the interaction between the white light of revelation and the cultural ideal of particular nations and epochs, the task of preaching the gospel is never more endangered than when these same schools are enfeebled, damaged or unproductive. At the same time, each and every theology is relative, 'seeing a dim reflection in a mirror' (1 *Corinthians* 13: 12), since its subject matter in creation and revela-tion, the infinite ocean of trinitarian love creating the world in the Word (*John* 1: 3; *Colossians* 1: 17) and recreating it in the blood of the Word made flesh and sacrifice (*Colossians* 1: 20), is so inexhaust-ible that it far outstrips all that can be said. Hans Urs von Balthasar always emphasised this disproportion. It is enough to look at the two

---

[22] *Analogy*, 204.

sets of 'clerical' and 'lay' theologians considered in volumes two and three, respectively, of *The Glory of the Lord* to be convinced of the point. Describing himself as a 'mind-friend' of Balthasar, Fr Noel Dermot O'Donoghue, O.D.C., assesses his theology in the light of this principle. He investigates the notion of theological aesthetics against the background of the classical tradition and of the philosophical doctrine on the transcendentals, indicates some 'absences and limitations', and suggests that his theological aesthetics can legitimately be termed 'orchestral imagination' which is 'a testament to that eternal beauty which is the imperial theme of the whole work'.

The Editors

1

HANS URS VON BALTHASAR: HIS CULTURAL AND THEOLOGICAL EDUCATION

Peter Henrici, S.J.

I

I should like to introduce Fr Balthasar to you from the standpoint of his cultural and theological formation. This, in turn, will show not only his roots in the Catholic tradition and in the culture of his time, but above all the striking originality both of Balthasar's figure and of his work – a work which includes much more than just the Trilogy, indeed, much more than the entire written work, vast though it is.

Born on 12 August 1905, in Lucerne, scion of an old patrician family of this city in the heart of Switzerland, Balthasar spent the first four years of gymnasium at the Benedictine college in Engelberg – an abbey in the heart of the mountains, not far from Lucerne.

Subsequently he moved to the Jesuit college at Feldkirch in Austria for another two years of secondary education – we do not really know why. Perhaps simply because – it was then 1921 – the borders were once again open and it was possible to study abroad: perhaps because he expected from the Jesuits a more rigorous and demanding formation than he could receive from the Benedictines.

Whatever the reason may be, in 1923, after having taken his school-leaving exam one year ahead of time, in Zurich, Balthasar took up the study of German literature, philosophy and, to a more limited extent, of Indo-European linguistics in Vienna, Berlin and Zurich for nine semesters. On 27 October 1928, he passed the rigorous examination for the Doctorate at the University of Zurich (which would be his 'home' university, since there is no university in Lucerne); at about the same time he gave the finishing touches to his doctoral dissertation on the *History of the Eschatological Problem in Modern German Literature* (which would be published in 1930), and on 18 November 1928, he entered the Jesuit novitiate, once again at Feldkirch.

After the two years of novitiate he spent two years studying neo-Scholastic philosophy at the Jesuit faculty at Pullach (near Munich), that is, from 1931 to 1933, dates which might evoke memories of political events. Finally, these studies were followed by four years of theology – also officially called 'scholastic' – at the Jesuit scholasticate at Fourvière, north of Lyons. On 26 July 1936, at the height of the Nazi period, he was ordained a priest by Cardinal Michael Faulhaber in Munich, and, after the conclusion of his studies with a Licence in Theology, he was to begin to work as a writer at the Magazine of the German Jesuits, *Stimmen der Zeit.*

This whole curriculum does not yet tell us a great deal. In particular, we have almost no knowledge of what must have been the most truly formative period for the young Balthasar: his studies at school and, later, of German literature. In fact, in his doctoral dissertation, an extract published as a kind of preview of what was later to be the monumental (and seldom read) *Apocalypse of the German Soul,* Balthasar appears as a man already formed.

Our ignorance, however, regarding the earliest cultural formation which Balthasar received does not have great repercussions; indeed, it is permissible to doubt whether a more detailed and more profound knowledge of those years would help us to understand better his later work. Balthasar's case is entirely unlike that of Karl Rahner, for example, whose theology requires a thorough knowledge of neo-Scholastic philosophy and theology. For such is Rahner's background and he continues to think in these categories and intellectual patterns. Nothing like this for Balthasar. Yes, one sees that he is well versed in the techniques of criticism and of literary interpretation; but the methods which he does use seem to be so 'non-technical' that it is not clear what a more thorough knowledge of them would contribute to a better understanding of the work. This work is unique, it is the basis of its own interpretation, and it is irreducible to 'dependencies' or 'influences'. This is one of the reasons why Balthasar, despite the fifty and more doctoral thesis which have already been written about him, nonetheless, continues to be one of the least 'thesifiable' authors.

Indeed, whoever meditates upon the years of Balthasar's formation often finds himself wondering whether this brilliant man, 'perhaps the most cultured man of our time' as the late Cardinal de Lubac[1] described him, really received and assimilated what is commonly called a 'formation'. Was he not rather a sort of autodidact, in spite of his more than twenty years behind school desks? What I mean is that he provided his own formation by reading very broadly and very deeply what he chose for himself to read.

There are several indications which support such a hypothesis. The first is his final school-leaving exam which he took a year ahead of time, because he had decided along with two other friends that he had studied enough. Thus, it seemed useless to him to finish the last year of school.

Then there is the fact that when Balthasar mentions his studies, he hardly ever names his professors, but speaks of some older friend who guided him in his choice of authors. He refers to only two professors from his years at university, Hans Eibl in Vienna and Romano Guardini in Berlin, but only to say that the first lead him to Plotinus and the other to Kierkegaard.[2]

Finally, we know that during the classes at Fourvière he stuffed his ears in order to be able to read in peace the *opera omnia* of Saint Augustine, of whom he was preparing an anthology.[3] That must not have been the first nor the last time he used a similar method of study.

Summing up the whole matter in Augustinian terms, it could be said that Balthasar seems never to have had 'teachers', but only 'mentors',[4] who stimulated him to find the truth by himself – not *in* himself, however, but in the great, indeed the greatest authors.

---

[1] 'Cet homme est peut-être le plus cultivé de son temps.' H. de Lubac, 'Un témoin du Christ: Hans Urs von Balthasar', in *Civitas*. Monatsschrift des Schweizerischen Studentenvereins, 20 (1965), p. 588.

[2] 'Vielleicht waren die Wiener Vorlesungen von Hans Eibl über Plotin, die mich faszinierten, während meiner Germanistikstudien der Umweg, auf dem ich dazukam, mich für die Theologie zu interessieren' (*Unser Auftrag*, Einsiedeln 1984, 31). 'Zu Meinem Unglück hatte ich, dessen Jugend in die Zeit der Kierkegaard-Welle fiel – Guardini erklärte ihn uns in Berlin – bei Kierkegaard gelesen, der Apostel Christi … sei einer, der sich für Christus totschlagen lasse' (*Mein Werk. Durchblicke*, Einsiedeln-Freiburg 1990, p. 46).

[3] *Aurelius Augustinus, Über die Psalmen*. Auswahl und Einleitung, Leipzig 1936, and *Aurelius Augustinus, Das Antlitz der Kirche*. Auswahl und Einleitung, Einsiedeln-Köln 1942.

[4] Augustinus, *De Magistro*, 14.

II

Balthasar often recalled with gratitude three of these mentors (perhaps the only ones whom he had). The first is the Viennese physician-psychologist Rudolf Allers,[5] who began as a student of Freud, then became a follower of Adler, and later converted to Catholicism. Allers was the brother-in-law of Lisa Meitner (who along with Otto Hahn discovered atomic fission) and a friend of Edith Stein and Fr Agostino Gemelli (the founder of the Catholic University of Milan). He was a translator of St Thomas and a specialist on St Anselm. In 1938 (after the Anschluss) he emigrated to the United States where for another twenty years he would teach philosophy at the Catholic University of Washington and at Georgetown University. It was while he was in the United States that he would publish the first complete and accurate critique of Freudianism: *The Successful Error: A critical study of Freudian psychoanalysis.*[6]

It was necessary briefly to evoke this figure, today undeservedly forgotten, because in his doctoral dissertation, Balthasar attributes to him whatever there might be of value in the work: 'Das Wertvolle, das sich unter diesen Ausführungen finden mag, ist in dieser Freundschaft gereift.'[7] Unfortunately, it is difficult for us to guess what these 'things of value' might be. Surely, it is not simply the fact that often in the evenings Balthasar and Allers, seated at the same piano keyboard, would play together one of Mahler's symphonies. If we may be permitted to conjecture, we probably see Aller's influence in the conviction that man must be treated as a whole, as a totality who finds his bearings in the light of values; that psychology has to have a basis in anthropology – of a Thomistic stripe – and

[5]   'Allers, der, von Alfred Adler herkommend, die wahre Communio in der Katholischen Kirche gefunden hatte, tat ein übriges, mich für echte Theologie zu interessieren.' On Rudolf Allers (1883–1963), cf. *Enciclopedia Filosofica,*[3] I, col. 192; *New Catholic Encyclopedia,* I, p. 325; H. Jugnet, *Un psychiatre-philosophe. R. Allers ou l'anti-Freud,* Paris 1950; R. Titone, *R. Allers, psicologo del carattere,* Brescia 1957; I. Collins, 'The Work of Rudolf Allers', in *New Scholasticism,* 38 (1964) pp. 281–309.

[6]   Rudolf Allers, *The Successful Error: A Critical Study of Freudian Psychoanalysis,* New York 1940.

[7]   Hans Urs von Balthasar, *Geschichte des eschatologischen Problems in der modernen deutschen Literatur,* Zürich 1930, VII.

that anthropology, in turn, must rely upon the insights of theology; that love is man's highest capacity, and that love is not the product of the sexual instinct but belongs to an entirely different order, the spiritual order that as such is also rare, although it is this spiritual love which makes man healthy even from the point of view of psychology.[8] But perhaps Aller's influence is detectable above all in the sort of philosophical and theological 'psychoanalysis' of the 'German soul' which Balthasar practises in his doctoral dissertation and, in an even more radical fashion, in the *Apocalypse*. This could well have been suggested to him by his conversations with Allers and by the 'psychoanalytic' mood which was then in the air in Vienna.

The other two mentors of Balthasar have no need of a long introduction. Erich Przywara,[9] the German Jesuit philosopher-theologian, was at that time the leading light of the Catholic dialogue with modern culture, whether secular or religious, in particular with Max Scheler and Karl Barth. This dialogue was deeply grounded in the classical metaphysics of Aristotle and St Thomas and in the spiritual theology of St Ignatius and of the Spanish mystics. Much has been written about Balthasar's dependence on the *analogia entis*, the pivotal point of Przywara's thought and his dialectic. However, there are two more formal aspects which specially deserve to be underlined. First, Balthasar was able to learn from Przywara how to read the 'figure', the mobile, dynamic *Gestalt*. The *Gestalt*, like a musical figure, is not something fixed or circum-scribable, but defines itself from its movement. To use Przywara's own terminology it is *über-in* ('transcendent-immanent'), *über-hinaus* (growing beyond), and *je-mehr* (always more). (Note that these constructions are all characterised by the comparative.) In the mature Balthasar this dynamic would appear in the Anselmian formula *quo maius cogitari nequit* (perhaps a reminiscence of his conversations with Allers). In the second place, Balthasar learned

---

[8] 'Gegner Freuds, hat er in freier Nachfolge Alfred Adlers den Blick für die mitmenschliche Liebe als objektives Medium menschlicher Existenz gehabt und mitgeteilt, in dieser Wende vom Ich weg zur Wirklichkeit voller Du lag für ihn die philosophische Wahrheit und psychotherapeutische Methode.' (*Mein Werk*, 70); cf. also the final chapters 'Die Liebe' and 'Auswrikungen und Umgestaltungen' in his manual: Die Psychologie des Geschlechtslebens. (*Handbuch der vergleichenden Psychologie* III). München 1922, pp. 462–500.

[9] On Erich Przywara (1889–1972) cf. Hans Urs von Balthasar, Introduction, in L. Zimny, *Erich Przywara. Sein Schrifttum*, Einsiedeln 1963, pp. 5–18.

from Przywara his method of presenting not only the exposition but also the critical discernment of the thought of an author by means of a 'collage' or 'mosaic' of his texts. By letting the author speak, Przywara is able to present what the author himself leaves unsaid. In a less extreme form – and with less strain – we find this same method in almost all of Balthasar's monographs – whether these be part of larger works or are works in their own right.

The last mentor is the one with whom Balthasar would feel in the most perfect harmony throughout his whole life. It was to be a friendship to death, based on mutual admiration and gratitude. Henri de Lubac,[10] only nine years older than Balthasar, was never his professor. However, living in the same scholasticate at Fourvière, de Lubac opened up to Balthasar his heart, his immense learning – and his collection of patristic files. It was he who introduced Balthasar to the study of the Fathers in whom, rather than in the desert of neo-Scholasticism, he was soon to discover true theology. De Lubac would confirm Balthasar in the rejection of a model of reality which envisioned two separate levels or two hermetically sealed compartments – nature and grace. De Lubac emphasised the only real end of mankind and of creation, namely, the supernatural, and consequently, the importance of the 'secular' and 'profane', or more precisely, the 'social' aspect of Catholicism. (Balthasar would later add to this the cultural.) *Catholicisme*, de Lubac's first great book, which has as its subtitle *Les aspects sociaux du dogme*, was to become decisive for Balthasar, who would translate it into German.

III

Until now we have had to proceed by means of conjectures, relying upon the sparse indications which Balthasar himself leaves us regarding the years of his formation. However, there is another source from which it is possible to draw information: his own books and other writings published in those same years or immediately afterwards; or, in any case, before he met Adrienne von Speyr in 1940. An accurate analysis of these writings would be extremely interesting; it could reveal to us what is most purely 'Balthasarian'

---

[10]   On Henri de Lubac (1896–1991) cf. Hans Urs von Balthasar, *Henri de Lubac. Sein organisches Lebenswerk*, Einsiedeln 1976.

in his later writings which were conceived under the influence of Adrienne. I am sure that this would not be a negligible amount; indeed, I would say *in nuce* almost everything. Here I will limit myself to using these sources simply for the sake of singling out some readings which seemed to have exercised a greater influence on the young Balthasar.

His readings, as we have said, were really boundless. In his dissertation there appear practically all of German literature and philosophy from the eighteenth to the twentieth century; in the *Apocalypse* there are, in addition, many non-German authors. What is most astounding is that Balthasar seems always to have read the *opera omnia*: he read the whole of Goethe (twenty-four or thirty-two volumes!), all of the Romantics, the entire corpus of Nietzsche. For the *Theo-drama* he would read, in the course of a single year, all of the dramatic literature of all times. This is, in its own way, an application of the principle of totality: the truth of an author manifests itself only in his entire work. Only in this way is it possible to perceive the author's 'figure'; for *Gestalt* in German means not only 'form' but also 'character'.

Which, then, are the 'figures' who made the greatest impression on the young Balthasar – the authors to whom he would be continually making reference? In his *Weizenkorn*, an early collection of aphorisms, he once wrote: 'Nothing gives as much pleasure as the possibility of drawing out of the farrago of history the four or five figures who, taken together, constitute, so to speak, the constellation of my idea and of my mission.'[11] We shall have to name here more than four of five, but as we shall see, all of them belong to that constellation. We can do no more than list them here, without a great deal of commentary.

In the first place, it is necessary to name the two authors of his life and of his soul, to whom Balthasar felt linked by 'elective affinity': Goethe and Mozart. It is not an accident that the last recognition which he received was the Mozart prize, which was conferred upon him by the Goethe Foundation at Salzburg a year before his death. Balthasar had already devoured Goethe in his first years at school and he would continually refer to him in order to explain his own style of thinking, which was characterised by totality and the self-

---

[11]   Hans Urs von Balthasar, *Das Weizenkorn*, Einsiedeln 1989³, p. 34.

manifesting 'Gestalt'.[12] Mozart, whom he discovered only towards the end of his musical studies, represented for him (as for Karl Barth) the *summum absolutum* of musical expression. Balthasar would come to know his *opera omnia* by heart, so that he would no longer need to play them nor to hear them played.

Plotinus and Kierkegaard were revealed to him during his university years as he himself has told us, and at the same period he must also have discovered Nietzsche. For the dialogue between Nietzsche and Kierkegaard (and Dostoevsky), that is, between the love of power and the power of love, would constitute the central pivot of the *Apocalypse* – a continuation, in that respect, of his dissertation.[13]

There is a third group of authors whom I would call the 'system builders'. First, Hegel, the symbol of the misdeeds of a pseudo-theological, all-inclusive systematic completeness which absorbs the creature in the divine synthesis. Next, St Thomas, whom he read and re-read at every stage of his formation and who remained the unattainable goal of a study which was never written. St Thomas represented for Balthasar the great alternative to Hegel, as well as the indispensable corrective, since a 'Summa' is in no wise a 'system'. I would also include St Augustine in the same group. Balthasar discovered Augustine under the influence of Przywara and, in his turn, would attempt to render him systematic (as he was to do later with Origen) in a collage of texts. Augustine was for him not so much the doctor of grace as the theologian of the mystical body and of the Church of saints and sinners, whose limits coincide to such a small extent with the boundaries of the visible Church. Finally,

---

[12] 'Es gibt ein Buch von Simmel, das heisst *Kant und Goethe*. Rahner hat Kant, oder wenn Sie wollen, Fichte gewählt, den transzendentalen Ansatz. Und ich habe Goethe gewählt – als Germanist. Die Gestalt, die unauflösbar einmalige, organische, sich entwickelnde Gestalt – ich denke an Goethes 'Metamorphose der Pflanzen' — diese Gestalt, mit der auch Kant in seiner Aesthetik nicht wirklich zu Rande kommt' ('Gesit und Feuer. Ein Gespräch mit Hans Urs von Balthasar', in *Herderkorrespondenz*, 30 [1976], p. 76. '... dies Gestaltsehen verdanke ich dem, der nicht abliess, aus dem Chaos von Sturm und Drang auftauchend, lebendige Gestalt zu sehen, zu schaffen, zu werten: Goethe, Ihm danke ich dieses für alles Hervorgebrachte entscheidende Werkzeug' *Ansprache in Innsbruck*, 22 May 1987, TMs. p. 2).

[13] Cf. in this connection the fine dissertation of J. Gesthuisen, *Das Nietzschebild Hans Urs von Balthasars. Ein Zugang zur Apokalypse der deutschen Seele*. Rome 1986.

still in this same group, there is Karl Barth. Fascinating in his radical christocentrism, and in his predestinationism of mercy, Barth was the interlocutor with whom Balthasar, as a Catholic, could not be in complete agreement, but by whom he was continually captivated. Barth was the well-mannered and grumbling friend of the Basle years.

The fourth and last group of authors, discovered at the theologate in Lyons, comprises some of the greatest among the Fathers of the Church. Irenaeus, the *genius loci* of Fourvière, the theologian of God's humanity, the anti-gnostic who for Balthasar was also the anti-idealist. In fact, idealism always represented for Balthasar the great seduction. 'Every philosophy which respects itself', he wrote in the *Weizenkorn*, 'ends in idealism; only Christianity opens up to it a path of superior realism.' In this perspective it is necessary to see also Balthasar's relationship with the other three Patristic figures to whom he would have liked to dedicate a trilogy (already in that early epoch he was interested in writing trilogies!) and whom he was able to present in various writings. First, Origen, the greatest, the most brilliant, who suggested to Balthasar the hope of an empty hell – and much more than that. Balthasar would present him in a 'collage' of texts which was to be his favourite work. Next, Gregory of Nyssa, perhaps the most philosophical of the Fathers, furnished him with another favourite theme, that of the non-sexual procreation in paradise. Gregory also appeared to him to have overcome German idealism and existentialist philosophy centuries before they made their appearance. Finally, Maximus the Confessor, upon whom Balthasar was to confer the status of systematic theologian in a synthesis elaborated twice under the title *Cosmic Liturgy*. For Balthasar, Maximus anticipates in his person the 'individual' of Kierkegaard, while his doctrine must be seen as a resume of the whole of ancient thought, and as the completion of that synthesis which German idealism was to attempt in vain.

Thus, whereas the *Apocalypse* had developed, in a grandiose epic drama, the immanentistic consequences of classical German philosophy as well as the existential choices which it faces, the never completed Patristic trilogy would have demonstrated the anticipated resolution of this drama in Christianity. In this light, the *Theo-drama* appears as the focal point towards which Balthasar's work tends.

IV

Yet we cannot and must not forget that for Balthasar his written works were and remained 'ein Nebenprodukt,' a by-product or a 'sideline', something secondary, produced 'faute de mieux'.[14] Balthasar saw his true work elsewhere.

Analogously, his true formation (call it 'theological or cultural') is to be sought not in the schools which he attended, not in the books which he read, nor even in the friends and mentors which he met, but elsewhere. He himself pointed out this 'elsewhere' to us when, at the end of his *iter* of formation, at his first Mass, he placed his priesthood under the words of the Eucharistic consecration: *Benedixit, fregit, deditque*: 'He blessed it, broke it and gave it.'

Everything which we have seen thus far, along with many other circumstances which I have not been able to mention, could be summed up under the heading *benedixit*: an abundance of gifts, talents and blessings received from God. But precisely because he was so exceedingly blessed, he had also to be broken, broken in pieces. At this point the divine formation in the life of Balthasar begins, a formation which was to remain permanent. Balthasar's life can be read as a series of fractures which succeeded one another at an ever more pressing pace from the earliest years of his life onwards: the move from the art-loving school of the Benedictines to the almost entirely unartistic Jesuit school; the religious vocation demanding immediate obedience, like a lightning bolt out of a clear-blue sky; the premature death of the mother whom he loved intensely; the desert of the novitiate and of six years of studying the most traditional and most insipid neo-Scholastic theology and philosophy; the unexpected mission to become the spiritual director of the mystic Adrienne; the calumnies which this mission would bring and, above all, the necessity of leaving on her account the Society of Jesus which had become his second home; the theological suspicions which hung over his teachers and friends at Lyons, and even over himself; a sort of banishment by the Swiss Church, without being incardinated in a diocese, for many years without

---

[14] 'Die zweite Voraussetzung ist die schlichte Wiederholung des vor zehn Jahren abgelegten Geständnisses: das Schriftstellerei im Haushalt meines Lebens ein Nebenprodukt und *faute de mieux* bleibt und immer bleiben wird' (*Mein Werk*, p. 76).

being recognised by the public, and without being called as a theologian to the Council; the years of Adrienne von Speyr's illness and slow death; the pain of finding that many of his disciples and friends were playing chief roles in the revolution 'movement' of 1968 in Switzerland; and, finally, as a last 'fracture', the cardinalate, which he accepted to please the pope, but which literally broke his heart. All of this is to demonstrate how right he was when, at his first Mass, he underscored with such insistence that *fregit* which (though I was eight years old at the time and did not know Latin) left an impression in me that has remained vivid throughout my entire life.

But the *fregit* had meaning only because it made it possible to be given, distributed, almost squandered. It is this other characteristic of Balthasar's formation which seems to me even more important. The 'grain of wheat' which Balthasar set as the title of one of his first books, which is also perhaps the most personal, not only must die to bear much fruit (*John* 12: 24) but even before that must be scattered in the field of the world. To be scattered in the field of the world, that is the mission, the 'task' which Balthasar recognised as his own.

Balthasar wished that the new religious community which he was to found with Adrienne be composed of lay men and women working in the world, in their secular profession as physician, architect, teacher, etc. This is a vocation whose essence is perhaps not adequately conveyed by the term 'secular institute'. For what was originally intended was a community which was at the same time more purely lay and more rigorously consecrated (with a true religious profession) than secular institutes normally are. Just as in his first works, particularly in the *Apocalypse*, he sought to recognise and gather together the *disiecta membra* of Christianity, even in the authors who are seemingly furthest from it, so also with his foundations, from the *Schulungsgemeinschaft* to the *Johannesgemeinschaft*, would he attempt to carry the Christian seed as far as possible into the world. The centre of the Church, as he said in one of his most pregnant formulas, is to be found where usuallly its periphery would be seen; that is, where it is fully present in the secular world, because it is there that the Church must give birth to Christ.

Such a lay and missionary concern can be explained once again from Balthasar's years of formation. Those were the years in which

German Catholics were becoming aware of the urgency of 'leaving the ghetto' to which the *Kulturkampf* had relegated them. The 'exit from the ghetto' had begun vigorously in the field of literature and the arts. The friends and mentors of the young Balthasar were leaders of this Catholic renewal, and his first works can be fitted perfectly into this context.

Later, at Basle, where he was chaplain of students, this was to become his programme of action: to form lay people for their action in the secular world – action which precisely in so far as it was lay was Christian. Balthasar's mission itself seems to have been in some fashion a lay one, in spite of his priesthood. In all of the recorded autobiographical testimony, Balthasar speaks only once about his vocation to the priesthood. It is precisely in that sole instance that Balthasar goes so far as to say that if he had at that time been acquainted with the secular institutes, then perhaps that would have been his true vocation.[15] The ecclesial mission of the layman in the world: this is the content of two of his (at that time) most famous and influential writings: *The Layman and the Consecrated Life* and *Razing the Bastions* – this latter title not so much because the walls become too narrow but in order to construct in their place 'boulevards' open in every direction. However, in these writings Balthasar also emphasises that the layman's mission will not be one of power and of domination; in this sense he was always as far removed as possible from every form of political Catholicism. In fact, he rather tended to withdraw his disciples from political engagement – indeed his mission will be a mission of losing oneself, like the grain of wheat and like leaven. It will be a mission characterised by *descensus*, by suffering endurance in which there re-emerges the indispensable *fregit*.

That which sustains this mission in the world and renders it truly ecclesial is contemplative prayer, the contemplative prayer to which the 'early' Balthasar[16] dedicated another highly successful book. Such contemplation was the principal obligation which Balthasar

---

[15] Wenn ich damals, als es nur darum ging, mich hinzugeben, schon die Lebensform der Säkularinstitute gekannt hätte ich wohl auch in einem weltlichen Beruf die Lösung für mein Problem finden können: mich Gott ganz zur Verfügung zu stellen. *Por qué me hice sacerdote* (ed.), J. e R. M. Sans Vila, Salamanca 1959, p. 31.

[16] Hans Urs von Balthasar, *Das betrachtende Gebet*, Einsiedeln 1955.

imposed on the members of the lay communities which he founded. And when, after the Second Vatican Council, the whole Christian people opened itself enthusiastically to the world, though rather triumphalistically and at times with secularising overtones, instead of following the path of contemplation and of Christ's kenosis, Balthasar felt it his duty to insist ever more emphatically on the contemplation which must be at the heart of the Christian mission in the world. Without this contemplation, the mission becomes dispersion and dissipation. Balthasar was to dedicate his Trilogy – the one which actually was written – to the contemplation of the Glory of the Lord who humbles himself and enters into the world, and to the drama of his passion in a world of sin.

This leads me to a final observation. Contemplation in the midst of engagement in the secular world, mission in the world and spirituality of descent are all terms which define Ignatian spirituality. 'Our holy father Ignatius' (as Adrienne and Balthasar called him following the Jesuit custom) was the true master of formation who remained hidden behind the entire human and divine formation of Balthasar, even in those respects where it seemed to be the work of an autodidact. A sign of this could be seen in the fact that already the doctoral dissertation and the *Apocalypse* appear to be marked by another Ignatian principle: both are works of spiritual discernment – a discernment which is not merely theoretical but which bears upon existential choices, whether of the authors whom he interprets or of the eventual readers of the works.

Thus it is possible to understand that Balthasar's written work was for him only a *Nebenprodukt*: something secondary and accessory in relation to his spiritual direction, his foundations, his courses of exercises, and to innumerable personal meetings.

Nevertheless, now that Balthasar does not speak to us any longer in *viva voce*, we rejoice that, in spite of it all, the *Nebenprodukt* turned out to be so rich.

2

THEOLOGICAL AESTHETICS

Breandán Leahy

A THEOLOGIAN OF BEAUTY

A passionate lover of Mozart's music, it is said that at the end of a long evening of discussions with university students in Basle, their young chaplain, Hans Urs von Balthasar would sit down at the piano and play for them from memory the Salzburg musician's *Don Giovanni*. Likewise, in his own student days, relaxing moments of friendship with Rudolf Allers, doctor, psychologist and theologian, were spent in playing together a Mahler duet. Later in life, music was the medium which enabled both Karl Barth and Balthasar to make themselves one with each other – a oneness that would then deepen in their theological insight. Indeed, a feature which marks Balthasar's theology is that whether it was the harmony found in music or in the paintings of artists such as Poussin or Grünewald, the cosmic catholicity and love of the 'whole' found in the works of an acquaintance like Paul Claudel, or the God-Nature religion of awe and form found in Goethe, music, painting, literature and drama were the keys in which Balthasar played his dialogical movement with some of the major figures in the western *Geistesgeschichte*.

And yet this dialogue ought not to be viewed as some luxurious leisure-land activity engaged in by an aesthete. Looking back on his life's work and outcome, he commented that the activity of being a writer was subordinated to the service of the cause of Jesus, the cause that concretely is the Church.[1] The 'origin' or starting point for his

---

[1] 'Another Ten Years – 1975', in John Riches (ed.), *The Analogy of Beauty: The Theology of Hans Urs von Balthasar*, Edinburgh 1986, pp. 222–33, especially pp. 223–24 (hereafter, *The Analogy of Beauty*).

dialogue was Jesus Christ. Being so immersed in the world of the arts, description of the greater immersion in the most original glorious light of divine revelation was, not surprisingly, etched out in artistic rather than scientific categories. But it was the 'origin' which prompted all his views on theological or ecclesial reform, including his project of elaborating a theological aesthetics. Attracted above all by the divine beauty of Christian revelation, Balthasar's overall concern in his theological aesthetics was that of winning back for theology the third dimension of glory – beauty (*pulchrum*), tracing its 'rays' wherever they were to be found. Accordingly, while never having held a university chair in theology it is valid to say that Balthasar is perhaps most immediately known today as the 'theologian of beauty'. And despite the limited nature of this description, the opinion can be ventured that it will be for his theological aesthetics rather than the Theo-dramatics or Theologics that he will be best remembered.

Just like Mozart's music with its light exuberant melody, Balthasar's theological aesthetics is basically simple in its central motifs, but tantalisingly subtle in its score. And here a caveat must be entered. The reader must tread slowly if he or she wants to join Balthasar in his odyssey of return to the beauty originating in divine revelation. Throughout his writings on this theme, almost *sotto voce*, the Swiss author is grappling with issues such as the relationship between nature and grace, thought and life, gospel and culture, fundamental and dogmatic theology. Likewise from the originality of divine revelation, he is trying to re-read the classical doctrine of the transcendentals of being and to reflect upon the Christian contribution to metaphysics in the modern world 'run aground on the sandbanks of a technological rationalism'.[2] Ultimately, he wants to outline a methodology for a theology which is nourished by an intense spiritual and ecclesial experience.

The aim of this chapter is to try and accompany the reader in seeing, hearing and touching the heart-beat of the theological aesthetics, so clearly a product of the spiritual-artistic biography of this Swiss theologian of beauty. We shall proceed as follows. Our first step shall be to distinguish briefly theological aesthetics from a theology which is aesthetical. To understand the dynamic pervad-

---

[2] See *Einfaltungen: Auf Wegen christlicher Einigung*, Munich 1969, p. 9.

ing our theme, we shall then indicate the core of theological aesthetics: a nuptial relationship centred in the cross. Here the form of Jesus Christ is most apparent and it is precisely this glorious form which the third section intends to present. Admittedly, we are only opening windows, as it were, to try and facilitate the reader's grasp of Balthasar's moves. In this section we consider the theme of the luminosity of Being, biblical revelation and mediations of the form. After this, we are ready in our fourth section to elaborate upon faith as a theologically aesthetic act. Finally, we shall mention the relevance of theological aesthetics for theology and the Christian life today.

THEOLOGICAL AESTHETICS OR AESTHETICAL THEOLOGY?

Knowing about Balthasar's love of music and painting (the former more than the latter),[3] drama and literature is only a prelude to an understanding of his theological aesthetics. True to a Barthian perception of things, he sees a world of difference between an aesthetical theology and a theological aesthetics. The former takes its conditions from the 'natural' world of aesthetic categories in general, the latter quite clearly wielding only categories of beauty as they emerge from divine revelation. This 'perhaps most cultured man of our time'[4] is not advocating the aestheticising of the mystery of Christ. His emphasis is not on the beautiful forms like poetry and epic, myth, lyrics, and hymns which are to be found in scripture. The theological aesthetics are not about theological rationalism. There is no question here of a self-constructed attempt to make theology or the Christian life more appealing.

In what sense then are aesthetical categories applicable in theology? Without prejudice to what will have to be developed more thoroughly throughout this essay, we can respond cursorily that in Balthasar's view analogues from created reality can be used in order

---

[3]   See Camille Dumont, 'Il Genio Musicale', in Karl Lehmann and Walter Kasper, *Hans Urs von Balthasar: Figura e Opera*, Casale Monferratto (AL) 1991, pp. 289–304.

[4]   See Henri de Lubac, 'A Witness of Christ in the Church: Hans Urs von Balthasar', *Communio* 2 (1975), pp. 228–49, especially p. 230.

to understand the aesthetic dynamic of divine revelation so long as we keep in mind that it is not univocal statements that are being made.[5] The reason why the area of worldly aesthetics can be a source of description in an analogous sense is quite simply that since God's 'great work of art' – the whole of salvation history – is in the midst of history,[6] the world symphony of every sound, word and beauty which speaks of love in the universe echoes the One Absolute Being who is disclosed to us in divine revelation as Love. The reciprocally-echoing transcendentals of finite being reverberate with the primordial echo of the divine triune Being who is love. Glory (*doxa*) as a theological transcendental exists in an indissoluble *perichòresis* with the philosophical transcendentals of being.[7]

Recourse to what happens in encountering the luminosity of being in a masterpiece of art, music or a breathtaking landscape can serve our understanding of faith as an aesthetic act within theological aesthetics. But, it cannot be emphasised enough, the transcendentally glorious is not to be reduced to the level of the inner-worldly and categorically beautiful. Balthasar keeps before him both the eastern tradition and the Fourth Lateran Council's doctrine of analogy: 'ever-greater dissimilarity however great the similarity' (*maior dissimilitudo in tanta similitudine*).[8] In a certain sense along with John of the Cross and Dionysius the Areopagite his theological aesthetics is a 'negative theology'. God can never be known positively because the divine is always greater, more mysterious than any scheme of ours. But, for Balthasar, a merely negative theology is not sufficient because it might be pejoratively understood in a gnostic and spiritualistic sense of searching beyond the revelatory form in the world which God established. Consequently, throughout his theological aesthetics, along with Anselm and Augustine, he never tires of seeing the divine glory as that than which nothing greater could ever be thought (*id quo maius cogitari nequit*)[9] and that which rationally one understands is incomprehensible (*rationabiliter*

---

[5] Cf. *Glory of the Lord*, I, 119 (hereafter, *Glory*).
[6] Ibid., p. 172.
[7] *Glory*, VII, pp. 242–43.
[8] DS 806.
[9] Anselm of Canterbury, *Prosl.* 3 and 15.

comprehendit incomprehensibile esse).[10] But, on the other hand, along with Irenaeus, Balthasar insists on the form of revelation which can be perceived and grasped. The Lateran Council's doctrine of analogy keeps the right balance:

> The basic form of the 'ever-greater dissimilarity however great the similarity' ... is irrevocable; but it can vary from being a philosophical 'negative theology' – in which God's Being remains infinitely hidden and unfathomable over and beyond all analogous utterances about him – all the way to being a 'negative theology' within the theology of revelation, in which God 'appears' unreservedly and, therefore, even in his ever-greater incomprehensibility really comes into the foreground and into the form that appears. God's incomprehensibility is now no longer a mere deficiency in knowledge, but the positive manner in which God determines the knowledge of faith.... This is the concealment that appears in his self-revelation; this is the ungraspability of God, which becomes graspable because it *is* grasped.[11]

In Louis Dupré's words, Balthasar's theological aesthetics is the science of the divine form as it stands revealed in Christ and, through that prism, reflected in the cosmos and history.[12] It is a concrete revelation in concealment. Balthasar himself sets out in summary fashion what a theological aesthetics purports to achieve. It sets up a doctrine of seeing the form of glory and a doctrine of rapture into the glory. The two abiding questions throughout are: (1) How can the free act of God's redemption be perceived (in a Kantian sense) in the world? (2) How do we cross over from our metaphysical systems into the free system of God?

---

[10] Anselm, *Monol.* 64.

[11] *Glory*, I, p. 461. Balthasar concludes that both Dionysius the Areopagite and John of the Cross kept both the apophatic and kataphatic approaches together and so he considers them the two most decidedly aesthetic theologians of Christian history. See *Glory*, I, p. 125.

[12] See 'Hans Urs von Balthasar's Theology of Aesthetic Form', *Theological Studies* 49 (1988), pp. 299–318, especially p. 300.

AT THE CORE OF THEOLOGICAL AESTHETICS: A NUPTIAL RELATIONSHIP IN THE CROSS

It is helpful at the outset to note that the doctrine of seeing and rapture central to Balthasar's theological aesthetics revolves around a core perspective: the God-world relationship as revealed (and concealed) in the nuptial encounter between Christ and Mary/ creation/Church. Congruent with Balthasar's ultimately Chalcedonian christological framework, revelation in the Christ event is viewed as the intimate encounter between the 'human centre' and the 'divine centre'.[13] It culminates as a nuptial encounter in what we might call a double ecstasy (*ekstasis*). In Dionysius the Areopagite's terms the divine *eros* goes out of itself in order to become man and die on the cross for the world.[14] Along with Bernard, Anselm and others, Balthasar sees the creaturely responsive going out in faith as primarily centred in the Marian/ecclesial self-surrender (*Hingabe*) in faith to God.

The cross is the place of the nuptial encounter where everything creaturely is reduced to silence only to be glorified in obedience. The human cry reaching up to heaven for glory is sheltered within a divine glory hidden in the cry which lies at the heart of the *Triduum mortis*. Jesus' cry, 'My God, my God, why have you forsaken me?', encloses both the basic philosophical question at the human centre: 'why is there something at all and not nothing?' and the cruciformed why-lessness of Christ's love reaching out to us from the divine centre.

Given the centrality of the nuptial dimension of the divine-human encounter at the cross, unlike Matthias Scheeben whose theological aesthetics he greatly admires in that it replaced the aesthetic theology of Romanticism with the outlines of a methodically founded theological aesthetics,[15] Balthasar does not want to draw too sharp a distinction between faith and reason, nature and grace. In positing a nuptial relationship between faith and reason, nature and grace, he follows Scheeben's intuition but, along with de

---

[13]   *Spiritus Creator*, Einsiedeln 1967, p. 71.
[14]   *The Divine Names*, IV, 13, London 1940, especially 105–6. See *Glory*, I, p. 122 and p. 217.
[15]   *Glory*, I, pp. 104–17.

Lubac, gives prominence to a continuity between nature and grace.

The nuptial simile expresses this continuity in that it reflects what Balthasar sees as a trinitarian ontology of love in terms of the reciprocity established by One of the Trinity coming on earth to suffer and die for us. The 'heavenwards' earth can be caught up into the 'earthwards' heaven because between Jesus Christ the Bridegroom and Mary-Church the Bride a new realm of being has been opened up. It is a trinitarian realm. In this context and not a Hegelian one, theological aesthetics is transposed from christocentrism into a final trintarian theocentrism.[16] It concerns our beholding and rapture into the eschatological nuptial realm with its trinitarian character. The locus of theological aesthetics is creation-humanity-history-Mary-Church taken up into the new trinitarian life granted in Jesus Christ, the Word made flesh.

Accordingly, the starting point for theological aesthetics is our encounter with this *Ursprunglichkeit* of love.[17] It is about our faith-experience of catching sight of the divine mystery ecstatically appearing before us in Jesus Christ, our rapture ecstatically into the triune communion which throbs at the heart of this mystery and then our going out of ourselves in ecclesial mission to the world. In a word, in catching sight (*Erblickung*) of the mystery of Jesus Christ, God draws you outside yourself, enrapturing (*Entzückung*) you within the triune love revealed in Jesus Christ, the Word made flesh, made form.

THE GLORIOUS FORM OF JESUS CHRIST

Already we are beginning to see that the glorious form of Jesus Christ is key to the theological aesthetics. Christ is his own measure. He claims to be the definitive appearance of God in history. And Balthasar invites us to see in the Christ-form how all is in proportion and harmony around the radiant centre of his relationship with God the Father in Spirit. Moreover, he claims that this figure which Christ forms has in itself an interior rightness and evidential power such as we find – in another, wholly worldly realm – in a work of art

---

[16] Cf. *Glory*, VII, p. 262.

[17] See Klaus Hemmerle, 'Das Neue ist älter: Hans Urs von Balthasar und die Orientierung der Theologie', *Erbe und Auftrag* 57 (1981), pp. 81–98.

or in a mathematical principle.[18] It is the archetype of beauty (*Urbild des Schönen*).[19] The splendour or radiance (*Veritatis Splendor*) of the Christ-form has an attractive power because in Christ we see what God's glory is but also how God's glory is, in Irenaeus' terms, man fully alive.

> What perfection and infinity really are for man, what emanation and encapsulation, self-surrender and being caught up really are, what 'transfiguration', 'deification', 'immortality' really are and what all the great words of aesthetics signify: it is in the Christ-form that all of it has its measure and its true context.[20]

Balthasar presents us with various entry-points into the perception of the glory of the Lord. In this section we want to take a brief glance at the notion of form itself, the phenomenon of the luminosity of being, biblical revelation, and the mediations of the form throughout time and history.

THE NOTION OF 'FORM'

Use of the notion of form[21] allowed Balthasar to bring together both the subjective and objective evidence of the glory (*Herrlichkeit*) of the Lord found in divine revelation. In his emphasis on form throughout the theological aesthetics he maintains an approach that tries to marry not only the objective structures of beauty such as the three elements outlined in Thomas Aquinas: form, harmony and radiance, but also the subjective structures in perception so prominent since the Kantian turning point in the concept of transcendentality.[22]

---

[18] *Glory*, I, pp. 465–66.
[19] Ibid., p. 477.
[20] *Glory*, I, p. 477.
[21] The concept of form (*Gestalt*) is one taken over from Plato and Aristotle, central in medieval ontology (Thomas Aquinas viewed all beauty as objectively located at the intersection of two moments called form and splendour, *species* and *lumen*), found also in the teaching about nature both in Herder and Goethe and, more recently, in the Berlin Gestalt school of psychology. See *Glory*, I, pp. 467–80; IV, pp. 28–39.
[22] *Glory*, IV, p. 35.

In emphasising form, Balthasar wants to concentrate us on 'the whole (*Das Ganze*), the totality, the unity of divine revelation and that is always at issue in Balthasar's theology. Hence he claims that no piece of divine revelation can be broken off the 'whole' or totality without destroying the 'whole'.[23] Form means a totality of parts and elements, grasped as such, existing and defined as such, which for its existence requires not only a surrounding world but ultimately being as a whole.[24] More than the parts we see and make out, it is the outer manifestation or expression of an inner-depth. It *is* this mysterious inner-depth in manifestation and expression.

It is with a sense of urgency that Balthasar says that seeing the form of revelation is a vital matter for Christianity today.[25] But use of the notion of form in theological aesthetics cannot be abstractly or generally described in some 'neutral' manner. In view of the unique application of the word 'form' to Jesus Christ Balthasar warns us to be careful in its usage.[26] Jesus Christ is a 'legible' form, and not merely a sign or an assemblage of signs, but his form can be seen for what it is only when it is grasped and accepted as the appearance of a divine depth transcending all worldly nature.[27] There can be no Husserlian bracketing out in some 'neutral' investigation.

We must allow the whole form to show itself in its own evidential power. That is why when he talks about aesthetics in revelation in terms of form, evidence, freedom, mystery, Balthasar prefers to use the expression 'super-' (*Über-*) forms, evidence, etc.[28] It has its own inherent power to attract and draw the beholder into unity with it. The Christian form unfolds itself in its own proportions, connections and balances. Upon comparison with any other worldly form of beauty, be it religious or otherwise, the uniqueness of the Christian form stands out. In his *The Glory of the Lord*, Balthasar tells us that his own project for a theological aesthetics echoes Karl Barth's theological aesthetics; he intends, however, to lead us more

---

[23] *Klarstellungen*, Einsiedeln 1978, pp. 17–25, especially p. 24.

[24] *Glory*, IV, p. 29.

[25] *Glory*, I, p. 132.

[26] Ibid., p. 432.

[27] Ibid., p. 153–54.

[28] See for instance, *Glory*, I, p. 432 and p. 480.

slowly towards the light of the beautiful form of the whole of revelation.[29]

THE LUMINOSITY OF BEING

It has been said that the Being-question is the dominating leitmotif of Balthasar's thought.[30] This is so precisely because of his constant wonder before the dominating disclosure of Being in the Word made flesh (*Verbum Caro*). He too shares in the Pauline awe before the disclosing 'Great mystery' (Ephesians 5: 32) of Christ and the Church, so thoroughly trinitarian in its nature. In his 'Christo-logic', Balthasar fits the world of being into Christ,[31] since God's incarnation perfects the whole ontology and aesthetics of created Being.[32] Clearly, it is Balthasar's trinitarian, christological, and ecclesial framework which lays the basis for his understanding of the analogy of being (*analogia entis*) within the analogy of faith (*analogia fidei*).

The christological revelation of the triune God acts, therefore, as a prism which explains the many 'colours of Being'. Following on from this and reminiscent both of the Heideggerian project of the rediscovery of Being which Balthasar acknowledges as the most fertile from the point of view of a potential philosophy of glory,[33] and also of Gustav Siewerth's metaphysics of childhood,[34] Balthasar

[29] See *Glory*, VII, p. 23. Unlike Barth, Balthasar allows of the analogy of being, and the aesthetic dimensions of faith as something in our present experience and not reserved to the eschaton.

[30] See John O'Donnell, *Hans Urs von Balthasar*, London 1992, p. 6. In a footnote (p. 9, n. 7) O'Donnell submits that the central insight of Balthasar's entire thought can be summed up in the proposition that Being is love.

[31] See Gerard Reedy, 'The Christology of Hans Urs von Balthasar', *Thought* 45 (1970), pp. 407–20.

[32] *Glory*, I, p. 29. Werner Löser calls Balthasar's perspective a 'theological ontology' embracing, outdoing and concretising the whole of Western philosophy in that it is a trinitarian ontology of Love. See Werner Löser, 'Unangefochtene Kirchlichkeit – universaler Horizont: Weg und Werk Hans Urs von Balthasars', *Herder Korrespondenz* 42 (1988), pp. 472–79, especially p. 477. See also Michael Albus, *Die Wahrheit ist Liebe: Zur Unterscheidung des Christlichen nach Hans Urs von Balthasar*, Freiburg 1976.

[33] *Glory*, IV, pp. 429–50, especially p. 449.

[34] *Metaphysik der Kindheit*, Einsiedeln 1957. See *Glory*, V, 613–34. Balthasar once commented that 'without him the fourth and fifth volumes of *The Glory of the Lord* would not have received their present form'. See 'In Retrospect', in John Riches (ed.), *The Analogy of Beauty*, pp. 194–221, especially p. 221.

often considers a type of 'trinitarian' reciprocal form in the luminosity of being. The inner dynamism found in the light of being is already preparing us for our perception of the glorious radiance in the super-form of Jesus Christ, the sacrament of the Trinity,[35] who discloses the mystery of Absolute Being to us. In everybody's encounter with Being there is an act of transcendence which gives rise to what he calls an inner-worldly aesthetic, a transcendental aesthetics which is oriented towards the transcendental theological aesthetics.

In considering the third transcendental of Being Balthasar states that the beautiful is above all a form, and the light does not fall on this form from above and from outside, rather it breaks forth from the form's interior. The ground of Being becomes luminous in its appearance (*Erscheinung*). The higher and purer a form, the more will light shine forth from its depths and the more will it point to the mystery of the light of Being as a whole.[36] The greater the degree of surrender to the mystery of the form of an entity encountered, the greater the degree of revelation, the deeper the depth of luminosity disclosed, but also the greater the mystery.

Epistemologically, revelation of Being takes place in the dynamic reciprocity of an inner and outer movement. Being's inner mystery is an inner oneness which also communicates outwards, and so unites the beholder with what is beheld but always in an ever-greater mystery. Almost a type of nuptial encounter, the dynamic of the openness of being and one's self-surrender to it is a movement of revelation and concealment, light and darkness. The more the oneness (the outer passing into the inner), the greater the mystery (the inner communicating ever more of its mystery outwards). A natural form such as, for instance, a flower, the face of an old man or a beloved, a masterpiece of art or music, can be seen for what it is only when the thing itself is perceived and received as the appearance of a certain self-opening of the ground of the depth of life contained in it. It is in the reciprocity of Being's openness and our self-surrender to the light which leads to revelation but always within the ever greater mystery of the light of Being.

[35] *Spiritus Creator*, p. 138.
[36] *Glory*, IV, p. 31.

In its groundless ground, Being proves itself in its disinterested gift and self-surrender, to be grace, beauty, love.[37] Already the primordial phenomenon in life, the awakening to Being which occurs in the interpersonal mother-child relationship, indicates how the 'paradise' of life into which one wakes is a luminous gift; being is experienced as grace, as love.[38] Although not before truth and good (because the transcendentals inhere in one another in a kind of *circumincession*), the mysterious beauty of love shows itself as the most original in the original mystery of Being, as its groundless ground.[39] If beauty were to be bracketed out, then the good and truth lose their evidence and are no longer binding.

Being understood as love and so primarily beauty is the reason why Balthasar reads the history of western metaphysics as a metaphysics of love. Transcendental aesthetics have always been present throughout history in myth, philosophy, religion and art, in that they point us to the divine. From Homer and Pindar, to Plato and Aristotle, to Plotinus and both the early and the late Christian period right up to the Renaissance and Baroque period, the intuition of the transcendentals as principles of Being, and therefore, beauty too, has been acknowledged in some fashion. Balthasar affirms that biblical revelation can and must enter into dialogue with transcendental aesthetics,[40] because they are oriented towards biblical revelation.

BIBLICAL REVELATION

The Swiss author's conviction that Christian revelation discloses the mystery of Being as triune love explains too why the primary analogue in human experience for the illumination of Being was not self-consciousness but the primordial phenomenon of the child awakening to Being through the I-Thou encounter. The greatest I-

[37] See Hanspeter Heinz on Balthasar's view of the love and beauty interpenetrating, *Der Gott des Je-mehr: Der christologische Ansatz Hans Urs von Balthasar*, Frankfurt 1975, especially pp. 21–28.

[38] See *Spiritus Creator*, pp. 13–20.

[39] *Theologik: Die Wahrheit der Welt*, Einsiedeln 1985, Vol. I, pp. 251–55. This was first published as *Wahrheit* in 1947.

[40] And consequently, two substantial volumes of *The Glory of the Lord* are dedicated to the realm of metaphysics in Antiquity and the Modern Era.

Thou encounter, however, in Balthasar's theological aesthetics is the God-humankind nuptial relationship as evinced in biblical revelation. Its centre is Jesus Christ. The biblical appearing of God confirms, includes, but also far transcends, the transcendental metaphysics in the new definite metaphysics disclosed by God. All categorical beauty, even the transcendental beauty of created being, is infinitely surpassed by the form of revelation (*Offenbarungsgestalt*).

Glory is a fundamental statement that leavens all of Scripture, yet it cannot be defined.[41] Two full volumes of *The Glory of the Lord (Herrlichkeit)* are dedicated to tracing this theme in the theology of the Old and New Testaments from the Pentateuch right down to the Johannine writings.[42] Balthasar understands the biblical experience of God as the experience of the invisible and unapproachable formless God taking form in world and history. It is in this form that we see the manifestation of God's glory.

And since God the creator is not to be contradicted in the working of God the redeemer but rather perfected therein, our finite created reality becomes the language of God in biblical revelation. Taking root in the concrete historical terrain of human thought, feelings, and imagination, biblical revelation always uses all these forms for its own expression.[43] In this sense, the form of revelation and the act of revelation are inseparable.[44]

To the primal tension between 'splendour' and 'form' proper to an inner-worldly aesthetics there corresponds at the highest biblical level a tension between the formless glory and its well-formed image and partner.[45] The whole movement of biblical revelation has as its goal to make image and glory coincide in Jesus Christ. And Balthasar seeks to understand the term 'glory' by relating it to the centre of the New Testament event of salvation itself. The 'One in whom the fullness of the deity dwells bodily' (*Colossians* 2: 9) came to build an extrapolation of the Trinity on earth. This he did through the cross. Biblical revelation is the witness to the covenant

---

[41] *Glory*, IV, p. 11.
[42] Both the introductions to the sixth and seventh volumes of *The Glory of the Lord* are well worth reading for the reader who wants to 'get into' his theological aesthetics without too much labour!
[43] *Glory*, VI, p. 21.
[44] *Glory*, I, p. 182.
[45] *Glory*, VI, p. 15.

dynamism striving towards fulfilment in the glory of the Crucified One and the collective ecclesial realm emerging from him. We shall outline some of the key features.

The Old Testament

Balthasar sees the whole journey of the Old Testament as a weaning from amorphous paganism and myth to the full form of Christ.[46] Accordingly, he sees the Old Testament itself as a chaotic event, a sphinx,[47] without form[48] because it transcends itself towards its centre found in Jesus Christ. The framework of the hypostatic union is in the making throughout the Old Testament. The quasi-personification of God's Word, Wisdom and Spirit indicate the incarnate dynamism of Old Testament (*Deuteronomy* 30: 14). Theophanies such as Sinai are intended to be understood as over-whelming events in which the living God becomes present.[49]

If in the human realm *kabod* means the resplendent weightiness or might of a being,[50] in the Old Testament notion of *kabod* glory and holiness are inseparable. God's glory is the manifestation of the weighty force of his divinity and God's call to his partner, his 'you', is to 'be holy, for I am holy' (*Leviticus* 19: 2). As the Old Testament moves toward the New, participation in the sphere of divine holiness deepens.[51] But the Old Testament *kabod* is ultimately a downward slope, a decrease in power and evidence of its presence. The aspect of revelation and concealment in finite being receives an

---

[46] *Man in History: A Theological Study*, London 1968, pp. 173–74.

[47] *Glory*, I, p. 628.

[48] *Glory*, VI, p. 403.

[49] Cf., ibid., pp. 18–19: p. 34. Looking at the Scriptural accounts of the particular manifestations of God's glory – Sinai (Ex 34–38), Isaiah's vision (Is 6: 5), the vision in Daniel 7, Tabor (Mk 9: 6), Stephen (Acts 7), Paul (Act 9: 4, 9) and John (Rev 1: 17) – Balthasar notes a type of death and resurrection experience as a constant in biblical revelation. In encounter with God's word the hearer and beholder falls but through the power of God's grace the human creature is put back on his feet by the spirit of God himself (Ex 2: 2). Every believer hears and beholds God in God and through God. The result of their visions is that the person goes outside himself to take on a mission.

[50] *Ibid.*, pp. 32–33.

[51] Balthasar views scholasticism's tendency to interpret the biblical *kabod* with the philosophical concept of *gloria* in the sense of honour, praise, fame, renown as too univocal an application of finite analogues to God (*Glory*, VI, p. 26, fn. 11).

unprecedented compression and intensification in Israel.[52] The whole dynamic of the greater opening of the Ground, the greater the mystery of the depths can be seen in Israel's history, chosen and elected in a covenantal love. The God of Israel showed himself in history as the ever more incomprehensible. Paradoxically, Israel is never surer of her God than when she appears to have been forsaken by him in exile.[53]

After the exile and the ruin of Jerusalem, with the departure of God's glory from the temple (*Ezra* 9: 3; 10: 18; 11: 22ff.) there are three forms of reaching out for it through a broadening of horizons: messianically into the future; apocalyptically into heaven, sapientially into the entire cosmos and history of the peoples of the world.[54] But God's ways are different. The fragments of the Old Testament itself lack a form that can harmonise so many seemingly irreconcilables.[55] Ruin, death and Hades must be taken up into the act of the covenant. This is granted only when God's Word (*dabar*) became flesh, when the eternal life took death (as judgment, ruin, hell) upon himself as a man, and made it past for himself.[56] In the absolute suffering of judgment and its overcoming in the rising of man to God, the imperfect Old Testament glory of God must display itself in the New Testament as the perfect glory of His love that overcomes all things.[57]

The New Testament
The term 'glory' occurs in the New Testament 116 times and the verb 'to glorify' more than sixty times. The grace and message of the New Testament, transcending all the statements about glory in the Old Testament, is precisely that God's glory can embrace transcendentally even the uttermost contradictions. God's glory was to be revealed in Jesus Christ's absolute obedience right to the point of the Cross and Hell.[58] The powerfulness in God's glory shines forth in

---

[52] *Glory*, I, p. 454.
[53] Ibid., p. 456.
[54] *Glory*, VII, p. 25.
[55] *Glory*, VI, pp. 402–414.
[56] Ibid., VII, p. 39.
[57] Ibid., p. 40.
[58] *Glory*, VII, p. 243.

complete powerlessness. The fragments of the Old Covenant which needed a synthesis find their form which only God alone could give in the inglorious form of a slave (Philipians 2: 6–11).

The New Testament 'glory' is the divine self-expression (word), self-representation (image), and self-realisation in the other (right-eousness a grace).[59] Otherness and concealment become the realm of expression and manifestation. God impresses his form on Jesus Christ who expresses the Father to the world and in this expression takes on all 'otherness' from God in order to impress it with his form of righteousness.

Our prophet, high priest, lamb of sacrifice, servant of God and Messiah is so as the righteous One made sin for our sake, *pro nobis*. The scandalous word of the cross, so much a Pauline theme (*Galatians* 5: 11; 1 *Corinthians* 2: 7; 1 *Corinthians* 1: 25) provides the wisdom of the Cross. And it is on the basis of the Pauline interpretation that the passion narratives of the Gospels are to be read. The post-Easter accounts show the redemptive character of the event already shimmering through its judicial character.

What happens in the New Testament is that the dust is blown off the original intention of God and his great act of judgment in the running of Jerusalem.[60] God's eschatological act of salvation in the New Testament in the cross and resurrection of Christ throws light on the Old Testament words of judgment. In Jesus' death, the Old Testament motifs of judgment and mercy come together because God's forsakenness reaches the extreme of the human sinful condition transforming the grounds for judgment into shibboleths of love. With the cross our sinfulness is unveiled for what it is. We see the truth of our condition. But this truth is enveloped in another unveiling – God's glory in the world shaping us to his glory as people fully alive. But to understand the New Testament glory fully, Balthasar leads us to John.

John

Out of the variegated panorama[61] of the Old and New Testaments Balthasar turns above all to the prologue of John's Gospel: 'And the

---

[59] Ibid., p. 318.
[60] See *Glory*, VII, p. 202ff.
[61] *Glory*, VI, p. 191.

Word became flesh and dwelt among us, full of grace and truth; we have beheld his glory, glory as of the only Son from the Father' (*John* 1: 14). The Synoptics begin by portraying the event of Jesus without using the concept of glory, but John lays claim once more to the word *doxa* wholly for the New Testament glory.[62] He captures the leap from the centuries-long dynamism of the Old Testament covenant with its varied *momentum* of divine presence: what it was oriented towards has come in the dramatic sudden sight of the incarnate dwelling of *kabod YHWH* among us. John unfolds the trinitarian kernel of the New Testament *doxa*.[63]

The incarnation and cross are inseparable as glorification in John's writings. Coming from the bosom of the Father, the Son's whole life is a glorification of the Father in obedience and powerlessness as he journeys towards his 'hour' of glorification in the cross. The theme of darkness and light reaches its climax in the Johannine faith which is able to see both God's kenosis in the Synoptics and the Pauline *doxa* of the risen Christ as a unity. The light of the risen glory is reached only through the darkness of the kenosis of glory. In John the raising up upon the cross and the raising up into glory are one single event, just as for Paul no one is raised up apart from the one who was crucified. It is in this sense that Jesus Christ is revealed in John as one who holds the keys of New Testament *doxa*.[64]

The Johannine inner nexus binding obedience and glorification is rooted in the life of the Trinity, the original glory. The farewell discourse on glory shows us Jesus requesting glorification from the Father. All his life had been a glorification of the Father through obedience. John invites us to see Jesus' 'formlessness' in the passion as a mode of his glory because it is a mode of his love to the end. It is in his deformity (*Ungestalt*) that we are to see the mystery of transcendental form (*Übergestalt*). His bearing of the world's sin (*John* 1: 29), or in Pauline terms, his being made sin for us (2 *Corinthians* 5: 21), is understandable only as a function of the glory of love, before and after and therefore also during his descent into darkness.

The resurrection is the glorification of the Son by the Father by virtue of the glorification of the Father by the Son in his death. The

---

[62] *Glory*, VII, p. 27.
[63] *Glory*, VII, p. 264.
[64] Ibid., p. 264.

Spirit who in Jesus' life lived over and in Jesus is breathed forth in Jesus' dying and with this the cruciform divine glory of the mutual love between Father and Son is set free for the world. The bridal responsive Mary-Church stands at the cross as the place where his new glory is to radiate in the world. The new Christ-Mary/Church reality born at the cross through the Spirit forms the original cell (*Urzelle*) of the Church. Here creation finds its place to glorify glory.[65]

With John's return to the beginning (*John* 1: 1; *John* 17: 21–23), beyond Sinai, with its dialectic of fire and smoke, lightning and cloud, light and darkness, we are brought to that which was the true purpose of God's disclosure in all the previous revelation of glory: his trinitarian love.[66] The Johannine writings present a journey from the primordial glory of the Trinity to the eschatological glory of the Trinity. In John's vision the Christian's penultimate experience is the tension between the present contemplation of God's glory and the eschatological hope of it.[67] Light and darkness, revelation and concealment mark the *chiaroscuro* journey of faith towards our eschatological participation in the final oneness of trinitarian glory. In Balthasar's view, the depth of John's vision of God's glory (*claritas*) in the unity of the incarnation, cross, resurrection and eschaton makes his theology the last word of the Bible.

What the whole of biblical revelation leads to is the measureless measure of love: the glorious form of Jesus Christ in the formed formlessness as the obedient one 'whom they have pierced' (*Zechariah* 12: 10; *John* 19: 37). It radically puts an end to all worldly aesthetics in that all classical notions of beauty as measure, proportion and harmony seem to crumble, but precisely this end marks the decisive emergence of the divine aesthetic.[68] The trinitarian radiance provides a new harmony, proportion and measure. What we have before us in the incarnation and cross is pure glory, whose character is a trinitarian dynamic of cruciform love. Balthasar writes of an almost 'theological three-dimensional plasticity' as part of the

---

[65] This theme would require much elaboration. See my own dissertation, *The Marian Principle in the Church in the Ecclesiology of Hans Urs von Balthasar*, Rome 1993.

[66] *Glory*, VII, p. 27.

[67] *Glory*, VI, p. 19.

[68] *Glory*, I, p. 460.

evidential force for the eyes of faith.[69] Theological aesthetics are to be based on the perfect proportion which Christ, through his obedience, has established once for all between heaven and earth in doing the will of the Father.[70]

MEDIATION OF THE FORM

Included in the glorious form of Christ is the fourfold witness to Christ from the Father, the Spirit, salvation-history and the cosmos. This attestation belongs to the very structure of form itself. But the mediations of the form throughout time and space belong to the Word and the Church.

Sacred Scripture as the Logos Body, in the Origenian sense, is the vehicle that impresses the Christ-form in the hearts of men. It is like a sacrament of the Holy Spirit which effects what sacred Scripture signifies.[71] The Church's mediation is exercised in many ways. On the one hand, she herself is a participation in Christ's bearing the guilt of world but she also proclaims the already realised redemption. The Church is the working of the risen Christ through the form of sacred Scripture and the form of sacrament.[72]

Both Scripture and the Church mediate what Balthasar speaks of as a communion of archetypal experiences of divine glory. We participate in glory through out sharing in these. The primary archetypal experience is Jesus Christ's experience of God. But the whole Old Testament experience of God, the Marian experience and the Apostles' eye witness experience flow into the Church as part of her mediational treasury. The four-fold layered Church (the Petrine, Pauline, Jacobine and Johannine) within the Marian archetypal experience is the realm in space and time through which we enter now into the anticipated experience of the eschatological glory between the Bride and Bridegroom.

---

[69] Ibid., p. 458. The Father is the Son's origin. The Father impresses His form on the Son who reveals God in the form of a servant to the world. The Holy Spirit, being the glory of God, enlightens the servant's form and-lets-its glory be seen. The Father witnesses to the Son as the Father's Word; the Son (and we in him) is transfigured by The Holy Spirit.

[70] *Glory*, VII, p. 262.

[71] *Glory*, I, p. 530.

[72] Ibid., p. 531.

FAITH AS AN AESTHETIC ACT

At this stage we are ready to look more directly at faith as an aesthetic act. How are we transported from our own metaphysical schemes to God's light? How is it that I am drawn outside myself to believe divine revelation? What makes up my *fides qua* as a total surrendering and adhering to Christ, the *fides quae*? In terms of 1 *John* 5: 9–10 we can speak of God's testimony as both an interior and exterior facilitating of our crossing over to God's free system. The glorious form of revelation with its own evidential radiance which we have looked at above was clearly stressed as an objective exterior testimony. But no-one comes to Jesus Christ unless the Father draws him or her (*John* 6: 44). It is only the Father's light shed on the Son that leads the believer into the unitive encounter with him. It is a light which also indwells the believer through grace. And all of this is the work of the Holy Spirit. But how can we articulate this process? In the following sections we shall look at some of the elements involved.

THE FORM IS CO-EXTENSIVE WITH GOD'S LIGHT-WORD

Once again we must return to the notion of form and take our investigation one stage further. The preface from the *Feast of Christmas* indicates that from and in the glorious form of Jesus Christ there streams forth an enrapturing light of the trinitarian life: '*Quia per incarnati Verbi mysterium nova mentis nostrae oculis lux tuae claritatis infulsit: ut dum visibiliter Deum cognoscimus, per hunc in invisibilium amorem rapiamur.*'[73] Stressing the objective nature of the form of Jesus Christ, Balthasar brings us to understand that this 'outward' light of the form of divine revelation also operates 'within'. Thomas Aquinas' notion of *inspiratio interna*, or the Augustinian teaching on *trahi*, our being drawn by love's gravitational pull within us, are seen by Balthasar as linked to the resurrection of Jesus Christ. The explanation is that the form instituted by

---

[73] 'Because through the mystery of the incarnate Word the new light of your glory has streamed into the eyes of our mind, so that while we are getting to know God visibly, we are caught up in love of the invisible' (translation my own). See *Glory*, I, pp. 120–21.

God himself in the forum of history died in history but rose up to God as form, a form which now, in God himself, has definitively become one with the divine Word and Light which God has intended for and bestowed upon the world.[74] The *lumen increatum*, the uncreated grace within us, has the form which Jesus Christ himself had in the public forum of history; the risen form is visible to the eyes of faith.

This explains too the readiness of the interior light which is wholly oriented toward the objective form of revelation so as to arrive at its content.[75] The form itself has shared in the process of death and resurrection and so has become co-extensive with God's light-Word. In Balthasar's view this makes the Christian principle the superabundant and unsurpassable principle of every aesthetics; Christianity becomes *the* aesthetic religion *par excellence*.[76]

The internal and external testimony therefore derives from the one glorious form of Jesus Christ. In other words, the external and internal should not be viewed in a dualistic fashion. Balthasar wants to avoid ways of reading the Christian form of revelation which would emphasise its signs, on the one hand, and interior light, on the other, to a degree where the historical facts seemed to be only pointers to a mystery behind them but separated from them. In divine beauty form and light are one. For Balthasar it is impossible to dissect the objective Christ into a form, whose sole property it is to 'appear' externally, and a formless light which is what remains for the existential interior dimension.[77] The *locus classicus* of Paul's theological aesthetics bears this out in that he identifies vision and rapture as united in a single process: 'And we all, with unveiled face, beholding the glory of the Lord, are being changed into his likeness from one degree of glory to another.'[78]

FAITH, REASON AND GRACE

Following on from what we have just seen, Balthasar points out that everyone is called to the vision of God in eternal life and therefore,

---

[74] Ibid., pp. 215–16.
[75] Ibid., p. 177.
[76] Ibid., p. 216.
[77] *Glory*, I, p. 216.
[78] 2 *Corinthians* 3: 18. See ibid., p. 127.

however secretly, everyone is placed by God's grace in an interior relationship to the light of revelation.[79] The divine grace predestined in Christ to be given to the whole world is secretly at work in the whole sphere of history and thus all myths, philosophies, and poetic creations are innately capable of housing within themselves an intimation of divine glory.[80] But while these other forms, religions, philosophy and art indicate an attitude of obedience toward the light of the self-revealing God they cannot be God's immediate self-witness in historical form and, pre-eminently, in Christ who, as an historical form, demands faith for himself.[81]

The 'interior master' works within us therefore to prepare us for all other instruction from outside whether it be from the Church, history or creation. Nevertheless, we are not exempt from the human effort of searching for the correct form of what we are to believe and, having found it, making the effort of integrating it existentially into our lives. After all, even in the case of a masterpiece, the mature observer of art can without difficulty give an objective and largely conceptual basis for his judgment.[82] Following Matthias Scheeben Balthasar writes of reason as fructified by faith. The *praeambula fidei* are drawn into faith as reason gives itself over to faith to be fructified. The light of grace works upon the reasoning subject bringing the person to suddenly see and believe. There is a moment when the interior light of the eyes of faith becomes one with exterior light of the form perceived and the beholder cries out: 'We have found …' (*John* 1: 45).[83] God is known in God.

Balthasar clearly admires Rousselot's inductive approach to faith in emphasising one's use of the 'eyes of faith', but it is Newman's 'illative sense' that he prefers.[84] An objective convergence of the

---

[79]   Ibid., p. 167.
[80]   *Glory*, VI, p. 21.
[81]   *Glory*, I, p. 168.
[82]   Ibid., p. 178.
[83]   Ibid., p. 190.
[84]   He sees Rousselot as too Kantian in that the synthetic power of the active faculty of believing remains one-sidedly a part of the subjective dynamism. In Balthasar's view he does not sufficiently attribute this synthesis to the efficacy of the objective evidence of the form of revelation. He agrees that one can use Kantian categories in asserting the subjective conditions for the possibility of the illumination of spirit prepared for and proportionate to objective evidence, we must be careful not to exaggerate to the detriment of God's own power (*Glory*, I, pp. 175–77).

fragments takes place under the prompting of grace. The condition for this convergence in grace is how much we live with 'enlightened eyes of the heart' (*Ephesians* 1: 18) through love. Love forms 'eyes of faith' (Augustine), faith that has eyes (Thomas Aquinas' *oculata fides*). In short, what we need is that evangelical 'simple eye' (*Matthew* 6: 22). Balthasar is clearly influenced here by the mystical tradition, such as that found in Eckhart and others, which speaks of the eye which sees God as the eye with which God sees himself. Only love can contemplate Love; only Love can arouse the love which can welcome Love. Love brings light and it is in God's light we see light.

The whole dynamic of light and darkness, revelation and concealment in Christ's form which we mentioned above, is also relevant here in that God's love would never allow us to be caught up in some violent manner. Consequently, out of love for us on God's part, there is a sense of hide and seek in God's revelation and our seeing the form. But, in the last analysis, Balthasar attributes blindness to the glorious form to our human sinfulness, our refusal to turn around, convert and see the light.

WITHIN THE MARIAN-ECCLESIAL ARCHETYPAL ACT OF FAITH

In discussing faith as an aesthetic act we need to read another important text. It comes from 1 *John* 1: 1–4. Lest we would wrongly interpret the *Christmas* preface quoted above in too individualistic a notion of faith Balthasar refers us to John's trinitarian and collective account of the dynamic of revelation and faith.

> That which was from the beginning, which we have heard, which we have seen with our eyes, which we have looked upon and touched with our hands, concerning the word of life – the life was made manifest, and we saw it, and testify to it, and proclaim to you the eternal life which was with the Father and was made manifest to us – that which we have seen and heard we proclaim also to you, so that you may have fellowship with us; and our fellowship is with the Father and with his Son Jesus Christ. And we are writing this that our joy may be complete.

Life-testimony, light, word and proclamation are the elements of an interior-exterior *collective* dynamic through which the Father draws us to faith. The collective dimension finds expression in Balthasar's theological aesthetics in his writings concerning the ecclesial communion with its Marian form.[85] Here we find the sphere for our reception of the divine life through looking away from ourselves and being caught up in a *fiat* of faith. Prior to our act of faith, accompanying it and embracing it the Marian-ecclesial collective realm of faith is a cosmos of grace and faith experiences.

The Marian *Ecce ancilla Domini* points to the distance between God and the human creature but her image radiates with the evidential power which comes from having been shaped by the glorious form of revelation.[86] She is the prototype of *ars Dei* fashioned from a human material which offers no resistance.[87] Because of Mary's role as the woman where all roads meet[88] and as representing all of humankind in consenting to God's work of art,[89] a key theme in Balthasar's writings is that the Church has a Marian centre. The communion perceived in the glorious form of Christ catches us up in a Marian participation in the trinitarian fellowship. This is not the place to develop this theme but it points to our act of faith as a participation in the primordial Christ-Mary/Church nuptial relationship we spoke of above. Our turning away from ourselves in faith is an 'ecclesiastication' in the sense that the fundamental response to seeing the form is to share in the feminine spousal 'we' of the mystical body embedded in the trinitarian glory.[90]

No one goes to God alone. No act of faith is merely individual. As we mentioned above what we find in the Church is a communion

---

[85] See for instance, *Glory*, I, pp. 362–65; *The Office of Peter and the Structure of the Church*, San Francisco 1986; 'Die marianische Prägung der Kirche', in Wolfgang Beinert (ed.), *Maria heute ehren*, Freiburg 1977, pp. 263–79.

[86] *Glory*, I, pp. 561–66.

[87] Ibid., p. 564.

[88] Ibid., p. 338.

[89] Balthasar cites approvingly St Thomas' dictum 'consensus virginis loco totius humanae naturae' *S. Th.* II, q. 30, a. 1, c and the other Aquinate dictum concerning Mary's consent radiating (*redundans*) on all of human nature. See *Sponsa Verbi*, p. 170 and p. 334.

[90] See Hans Meuffels' work, *Einbergung des Menschen in das Mysterium der dreieinigen Leibe: eine trinitarische Antropologie nach Hans Urs von Balthasar*, Würzburg 1991.

of faith experience in which we can share. And it is the Holy Spirit, the personification of reciprocal Love in the Trinity, who links the past, present and future in our fundamentally Marian-ecclesial faith experience. The third divine person is the Spirit of God's objective revelation in Christ and also the Spirit of the objectivisation of the Christ-form in the form of the Church – her offices, charisms and sacraments – as well as the Spirit of the Marian-form of Christian subjectivity as faith, hope and love.[91]

Even in the fulfilment of the threefold unity found in the economy of salvation – God in himself, God coming to us and God in our midst[92] – the final *visio beatifica* will be no mere individualistic or formless achievement. The Book of Revelation indicates how the eschatological nuptial interpenetration between the Spirit-guided Jerusalem above descending to earth and Marian-formed earth ascending to heaven will be a cosmic hymn in unison to the glory of God. In this cosmic, collective vein, Balthasar writes that the world will be the end sacrament of the whole triune God revealed in the world of transfigured creation.[93] It will be Christ himself in us standing before the Father and, in us Christ will be in the Father.[94]

THE SACRAMENTALITY OF OUR FAITH JOURNEY

We live by faith in the dawning of divine I-Thou-We in the worldly and creaturely I-Thou-We of human fellowship.[95] The whole incarnational and sacramental structure of redemption and grace which imparts the trinitarian grace of Christ is oriented towards making us members of a Marian bridal people.[96] In the light of this and following the patristic tradition Balthasar maintains that faith can be experienced. But not in an experiential certainty deriving from *sola fides* nor in some vague sentimental manner. Taking the German word for experience *Erfahrung* which includes the notion of journey, Balthasar comes to a scriptural explanation of faith as the

---

[91]   *Glory*, I, pp. 195–96.
[92]   *Die Wahrheit ist symphonisch: Aspekte des christlichen Pluralismus*, Einsiedeln 1972, p. 56.
[93]   *New Elucidations*, San Francisco 1986, p. 103.
[94]   *Credo*, Edinburgh 1990, p. 41.
[95]   *Glory*, VII, p. 432.
[96]   Cf., *Sponsa Verbi*, Einsiedeln 1971, p. 162.

journey out of ourselves in striving forward towards the goal of
heaven. Being schooled in our faith we strive towards that which
belongs to the future but sharing already in the great eschatological
gift of the Spirit: joy.[97]

The journey of faith involves the whole person – intellect, will,
soul and body, all our senses. Along with Jean Mouroux,[98] Balthasar
sees the Christian experience as a progressive entrance of the believer
into the total reality of faith and the progressive realisation of this
reality. Seeing, hearing, touching must form part of the normal
faith-relationship with God. Echoing Irenaeus and other early
Fathers of the Church, Balthasar wants to avoid a gnostic-like
spiritualism which would want to by pass the senses in our journey
to God. Although the senses have to be healed because of the fall
Balthasar sees in Christ's institution of the sacraments the value of
the senses and the incarnational dynamism in the Christian life of
faith. The great sacrament in my journey to God is the *neighbour* for
whom Christ died.[99]

While recognising that the mystical charism has a particular mission
in the Church, Balthasar sees a certain unity between the mystical
experience and the ordinary faith experience of believers.[100] But mysticism should not be understood as a breaking beyond form to God's
essence. The senses can be mystical in our journey to God as evidenced
for example in the *Spiritual Exercises* of St Ignatius of Loyola. Above all
it is the Marian experience which shows us the mysticism of the ordinary
believer. Mary's motherhood in the flesh through her faith provides the
best image we have to vindicate the sensory aspect of faith. The glorious
form of Christ must be shaped in our whole being.

TOWARDS A REDISCOVERY OF THE AESTHETIC
DIMENSION IN CHRISTIAN LIFE AND
THEOLOGY

The main concern all along in Balthasar's theological aesthetics is to
bring about a rediscovery of the authentic contemplative aesthetic

---

[97] *Glory*, VII, p. 19.

[98] *L'Expérience chrétienne: Introduction à une Théologie*, Aubier 1952.

[99] See especially *Glory*, VII, pp. 432–84; *The God Question and Modern Man*,
New York 1967, pp. 142–55.

[100] See *Glory*, I, p. 300.

dimension so central to Christian life and theology in the patristic and medieval era, and which has been lost in both Protestant and Catholic traditions.[101] The Reformation and the consequent modern philosophy have given prominence to the word, the concept, the idea rather than the sight, rapture, beauty. To concentrate only on the Word and blind obedience in some form of dialectical theology seems unbiblical to Balthasar. But Herder and the whole of Romanticism gave rise to what Balthasar considers too aesthetic a theology. Since Matthias Scheeben there has been a move away from that towards something more refined and credible as a theological aesthetics.

Balthasar points to people like E. W. Gulin, Johannes Weiss, Karl Barth and Dietrich Bonhoeffer as representatives in Protestant theology who proffer pathways back from Luther and Kierkegaard to a rediscovery of the authentic dimension of beauty in the New Testament. In one of his letters from prison Bonhoeffer wrote:

> Perhaps – it almost seems so, today – it is only the concept of the *church* that will be the source of the rediscovery of the free space for the freedom of art, education, friendship, and play; so that one should not banish the 'aesthetic existence' (Kierkegaard) from the realm of the church, but precisely give it new foundation *in* the Church?[102]

To give this new foundation by returning to the origins in divine revelation in order then to trace out rays of its glorious form is what Balthasar aimed to do. Along with Romano Guardini who introduced him to Kierkegaard, Balthasar believes in reform from the

---

[101] See Balthasar's introduction to *The Glory of the Lord* in *Glory*, I, pp. 17–127. In Balthasar's view the loss started in the Medieval period but has burgeoned in particular since the Reformation with its stress on the obediential Word dimension of revelation and the concomitant dialectical theology (*Deus sub contrario*) with its refutation of any shimmering of Neo-Platonic philosophy in Christianity. While the names of Luther and Kierkegaard are associated with the loss of theological aesthetic, Balthasar also faults some Catholics like François René de Chateaubriand and Alois Gügler who tried to offer apologetics in aesthetic categories. Their categories derive from Romanticism and the Romantic aesthetic theology with its love of biblical poetry, art and liturgical aestheticism.

[102] *Widerstand und Ergebung* (1951), p. 136 (letter of 23.1.1944). See *Glory*, VII, pp. 20–21.

origins.[103] He was convinced that giving the aesthetic a new foundation in the Church is an extremely important cultural project for
today especially since in German Idealism (especially Hegel) and its
sequel 'glory' has collapsed into the beauty of the world and has
ultimately become a prayerless self-glorification of the finite spirit
taking control of everything.[104]

A primary task for Christians today therefore is to be the
responsible guardians of glory. In descending to the heart of the
biblical glory of the incarnate God who gives the Spirit,[105] the
guardians of glory can accomplish and exemplify in their lives the
inalienable experience of Being. Accordingly, as well as offering the
biblical glory, Christians can offer to the world the metaphysical
depth of being, once thought lost and now again drawn forth from
scriptural revelation.

The experience of glory must be lived, thought through and
formulated for our time anew. It is in this sense that Balthasar
repeatedly contends that the Church's life, above all the mutual love
of Christians, should be a source of hope to the world.[106] And all to
God's greater glory because their mutual love is a theophanous source
of light in which others will see Light. Through their reciprocal love
the glory of the God-among-us can shine forth in that the inner form
of Christian love is the crucified dying to oneself for love of one's
neighbour. What radiates therefore in mutual love is the glorious
crucified form of trinitarian love, disclosing the meaning of Being.
God's demonstration of his glory is always necessarily answered by
glorification (doxology) of God.[107] It is the glorification of God's glory
in the liturgy of life.[108] Accordingly, Christian mutual love is an act of
praising God not as an external praise; it has also an inherent
relationship to the essential glory of God.[109]

---

[103] See Balthasar's work on Guardini, *Romano Guardini: Reform aus dem
Ursrpung*, Munich 1970.

[104] *Glory*, IV, p. 643.

[105] *Glory*, VI, p. 23. See Andrew Louth, 'The Place of *Heart of the World* in the
Theology of Hans Urs von Balthasar', in John Riches (ed.), *The Analogy of Beauty*,
pp. 147–63.

[106] See *Love Alone: the Way of Revelation*, London 1968; 'Love as Custodian of
Glory', in *Glory*, V, pp. 635–56.

[107] *Glory*, VI, p. 24.

[108] *Glory*, VI, p. 25.

[109] *Glory*, VII, pp. 389–484, especially p. 399.

If this experience deriving ultimately from the momentum of the glory of divine love as experienced in the reciprocity of Christ and the Church is reflected upon as theology, then the *kabod* moves methodologically also into the midpoint of theology.[110] In Balthasar's vision all dogmas are only aspects of the one, indivisible, good and beautiful truth of God.[111] A theologian must keep his or her eye on the surpassing brightness, where the glory flares out.[112] In order to do so the 'locus' for theology in Balthasar's view is within the ecclesial-bridal encounter between the divine and human which centred on the Cross. In theology one enters into a creative fructification by a divine 'light' which cannot be self-constructed. It is given as gift but within the sphere of cruciform reciprocal love.

Theology is a self-surrender to the glorious form and within its light or radiance unfolding the mysteries of faith. What emerges from the theological aesthetics is that the *Fides quaerens Intellectum* is a contemplative, receptive, opening to and entering into the mystery of the Godhead through the Word-light as form perceived, entered into and incarnated. The *Intellectus quaerens Fidem* is the formative, creative aspect emerging from the Holy Spirit as *Spiritus Creator*, overshadowing the beholder with the new light which draws forth new forms in theology. It is no surprise that Balthasar tells us that theological and pastoral knowledge and understanding have been placed deep within the spiritual womb of feminine contemplation.[113]

Looking back over history, there have been many methodologies within this perspective. There have been many styles of the theological interpretation of God's glory. Some spoke more directly to one age than to another, some defunct have come to life again like Irenaeus', whereas some like Augustine's, Anselm's and Pascal's provide leaven for all ages.[114] If the whole of the form of Christ is constantly held in view, methodologies complement each other.[115]

---

[110] Cf. ibid., p. 113.

[111] Ibid., p. 243.

[112] Ibid., p. 18.

[113] *Sponsa Verbi*, p. 173.

[114] *Glory*, VI, p. 21.

[115] Balthasar maintains that after Thomas Aquinas theology became so specialised that few official clerical theologians were able any longer to treat the radiant power of the revelation of Christ (see *Glory*, II, pp. 11–17). Accordingly in his volume on what he calls 'lay styles' he turns to names such as Dante, Pascal, Péguy, Hopkins, Soloviev, Hamann and John of the Cross.

Greek symbolic theology, for instance, sees mainly the glowing centre-point of God's epiphany. Western theology, on the other hand, emphasises the various rays which provide paths leading to the midpoint.[116] But both are complementary.

Balthasar's theological aesthetics is a meeting point of complementarity between the past, present and future. Focus on the rays of glory was perhaps most evident for him in the writings of the Church Fathers. It has been suggested that tridentine theology attains its final, perhaps most beautiful expression in *The Glory of the Lord*.[117] But it has also been commented that through his attention to aesthetics Balthasar stands in many ways closer to current forms of critical theology than is generally recognised.[118] The theological aesthetics are evidently a creative point of dialogue. And this is where we can appreciate better why Bonaventure is clearly so important a model for Balthasar. In a marvellous article in the second volume of *The Glory of the Lord* Balthasar praises this theologian who not only spoke often of beauty but gave expression to his innermost experience of the beauty in divine revelation in new concepts that were his own.

Of all the great scholastics Bonaventure is seen as the one who offers the widest scope to the beautiful in his theology.[119] Immersed in the Great Tradition found in Augustine, Bernard, Anselm, Denys the Areopagite and even Joachim of Fiore, the disciple of Alexander of Hales' theology was born in the overpowering realm of rapture which opened up for the Church also in the Franciscan charism of poverty. All the main themes of Balthasar's theological aesthetics are found in Bonaventure. The Swiss theologian too is

---

[116] *Glory*, VII, p. 18.

[117] Louis Dupré, 'Hans Urs von Balthasar's Theology of Aesthetic Form', *Theological Studies* 49 (1988), pp. 299–318, especially p. 314.

[118] Leo O'Donovan, 'God's Glory in Time', *Communio* 2 (1975), pp. 250–69, especially 268. Jeffrey Kay notes a surprisingly close association of Balthasar with people like Jung, Ricoeur and Lonergan. He contends that possibly Balthasar's theological aesthetics and its attention to symbols will help to draw contemporary theology away from the temptation to settle down in Enlightenment hermeneutics at just the time when non-theological thought is making a second Copernican revolution into a post-critical hermeneutics. See his article, 'Hans Urs von Balthasar: A Post-Critical Theologian?', *Concilium* 141 (1981), pp. 84–89, especially p. 84.

[119] See *Glory*, II, pp. 260–362.

convinced that since theology is so united to the visible form of the incarnation it must not be just a purely theoretical speculation but rather an aesthetical experience. It must be open existentially, ecclesiologically, and meditatively. It is especially in experiencing, living and praying the mystery of the cross that we enter into the trinitarian mystery which is the glory of God. In the case of Bonaventure it was consideration of the stigmatisation of St Francis on Mt Alverna where the beauty of Wisdom appeared to Francis in the form of the crucified seraph that provided him with his nuptial and trinitarian theology.

The last word in a theological aesthetics concerning Christian life and theology is that with the crucified Christ we are transported in an ecstasy of love from this world to the Father.[120] But not in a world-escaping sense. From the glory of 'Tabor' we descend to give our contribution to the realisation of our Lord's prayer: 'that they may all be one, even as you, Father, are in me and I in you, that they also may be in us, so that the world may believe that you have sent me' (*John* 17: 21). Christians owe to the world the witness of mutual love in Christ as the only effective apologetics for the truth of Christianity.[121] Balthasar agrees with Bonaventure that only those who know and live the glorious trinitarian mystery are 'true metaphysicians'.[122]

CONCLUSION

We have attempted to introduce the theme of Balthasar's theological aesthetics. Various motifs running throughout his aesthetics have been mentioned with a view to drawing closer to what the 'whole' form of Christ means for theological aesthetics. In him crucified and forsaken radiates the glory of the Trinity and within a 'Christo-aesthetic' measure all worldly being can be read anew. Faith is perception of the form and transportation in rapture into the new Marian-ecclesial reality, the place today where Christ's radiance shines out.

Together with Adrienne von Speyr, Balthasar felt urged to bring the beauty of Christ, of the life of the Trinity, from the closed

---

[120] *Itinerarium mentis in Deum*, 7,6.
[121] *New Elucidations*, p. 100.
[122] *Glory*, II, p. 278.

convented worlds of consecrated environments out into the midst of the world. And this he did by the foundation of a secular institute, *Die Johannesgemeinschaft* (where the mutual love of Christians could be a divine-human beauty in the midst of the world having itself an evidential power to convince), an editing company (searching out those rays of glory wherever something original blossomed in history), and by translating from and dialoging with Spanish, French, Latin and Greek writers, thinkers and mystics who bore witness to the glorious radiance of the 'whole'. But it is his theological aesthetics which are clearly a major contribution to the Church in terms of intuitions, directions, and hints as we approach a new millennium and a new evangelisation.

Louis Dupré has pointed out that Balthasar provides an approach to theology that, though not entirely new has never been attempted in such a sustained, comprehensive manner.[123] A proverb from Kenya, however, says that 'no one head alone contains all the wisdom'. Balthasar would clearly recognise this:

> Our whole attempt to restore to theology the third dimension of glory – alongside the dimensions of the true and the good – must itself remain a fragment, and at best it can serve as a stimulus to do new homage to the incomprehensible mystery of divine love.[124]

Others have to take up and develop his project. He himself was certainly aware of the ecumenical dimension.[125] The dogmatics of the Orthodox, Evangelical and Catholic churches in each case has its centre in the concept of the *Gloria Dei*. Accordingly he maintained that a fruitful dialogue can only be carried out by starting from this common centre.[126] That remains to be done since, unfortunately, he never wrote the last volume of *The Glory of the Lord* which was intended to be an ecumenical one. Likewise he

---

[123] 'Hans Urs von Balthasar's Theology of Aesthetic Form', *Theological Studies* 49 (1988), pp. 299–318, especially p. 300. See also Thomas O'Meara, 'The Aesthetic Dimension in Theology', in Diane Apostolos-Cappadona (ed.), *Art, Creativity, and the Sacred*, New York 1988, pp. 205–18.

[124] *Glory*, VI, p. 27.

[125] *Glory*, IV, p. 17.

[126] Ibid., pp. 26–27.

wanted to consider Christian art and the relationship between the theologically beautiful and inner-worldly beauty as a question with regard to Christian art.[127] That too remains to be discovered in all its implications for Church expressions of life and not just artistic representations.

Hopefully, at the end of this chapter we have come to a clearer grasp of what it means to say Balthasar is a theologian of beauty. Perhaps we can conclude by attributing to Balthasar what Alexander Solzhenitsyn said about Dostoevsky:

> Could it be that the old trinity of Truth, Goodness and Beauty is not just a well-worn cliché to be trotted out on official occasions, as it appeared to us in the days of our conceited materialistic youth? If the tops of these trees merge, as the sages of old used to say, but the too obvious, too straight shoots of Truth and Goodness are choked, felled, suppressed – then may not perhaps the fantastic, unpredictable, unexpected shoots of Beauty fight their way through and soar up *to the same place*, and thus achieve the task of all three?
>
> And in that case will not Dostoevsky's words 'the world will be saved by beauty', turn out to be no slip of the tongue, but a prophecy. For *he* was granted extraordinary vision, he was amazingly inspired.[128]

Yes, Balthasar would only add that the inspiration will come from the theological trinitarian beauty radiating from the risen, crucified and forsaken Christ.

---

[127] Ibid., p. 27.
[128] Alexander Solzhenitsyn, *'One Word of Truth': The Nobel Speech on Literature, 1970*, London 1972, pp. 6–7.

3

THE BIBLICAL BASIS OF GLORY

John Riches

In the Preface to his Latin Writings, published in 1545,[1] Luther describes the painful route by which he came to know God, no longer as a terrifying and avenging God, but as a God of mercy and grace. The stages along that route are marked out by his own lectures on different books of the Bible, first the Psalms and then Galatians and Romans. As is well known he records how it was the verse: 'In it the righteousness of God is revealed' (*Romans* 1: 17) which caused him great anguish, for he understood it, as he had been taught by the schoolmen, to refer to the formal or active righteousness of God, that is to say righteousness considered as a characteristic of God himself and his actions *ad extra*. On such a view, the Gospel merely added to the terror which the law of the Old Testament already struck into his heart. Was it not enough that the law should bring home to sinful men and women the enormity of their failings and the inevitability of God's wrath which they occasioned, without the gospel reinforcing this by publishing again the righteous nature of God? But Luther did not abandon the struggle. If he hated the God which such an interpretation of Paul presented him with, he was the more determined to discover what it was that the Apostle had intended by those words, specifically by his use of the genitive *theou* in that clause. It was, says Luther, eventually from paying attention to the context of those words that illumination came. It was Paul's reference to Habakkuk, 'He who through faith is righteous shall live' that showed him that Paul was using the genitive to refer, not

[1] In J. Dillenberger (ed.), *Martin Luther: Selections from his Writings*, New York 1961, pp. 3–12.

to the righteousness by which God himself is righteous, but rather to the 'righteousness with which merciful God justifies us by faith,', the gift of righteousness which he bestows out of his mercy. Now, that is to say, he understood the genitive as referring not to the formal or active righteousness of God, but, in the schoolmen's phraseology, the passive righteousness. It was this strictly grammatical insight which brought release and joy to Luther: it was for him 'the gates of paradise'. Immediately from memory he ran through the writings of Paul, re-construing the genitives: 'the work of God, that is, what God does in us, the power of God, with which he makes us strong, the wisdom of God, with which he makes us wise',[2] like indeed an explorer who at long last reaches his goal and runs delightedly about, simply savouring the strange, new world which he has at long last entered.

This account of the work of the biblical theologian, for that is what it is, has been enormously influential. It is not difficult to trace its reception in our century both by Barth and by Bultmann. But it is perhaps useful to draw out certain features of this account, which whatever its historical accuracy, has informed the practice of biblical and exegetical theology.

For Luther, we have seen, it is the search for Paul's intention which ultimately governs his search for the 'plain meaning' of the text. The 'plain' meaning of the text is not something that is necessarily lightly won; it may be discovered, at least on occasion, only by stripping away inherited readings of the text which obscure the original intention of the author. Nevertheless, for Luther the 'original meaning', or, at least, the new reading which he wished to offer, was still something which emerged out of his own vigorous debates with traditional, received understandings of the text. However much he may wish to set aside Mediaeval readings of the text, he is also eager to show his continuity with Augustine. Nevertheless it is clear that for Luther, the struggle for Paul's intended sense was conducted with the full resources of humanist philology. The central religious experience of the Protestant Reformation was a 'grammatical' experience, and this has been reflected in the extraordinary treasury of biblical scholarship which the Lutheran tradition has given to the world. (This by way of corrective to the currently modish attacks on 'Lutheran' interpretations of everything.) But, it is important to notice that Luther's wrestling with the sense of Romans 1: 17 is not an isolated phenomenon; it is part of his sustained attempt to read the Scriptures, of which his work on the Psalms, and importantly here, his understanding of Paul's use of the Old Testament are integral parts. He is a biblical theologian, interested in the meaning of the Bible (singular!) for all his focus on the original intention of particular writers. This will set up a tension between the sense of particular utterances in particular books and the sense of the whole, a tension which Luther will tackle in his own vigorous way, but which will leave a difficult legacy for those who follow him.

Of course this picture of the work of the biblical scholar is only one among many, however influential it has been. It presents us above all with the story of the achievement of a major shift in cultural perspective. It marked the birth of a new world. But if Luther had opened the gates of paradise, he was arguably less effective in describing the territory which lay within. Indeed the metaphor is misleading; Luther did not so much discover a new world simply for the entering and enjoying. He discovered new concepts which would enable him and those who worked with him on the biblical texts to create new worlds, some of which would seem strange even to Luther himself. The work of other Reformers, notably of John Calvin, would then lie more in elaborating the ground rules of this new world, than in describing what Luther has discovered. But, and this is of the greatest significance, this was not how they or indeed others after them would see it. They saw themselves precisely as discovering the kind of world that God had – always – intended and indeed had communicated effectively through the biblical writings. (Hence for Luther the importance of the 'plain' meaning of Scripture and his insistence on 'what stands written'). This explains both the Reformers' passionate attachment to the original intention of the author and the bitter conflicts which arose between rival Reformation groups as they discovered how different were the worlds which they severally delineated. How could paradise be divided?

I raise all this by way of introduction to a discussion of the interestingly different kind of biblical theology which is offered by Hans Urs von Balthasar's concluding two volumes of *The Glory of the Lord*. Appearing in German first at the end of the sixties,[3] it has

---

[3]   *Herrlichkeit. Eine theologische ästhetik*, Bd. III, p. 2, *Theologie*, Teil I, *Alter Bund*, Einsiedeln 1967; Teil II, *Neuer Bund*, Einsiedeln 1969.

so far made little impression on the scholarly world, despite the glaringly obvious lack of any serious successors to Bultmann's *New Testament Theology*[4] of 1948. Nevertheless there are I believe ways in which this most idiosyncratic of biblical theologians may contribute to the present revival of interest in the enterprise of biblical theology and these are related partly to his determination to reinstate aesthetics in theology, partly to his willingness to see biblical theology as an enterprise which is necessarily engaged in dialogue with the theological tradition. As his work is far from familiar, even to those with an interest in theology and aesthetics, let me begin with a brief introduction to the present two volumes.

It is Balthasar's contention that theology, both Protestant and Catholic, has since the Reformation steadily turned away from aesthetics, conceiving God that is to say principally as good and true, only secondarily and infrequently as beautiful, the fulfilment of human desires.[5] In so doing, it has turned its back on central aspects of the Bible and the tradition: the sense of beauty and glory which pervades the Psalms, the prophets and the Patriarchal narratives; the confession of the strange and wholly unprecedented glory of the crucified and risen Lord, which is to be found in measure at least in Paul and the Synoptics, most clearly in the theological vision of the Fourth Gospel. Such a sense of beauty did indeed find a place in the great works of the theological tradition, as Balthasar has impressively shown in the first volume of his *Studies in Theological Style*.[6] But in the later stages of theological history, it is the lay theologians, the poets, philosophers and playwrights who have kept the vision alive: Dante, Pascal, Hopkins, Soloviev, Péguy and others. Among modern theologians of stature it is only Karl Barth who has devoted time and attention to it, and it is, among his contemporaries, from Karl Barth that Balthasar has learnt most.[7]

To speak of the aesthetic dimension is to focus on the manner in which an object appears and, correspondingly, on the manner in which it is sighted. Beauty,[8] to Balthasar, is intimately related to

---

[4]   English edition, London 1955.
[5]   See e.g. *The Glory of the Lord*, I, passim.
[6]   *The Glory of the Lord*, II, 1984.
[7]   Cf. above all in his *Karl Barth. Deutung und Darstellung seiner Theologie*, Cologne 1951.
[8]   The matter is most fully discussed in *The Glory of the Lord*, I, 1982.

form. The artist's vision of beauty cannot be separated from the figure in and through which it is expressed. There are no external criteria which can be brought to judge the beauty of a work of art: the work must have its own *Evidenz* (evidential force), confronting the beholder, as it does, with its sheer otherness, its irreducibility. But, paradoxically, such radiance will only be grasped by those who have eyes to see, who have been to school with the works of the great artists and learnt to read the figure, the *Gestalt* of a work of art, its measure and proportions. The 'truth' that is to say of a work of art lies in its rightness, the fact that the Jupiter Symphony could not be otherwise, is perfect as it is; and it is in this that its power to delight and restore lies. But such truth is not for all; it is only those who have been caught by such beauty, have had their eyes opened, have 'the eyes of faith' who in fact see, who are filled.

Such talk of beauty and form may indeed seem a far cry from modern theology. To many it will sound strangely frivolous, diverting attention alike from the pressing moral issues of world poverty and injustice and the intellectual challenges which have been forced on Christian theology by the development of the sciences. But it is precisely Balthasar's contention that beauty is one of the fundamental determinations of Being, that the aesthetic vision is a vision of reality, of the way things are. It is not therefore an optional aspect of theology; it is essential if we are not to lose sight of Being altogether. Without it, theology may degenerate into a chilly, over-serious moralism; while metaphysics, divorced from its fundamental sense of wonder will cease to command attention at all. Being is in risk of being forgotten altogether. And in his two volumes on *The Realm of Metaphysics*,[9] he has attempted to show, with enormous erudition, how the myth makers and poets and philosophers have caught sight of Being, have themselves been possessed by a vision of the terrible beauty of the gods, of ultimate reality, which they have expressed in the rich treasury of Antiquity and its modern mediations.

And it was at this point that Balthasar had to meet the sharpest opposition from his mentor and friend, Karl Barth. If we press the analogy between the poetic, mythical vision of Being and the glory of God which is sighted in the Bible are we not in danger of reducing

---

[9]   *The Glory of the Lord*, IV & V, 1989, 1990.

the revelation of the divine Word to a mode or variation of human apprehensions of reality, confusing the work of men and women with the work of God? Certainly it was this anxiety which had earlier led Karl Barth to claim that the doctrine of *analogia entis* was the work of the Anti-Christ and the only serious reason for not becoming a Catholic.[10] Nor were Balthasar's subsequent attempts to dissuade him by any means successful.[11]

Thus in approaching Balthasar's final two volumes of *The Glory of the Lord* we must be at least aware of forces which pull at him in different directions. On the one hand his whole enterprise is concerned with re-instating aesthetics to its proper place within theology. And this means being alive to the analogies between expressions of the divine glory in the Bible and works of the poets and myth makers of ancient Greece and Rome, with all the attention which they gave to form and proportion. On the other he has been put on his mettle to show that what is indeed perceived in the Bible is *totaliter aliter*, a vision where the dissimilarities to the visions of Antiquity are always immeasurably greater than the similarities.

Balthasar is at some pains to insist that his study of glory in the Old and New Testaments is in no way an attempt at providing a complete biblical theology. In some ways indeed it is more like his earlier studies of theological styles, where he was attempting to show the place that aesthetics occupied in the tradition before its deposition, at least from the official schools. Thus in the Old Testament volume we are treated to a series of studies of the portrayal of the divine glory, from its almost physical manifestations in the Patriarchal narratives through to the visions of future appearances in the apocalyptic seers. Such portrayals are properly speaking aesthetic not least because they present the glory, the weight and majesty of God, as perceived through sight: whether it be the seeing of the physical events of the burning bush, Isaiah's vision in the Temple, Ezekiel's vision of the chariot, or the apocalyptic seers' visions of the future appearing of the Almighty. There are elements in the Old Testament, constitutive elements indeed, whose similarities to the world of the Greek myths, of Homer and Pindar, or indeed to later

[10] *Church Dogmatics*, I/1, *Xf.* Edinburgh 1975, p. xiii.
[11] Cf. Balthasar's remarks in the preface to the second edition of *Karl Barth*, Cologne 1962, which Barth was by no means happy to accept.

Jewish traditions of Zohar mysticism are not to be denied, but which are fastidiously avoided by a Christianity purged of mysticism, where faith is schematised in terms of obedience to a prophetic word conceived of primarily in moral terms. Balthasar does not, for all that, overlook the powerfully moral dimension of the vision of God's *zedekah* in the Old Testament. Such visions spring out of the covenant between God and his people, a relationship which guides and governs the whole life of the people and is therefore in the deepest sense moral. And in this covenant there is seen something of that loving condescension by which God binds himself to his people, risking as it were his own glory by linking his name with a people who may betray and dishonour him. And yet the people of the covenant is intended precisely to show forth his glory to all the nations, to be holy as he is holy. And such holiness lies in faithfulness to the divine will and law.

But of course those who read the Old Testament from the viewpoint of the New conceive of it as only part of the story of the manifestation of God's glory. For Balthasar the question of the relationship of the two covenants is posed in terms of form and fulfilment, as indeed in the theology of Irenaeus. God's glory is perceived in and through the particular *Gestalt* which is constituted by the relationship of the two covenants. Already in the later books of the Old Testament the vision of God's glory becomes fragmented; there is a loss of the sense of the reality of the covenant, a looking to something which is yet to come. And this sense of fragmentedness, of the questionableness of existence in the face of death is brought even more sharply to expression in subsequent apocalyptic literature. So the fulfilment is not achieved by a process of steady development to a final climax: rather there is a sharp break between the two covenants, a caesura which could in no sense have been anticipated. The Word of God himself enters history in order to restore the broken relationships between God and his people. And such a coming involves both judgment and restoration; the breaking of relationships and their refashioning, the emergence of a new covenant where the Son unites in himself the unconditional love of God and the response of restored humanity, the birth of a new world in which people can live anew in praise of his glory.

It is then this central event of the Word becoming flesh which holds the two covenants together, by way of on the one hand anticipation and on the other, response, witness. This is reflected clearly in the design of Balthasar's second volume. If the first volume presented an account of the developing – and fragmenting – vision of God's glory in the old covenant largely by following the order of the Old Testament Writings, the second can no longer sustain the design. What is abandoned is not so much the salvation historical schema. The caesura must be marked, and marked in its due place. But it cannot be grasped simply in terms of the subsequent New Testament accounts of the glory of God in Christ: these are reserved for the second and third parts of the volume. Before them Balthasar sets a section which he entitles indeed *Verbum Caro Factum,*[12] but which is in no sense a straight interpretation of Johannine theology. It is rather his own creative attempt to point to the central reality which as it were holds together the two covenants. It is the centre to which the old covenant, almost unwittingly leads up; it is that which is reflected on, worked out, brought to expression (*ausgewortet*) in all subsequent biblical theologies, whether those of the New Testament itself, or in later theologies which continue the process begun in those writings.

Thus for Balthasar the New Testament writings are not the ending of the Old Testament, which without them would be incomplete, lacking a fitting 'closure'; rather in the word-less death of the Word made flesh, the glory of the Old Testament is gathered up, recapitulated in such a way that it can then flow out in the fulfilment of the New. The New Testament is not the last chapter in the Old: it marks the beginning of the new world which springs from the divine kenosis of the Son. And the fullness which is imparted is not 'given by measure': it is the inexhaustible glory of the divine self-giving which is only properly reflected in the multiplicity of the New Testament witnesses and of subsequent biblical theologies.

The first part of the volume, in which Balthasar addresses himself to the event of the incarnation is not, it has to be said, in any way easy to characterise. In one obvious sense he is attempting to describe theologically the coming of the Word. In this he starts by relating its coming to that which has gone before, to the 'fragments of the old covenant', to the figure of the Baptist.[13] This is followed

[12]   The Glory of the Lord, VII, pp. 33–235.
[13]   Ibid., pp. 33–76.

by some illuminating theological reflection on the nature of biblical
theology, to which we shall return, by a section entitled simply
'Word-Flesh'.[14] It is in effect a theological account of the life of Jesus
which presents it under the three heads of claim (*Anspruch*), poverty,
and self-abandonment, portraying the progress of the authoritative
Word into increasing powerlessness and abandonment. There
follows again a more generally reflective section, this time on the
theology of time and salvation history,[15] which contains surely one
of the most original discussions of eschatology, drawing out with
great sensitivity the implications of the different stances of Dodd,
Bultmann, Cullmann and others. And then in a final section,
entitled 'The Momentum of the Cross' (*Wucht des Kreuzes*[16]) the
final confrontation with the godlessness of the world is reached, and
we are offered a concluding meditation on the kenosis of the eternal
Son, his taking upon himself the 'concrete human destiny'[17] which
is wholly opposed to God, to life, to the very nature of the Word
himself. The Word becomes word-less; he who was eternally related
to the Father enters the God-forsakenness of hell.[18]

Of course a mere sketch of the contents of this section can hardly
indicate the way in which the outline is filled out. Reading Balthasar
is often like reading Thomas Mann at his most allusive, say in *Doktor
Faustus*. He is a man so deeply engaged in dialogue with the
metaphysical tradition, the theological tradition, recent biblical
scholarship, literature and drama, with those sympathetic to him
and those whom he passionately opposes, that only the closest
reading of his text will do justice to it. And that is the first point to
notice. For him the biblical texts feed naturally into the theological
tradition, are at least analogically related to the metaphysical tradition and the traditions of European letters in such a way that a
dialogue between them is in principle possible and to be expected.
And this distances his work immediately from so much that stems
from the Protestant rejection of metaphysics (notably I suppose by
Ritschl) and the consequent attempt to set biblical theology up as an

---

[14] Ibid., pp. 15–161.
[15] Ibid., pp. 162–201.
[16] Ibid.,pp. 202–35.
[17] Ibid., p. 212.
[18] Ibid., pp. 228–35.

alternative and epistemologically distinct mode of discourse about God, one where indeed the moral would have the primacy over the metaphysical and the aesthetic. For Balthasar it is a fundamental assumption that the biblical texts do address themselves to the perennial questions of the mystery of the universe, of the existence of evil, error and suffering, of the root of evil within the human will and the manner of its overcoming, of justice, restitution, judgment and mercy, and that they can do so in a way that is at least analogous to that of the people, the mythmakers and even the philosophers.

And belief in the possibility of such dialogue with the theological and metaphysical tradition also of course sharply separates him from those for whom the 'cultural gap' between our appropriations of the biblical traditions and the writings of the New Testament themselves is so great that a complete shedding of our own cultural skin would be necessary before we could adequately begin to apprehend their meaning. Not that Balthasar seriously considers such objections: for him the validity of his own position must lie in the fruitfulness of his method, his ability to draw illumination from his continuing dialogue.

But what indeed of the content of this first part of the volume? Where indeed does it come from? How does it relate to other attempts at a biblical theology? The section 'Word-flesh' has a particular interest. It draws on theses from (then) recent discussions of the historical Jesus (the so-called 'New Quest') and yet clearly weaves them into a schema of his own devising, for all that its elements are individually drawn from the Bible. Thus the section on Jesus' claim[19] draws freely on work by Bornkamm, Käsemann, Fuchs and Schweizer. The claims to authority which Jesus makes in the antitheses on the Sermon on the Mount and his ability to see into people's hearts are taken as at least indirect confirmation of the church's confession of him as eschatological Word and Judge. That is to say, like the theologians of the New Quest (and like more recently R. Morgan), Balthasar is ready to allow faith's understanding of the Word to be filled out, deepened by historical critical enquiry into the biblical traditions. Like them too he is unwilling to take his overall schema from such enquiries, arguing that proper understanding is only possible from the perspective of faith. Where

---

[19] Ibid., pp. 115–29.

however they differ is in the way that they would each explicate the phrase 'faith's understanding of the Word'. For Bornkamm, Käsemann and Fuchs faith is to be understood primarily in (Lutheran) terms of obedience to the Word of the kerygma, that is to say the proclamation of the gospel. It is a willing acceptance of the call to decision, an abandonment of one's attempts to find a meaning for, to justify one's own life, and a thankful acceptance of the new life which flows from the gospel. Thus faith knows the Word primarily as 'address' (*Anrede*), that which judges, challenges human pretensions and restores men and women to a life lived out in trust in God. In this of course the mythological language of final judgment is abandoned in favour of an anthropological (existential) account of the effect of the Word on those who hear. Judgment is present now in the words of Jesus, as it is present in the proclamation of the Church.

It would be easy to misunderstand what Balthasar has to say at this point as simply a re-affirmation of traditional mythological eschatology over against the existential interpretation of Bultmann and his followers. It is undeniable that he wants to hold on to the eschatological language of future judgment but equally clear that he does not want to do so in any simple, literalist sense. He quotes with approval Marxsen's dictum that such 'implicit' christology always expresses more than any so-called explicit christology, 'because the momentum of this claim can never be equalled by any formulation of it in words'.[20] He wants to give due weight to both present and future eschatology and not to resolve that tension by reducing judgment to an event within the lives of believers. All this, as the later discussion of the momentum of time will make clearer, because for him the coming of the Word is an event in history which gives meaning to history as a whole, which answers the fundamental mystery of the world's ills, and which cannot therefore properly be reduced to particular historical events, however much it may have concrete implications, may bear fruit in the lives of believers. And for that reason too the 'story' of the coming of the Word cannot be exhausted by discussion of the claims which he makes but must press on to explore the paradox of the Word made flesh, of his being stripped of his power and freedom as he freely accepts his deliverance

---

[20] Ibid., p. 121.

into the hands of wicked men, into the grip of the powers of darkness, that the divine will for the world may be done.

This brings us to the final section of the first part, 'The Momentum of the Cross'. Here most obviously, Balthasar is in dialogue with the theological tradition. But again it might be said with some justice that it is a dialogue which is at the least idiosyncratic, choosing with whom he will engage, laying his emphases where he will. His christology draws heavily on the quite recent tradition of kenotic christology, and develops it in creative and imaginative ways. The final section without question is deeply indebted to Adrienne von Speyr's visions of the descent into hell which she received regularly on Holy Saturday and which have had a profound effect on Balthasar's theology.[21] For it is in the descent into hell that Balthasar sees revealed the mystery of the Trinity and in it too that he finds the only possible answer to the ultimate riddle of how a loving, sovereign God could allow the misery and suffering and evil which inflicts our world.

All of this may indeed seem a very long way from sober exegesis of the biblical texts and is certainly quite without precedent in recent works of biblical theology. Is there anything that we can learn from it? It may help first to bring out some of the dissimilarities and perhaps surprising similarities between von Balthasar's work here and the kind of biblical theology which we described at the beginning of this essay. At the very simplest level both Luther and he are seeking a comprehensive understanding of Scripture which will enable them to live out of the Christian tradition which has become ossified and restrictive, even oppressive. (It is important to recall that Balthasar's early work was the subject of much official criticism, and that even though he may have come to be regarded as a conservative, the foundations for his major work were laid when he was active among those who were working to break down the defensive bastions of the church.) More, both men write with quite specific theological, moral problems in mind: Luther the terrible moral anguish which was caused by the Babylonian captivity of the Church; Balthasar deeply wounded by the breakdown of European civilisation and the appalling atrocities with which that was accompanied, possessed almost by a sense of pervasive evil in the world.

[21] See Balthasar's account in *First Glance at Adrienne von Speyr*, San Francisco 1981.

There is no doubt of the ultimate seriousness of Balthasar's writing at this point, nor of the way in which Adrienne's terrifying visions of hell inform his treatment of christology and soteriology. But the comparison with Luther raises a key question. Luther's account focused on the interpretation of biblical statements about God's justice. His struggle to discover Paul's intended meaning in such passages provided him with a key which would successfully unlock a wide range of passages and show him Scripture in a new light. By contrast Balthasar brings to the text a set of powerful religious experiences (Adrienne von Speyr's visions of Holy Saturday) and uses them as the key to the understanding of central passages about the incarnation and passion, indeed as a guide to that central mystery of the Word become flesh which the Biblical texts themselves witness to and reflect on. Yet it can hardly be said that the *descensus* motif (unlike, arguably at least, Paul's treatment of justification) plays a central part in the New Testament, even if it might be said that it serves to point to a gap in the admittedly quite schematic Christian narrative of salvation, one which Balthasar fills out with great virtuosity.

How illuminating is this contrast between an historical, grammatical search for Paul's intended sense and a virtuoso performance of the text by Balthasar, redolent as it is of discussions which have developed within theological circles only since the publication of the present volumes? On the one hand it does I think represent quite accurately the sense in which Balthasar sees himself doing biblical theology, namely as an extension of the reflection on the *verbum caro factum* of which the New Testament books are the font and also prime exemplars.[22] In that sense his theology is indeed a performance of those texts with their quite specific referents in the life, death and resurrection of Jesus, however elusive any account of that might be. On the other hand, to press the contrast between 'performance' and the search for the original meaning of the texts too far would be mistaken. For Balthasar it is clearly vital that any reading that he offers should be guided by, certainly should not conflict with the

---

[22] Ibid., pp. 103–14: 'theology in the Bible can have no fundamentally different form from later theology in the Church: each is an interpretative act of standing and circling around a mid-point that can indeed be interpreted, but is always in need of interpretation and *has never been exhaustively interpreted*', p. 103, my italics.

central claims made by those texts, precisely because they do refer to a central mystery, are not simply meaningful in and of themselves. But, and this again distinguishes his position from much recent Protestant biblical theology, he would not claim that the biblical texts give either a uniform, or indeed any exhaustive account of that to which they refer. Central though their witness is, they are always to be seen as mediating, through their various 'theologies' the central, inexhaustible and always greater glory of the wordless Word. And that mediation comes precisely as those texts interact with the life of the various communities which accord them authority, a hearing. What indeed Balthasar brings to their interpretation from Adrienne is not a purely extraneous set of theological ideas and visions, but ones which have grown immediately out of her extraordinarily intense meditations on the *Triduum Mortis* and which provide a link with the torn and bitter experience of the present century.

This may perhaps also help to pave the way out of a dilemma to which I alluded in the introduction. Luther suggests that his discovery of Paul's meaning in *Romans* 1: 17 had unlocked the gates to paradise, giving him a key to the whole meaning of Scripture and therefore allowing him to discover the divine will and purposes. But of course the Reformers who followed him gave very diverse accounts of the new world whose gates Luther had unlocked. One way of describing what had happened here would be to say that what Luther had done was to grasp certain concepts which would become the basis for a new family of Christian communities, rather than for a single church. Such concepts, that is to say, function as means for constructing new social worlds. And clearly there is truth in such an account and it enables us to discern the unity and diversity between the different historical communities which have taken their lead from Protestant biblical scholarship.

On the other hand such a view may seem to give a rather minimal account of the unity of such bodies, and to fail indeed to deal adequately with the question how far such common basic concepts, together with their diverse elaborations, refer to the divine will and purposes (which they were certainly held to do). What Balthasar's emphasis on the inexhaustibility and transcendence of the *verbum caro factum* does is to point to the ground of the unity of such diversity in the referent itself to which our concepts and their elaborations can only ever approximate. In this sense Balthasar's biblical theology (sometimes, it has to be said, somewhat *malgré lui*) provides a fruitful basis for an ecumenical theology – one which arguably is more satisfactory than Luther's search for the plain meaning.

One further point of comparison may be made and referred to contemporary debates. Luther's study of Paul was rooted in a wider search for the meaning of the whole of Scripture. At the same time his emphasis on the *pro me*, the sense in which scriptural terms and concepts were to be understood in the light of a specific experience of divine judgment and grace became itself a critical instrument by which the Bible itself could be judged and passages which were found wanting could be relegated to the margins or indeed dismissed from the canon altogether. Balthasar's theology allows for a far greater diversity in the biblical visions of God's glory, and allots such diversity, fragmentedness, a place within the overall *Gestalt*. Such an enterprise with its emphasis on the overall *Gestalt* might be thought however to be vulnerable to another charge, namely of imposing on the openness of the Hebrew Bible a closure, which it precisely and characteristically lacks. Such charges have been made against the Christian Bible and indeed much recent exegesis by Gabriel Josipovici,[23] who argues strongly for the radical openness, the resistance to any schema of fulfilment, of the Hebrew Bible, specifically of its narratives.

Perhaps enough has been said to show how far Balthasar's theology might be thought to be vulnerable to such a charge. Clearly there is a sense in which he claims that the revelation of the Word made flesh is a final revelation of God's glory which therefore surpasses all other manifestations. But he is firstly at great pains not to suggest that there is a simple relationship of promise and fulfilment between Old and New Testaments. The manner in which the Word made flesh fulfills the visions of God's glory in the Old Covenant is wholly unexpected, outstripping all that might have been imagined. Above all it occurs in an event which is wordless and which only subsequently liberates the images of the Old Testament to give expression to what is achieved in that event: the overcoming of death, the bounds of mortality:

---

[23]   *The Book of God*, Yale 1988.

That which is Christian is anthropologically significant (in relation, that is, to what is already given in Israel), or it is nothing at all. It solves the unbearable contradiction that runs right through the very form of man: that he, knowing and touching what is immortal, yet dies; if it does not solve this, then it solves nothing at all. Therefore its truth does not lie primarily on the level of what may be looked at, the comparison between the form of the promise and the form of the fulfilment, but on the level of an invisible collision of the absolute weight of God with what is other, with that which has nothing in common with God. Only when this inconceivable event takes place, is the world of images liberated – what the old covenant still owes us, is possible only on the basis of what is unimaginable, so that the images … which surrounded the unconstructible midpoint, and which could not bring themselves together to make a credible whole form, suddenly crystallise and become thereby comprehensible both in themselves (as images of the Old Testament) and in their transcendence to the New Testament unity that gives them meaning.[24]

The figure of the crucified, dead Christ is a wholly strange figure of glory which – precisely as wordless – defies exhaustive interpretation. This is not closure in the sense of bringing the movement of the Old Testament to a term, giving it a rounded meaning in virtue of its conclusion in Christ. It is a radically new beginning which can nevertheless be seen to have its roots in the 'fragments' of the Old Testament as they are drawn together and 'handed over' in the figure of the Baptist. Moreover, the sense in which this vision of the glory of the incarnate Word 'fulfils' is also resistant to the notion of closure, if by that is meant the setting of a limit to the possibilities of human existence and, indeed, knowledge. This is clear in Balthasar's insistence on understanding fulfilment as something which inaugurates a new life of inexhaustible richness lived out of the contemplation of the divine glory: *in laudem gloriae*. It is also importantly to be seen in his treatment of Christian universalism,[25] where he stressed the continuing struggle between God in Christ and men and women in an *Agonie* which is genuine only because of its open outcome.

It is unlikely that any one will follow Balthasar slavishly in the development of a biblical theology. Nor would he have wished it. What he has given us may, however, be a constant source of disturbance. He reminds us of the rootedness of the biblical texts in the deep and fundamental questions of human existence – and in the articulations of those questions in myth and philosophy. He reminds us of the centrality to the Christian Bible of an *event,* that which can only subsequently be expressed in words and which by its very nature as it crosses the boundaries between death and life can never be fully grasped in human language. He sets the task of biblical interpretation firmly back into the long tradition of biblical theology, asserting in his own way the predominance of 'literary' readings of the texts over purely historical critical ones, and allowing those readings to be deeply informed both by the reader's own apprehensions of the human predicament and by the 'eyes of faith'. And he underlines the inexhaustibility of the glory and transcendence of God in the Old and New Covenants which holds out its own promise and spurns all attempts at systematisation and reduction. It is an invitation to explore the 'strange new world of the Bible' which from the start encourages us to expect richness and variety, as the divine glory bears fruit in the lives of its beholders.

4

THE FATHERS: THE CHURCH'S INTIMATE, YOUTHFUL DIARY

Deirdre Carabine

Epiphanius relates that Origen wrote more than 6,000 volumes; Jerome supports this claim, adding, perhaps with some measure of despair, that Origen wrote more than any individual could ever read! Balthasar is, in this sense at least, following in the footsteps of the Patristic author with whom he felt most at home. He began theology with Origen – whom he regarded as more important than Augustine[1] – and it was his Origen anthology, *Geist und Feuer*, which gave him most joy.[2] Balthasar's preoccupation with Origen and the whole tradition of Origenism is evident even in his mature works; one reason he gives is that in attaching such importance to the resurrection and ascension, Origen's theology is not one-sided, but 'simply a real theology'.[3] Of the man who was condemned by Justinian I in 543, Balthasar was a most loyal champion.

The whole movement of the return of theology to Patristic sources, inspired by Henri de Lubac, can be seen as opening a window on what Balthasar describes in another context, as the grumpy, super-organised, super-scholasticised Catholicism and the humourless, anguished Protestantism.[4] In the 1940s de Lubac,

---

[1] *Rechenschaft 1965*; English translation, *In Retrospect*, in *The Analogy of Beauty: The Theology of Hans Urs von Balthasar* (ed.), John Riches, Edinburgh 1986, p. 220. (Hereafter abbreviated as *R.*)

[2] *Origen, Geist und Feuer. Ein Aufbau aus seinen Werken*, Salzburg 1938.

[3] *Die Gottesfrage des heutigen Menschen*, Vienna 1956; English translation, *Science, Religion and Christianity*, London 1958, p. 99. (Hereafter abbreviated as *SRC.*)

[4] *Herrlichkeit*, 1, *Seeing the Form*, Edinburgh 1982, p. 494. (Hereafter abbreviated as *H.*)

Daniélou and Balthasar, among others, embarked upon a veritable
frenzy of Patristic studies, almost it seems as if vying with each other
to publish first. Balthasar published his study of Maximus in 1941
and his works on Gregory of Nyssa and Origen in 1942 and in 1957
respectively.[5] However, this very prolific period of Patristic studies
prompts the question why twentieth-century theologians thought
it worthwhile to delve into the far distant past of the Church's
history. In the first place, they reached the very wise conclusion that
many problems which the contemporary age regards as without
precedent had already been raised by writers in the past.[6] In the
second place, they understood that the treasurers of revelation were
bound as much to the past as to the present and future and were,
therefore, worth preserving. 'For Patristics meant to us a Christendom which still carried its thoughts into the limitless space of the
nations and still trusted in the world's salvation.'[7]

In the introduction to *Présence et Pensée*, Balthasar gives a very
specific answer to the question, why study the Fathers? He employs
an architectural analogy to demonstrate a general and universal law:
a Greek temple, a Romanesque church or a Gothic cathedral each
merit and evoke our admiration because they are testimonies to an
incarnate truth and beauty in their own period; the same law holds
true for theology. However, the mere evocation of admiration does
not itself mean uncritical acceptance, for just as the literal modern
reproduction of the temple, church or cathedral is not only anach-
ronistic but evokes horror, so too, we cannot simply exhume the
Fathers, transmit them literally and adapt their solutions to modern
problems. What Balthasar advocates rather, is an imitation of the
Fathers' attitude of intimate reflection, which he believes is a
prelude to a truly fruitful spirituality. He wants to penetrate the
spirit of their thought, 'jusqu'à cette intuition fondamentale et
secrète', which directs the expression of their thought.[8] He employs
another analogy to express his intention and meaning, one which is

---

[5]   *Hoehe und Krise des griechischen Weltbilds bei Maximus Confessor*, Friburg
1941; *Essai sur la philosophie religieuse de Grégoire de Nysse*, Paris 1942; *Parole et
mystère chez Origène*, Paris 1957.

[6]   *Glaubhaft ist nur Liebe*, Einsiedeln 1966; English translation, *Love Alone The
Way of Revelation: A Theological Perspective*, London 1968, p. 123.

[7]   *R.*, p. 195.

[8]   Ibid., p. xi.

itself apt although not wholly fortuitous: we can think of the Fathers of the Church as a man would think of the profound intuitions of his adolescent years – as they are part of himself even though he himself has changed. The documents of the Fathers can be thought of as the Church's intimate youthful diary. However, it is not clear that Balthasar was aware of the consequences of applying his analogy further, in implying that the Church has grown out of its Patristic past. However, the analogy is fruitful in the sense that the documents of the early centuries of the Church cannot be regarded as one might regard a stamp collection or butterfly collection, for it is our history we are dealing with, that which we once were. In this way, all that has gone before is in some sense mysteriously present in the depths of our being.

And yet, even though Balthasar does not advocate a literal transposition of Patristic solutions to contemporary problems, nevertheless, we find that his early scholarship was never far from his thoughts, for it was the backdrop against which his mature work emerged. Although I will be concentrating almost exclusively upon a number of closely-related Patristic themes in Balthasar's writings, at this point I note that the entirety of his works is laden with Patristic themes. For example in the section, 'The Experience of Faith' in *Herrlichkeit* I, Diadochus of Photice's theology of experience and discernment of spirits (which is set over against the Dionysian notion that God is beyond all human experience and the Patristic concept of *apatheia*) is regarded by Balthasar as one of the high points of Patristic literature and superior even to the Ignation rules outlined in the *Exercises*.[9] The working out of a theology of experience is closely linked with the doctrine of the spiritual senses, especially the notion of the 'spiritual eye', a theme which is ultimately derived from the Platonism of Origen, and one which Balthasar traces in both Irenaeus and Augustine in *Herrlichkeit*, II. Balthasar's recurrent proclamation of the mysterious element in being (although Heideggerian in tone) is a theme upon which Gregory of Nyssa places considerable emphasis. Balthasar's insistence upon the wholeness of the human response to God immediately recalls the famous sentiment of Irenaeus: *gloria Dei vivens homo*; the affirmation of this concept in Augustine (Balthasar

[9]   See p. 275ff.

regards the Augustinian interpretation of the beatific vision as 'a notable victory of Christian thought over Platonism')[10] and the consolidation of this concept in Maximus the Confessor in the light of Chalcedon.[11] Indeed it was through a Patristic inspiration that Balthasar found the impetus for attempting to re-insert the idea of beauty into the arteries of theology. His emphasis on the fundamental concept of *doxa*, an emphasis which is typically Ignatian and one which permeates the whole of the Greek Patristic period, would have been strengthened by his initial reading of Origen's *De principiis*.[12] Finally, Balthasar himself, in the true Greek sense of the word, *hymneo*, calls his first theological work, *Das Herz der Welt*, hymns of contemplation on the cosmic Christ.

However, the revitalisation of theology from an aesthetic perspective, especially with regard to Balthasar's Patristic sources, at once leads to a major problem, at the centre of which lies Platonism especially in its Neoplatonic development. The Patristic employment of many Neoplatonic categories and themes does not, at least for the Fathers themselves, pose the question of the relationship between philosophy and theology, but it is a question which causes a certain amount of tension in Balthasar's own writings. We observe him time and time again attempting to fix the boundaries and establish strict lines of demarcation between the two disciplines. Of course Balthasar's underlying pre-occupation with the roles of theology and philosophy must be understood in terms of modern and contemporary scholarly trends, but it is a theme which he pursues with vigour. His basic assertion is that philosophy cannot penetrate beyond the boundary of revelation, that it cannot attain to the God of love.[13] However, while philosophy cannot penetrate revelation, we find that theology can quite cheerfully, almost triumphantly, carry off, in Patristic terms, the *spolia Aegyptiorum*, the *spolia Platonicorum*.[14] Although Balthasar is not slow to ac-

---

[10] *H.* II, *Studies in Theological Style: Clerical Styles*, Edinburgh 1984, p. 138.

[11] See *H.* II, p. 165.

[12] Origen himself comments that the whole world is too small to contain all the books that might be written on the glory and majesty of the Son of God, *De principiis* II, vi, 2.

[13] In Maximus we find that the meaning of Trinity and Incarnation cannot be understood through rational demonstration but must be explored with faith, see *Cent. theol.* II, 36.

[14] *H.* IV, *The Realm of Metaphysics in Antiquity*, Edinburgh 1989, pp. 320–22.

knowledge the massive debt owed by the Cappadocians to Plotinus,[15] we can nevertheless detect in his later works, with respect to certain themes, a deep-rooted suspicion of Neoplatonism.[16] Again, although Balthasar validates the Dionysian aesthetic, and indeed champions Dionysius against the general current of German thought since the pioneering work of Koch and Stiglmair, he is not at all comfortable with the Areopagite's supra-experiential apophatic approach to the divine nature. Balthasar would most certainly agree with the sentiments expressed by Tertullian: 'what has Athens to do with Jerusalem?' for he remarks, 'Israel does not philosophise'.[17]

It is, therefore, the Neoplatonic elements in the Fathers – which for them was by no means an uncritical acceptance of philosophical sources – which Balthasar ultimately finds problematic. I hope to show how his own adoption of certain Patristic themes is always qualified, always transformed so that (following the example of Maximus) any dubious Neoplatonic or Dionysian elements are filtered out. I would like to do this by concentrating specifically upon two themes: *katabasis* and *anabasis*, (*kenosis* and *theosis*), and the great Cappadocian concept of the incomprehensibility of God. The descent of the Son and the corresponding ascent of humanity, which can be understood within the broader context of proodos and epistrophe,[18] is expressed by Irenaeus and taken up by Athanasius and the Cappadocians: 'God became man, so that man might become God'. What does Balthasar make of these two most Patristic of themes?

I begin this discussion with a very brief outline of Balthasar's understanding of Incarnation as both manifestation and concealment in order to situate his transformation of the concepts of ascent and *theosis*. The second part of this paper will be concerned with his employment of the Cappadocian theme of transcendent unknowability.

[15] *H.* IV, p. 291.

[16] *H.* I, pp. 119, 123, 137, 195, 217 and 551; Balthasar regards Origen as having brought to the static philosophy of Plotinus an eschatological dimension, see *H.* IV, p. 344.

[17] Tertullian, *Praescrip.* 7, 9: see *Klarstellungen. Zur Prüfung der Geister*, Friburg 1971; English translation, *Elucidations*, London 1975, p. 30. (Hereafter abbreviated as *Eluc.*).

[18] According to Balthasar, this was one of the three great themes of Antiquity which passed into Christian thought, the others being *eros* and beauty, see *H.* IV, p. 321.

INCARNATION: MANIFESTATION AND CONCEALMENT

Balthasar's understanding of the central mystery of Christianity is most expressly summarised in the first 'Preface of Christmas':

> In the wonder of the incarnation your eternal word has brought to the eyes of faith a new and radiant vision of your glory. In him we see our God made visible and so are caught up in love of the God we cannot see.[19]

Herrlichkeit itself can be regarded as a commentary on this text which echoes Origen's expression of the self-revelation of God as the visibility of *doxa*:

> so that we who were unable to look upon the glory of that marvellous light, when placed in the greatness of his Godhead, may by his being made to us brightness, obtain the means of beholding the divine light by looking upon the brightness.[20]

One of Balthasar's recurring themes is that the self-revelation of the glory of God is not something which somehow leaves behind it some aspect of the Godhead as unknowable and untouchable. It is not the case in this supreme condescending (*katabasis*) that in Christ only certain aspects of God are disclosed while other aspects remain hidden.[21] Both the Son and the Father are revealed fully and are known entirely, not partially. Christ is, as Irenaeus says, the visibility of the invisible, a theme echoed many times by Maximus: 'God the Father is by nature present entirely and without division in the entire divine *Logos*'.[22] In this respect it is very clear that Balthasar would not accept the Cappadocian understanding of the distinction between *ousia* and *energeiai*, by which they understood God to be

---

[19] Quia per incarnati Verbi mysterium, nova mentis nostrae oculis lux tuae claritatis influxit: ut dum visibiliter Deum cognoscimus, per hunc in invisibilium amorem rapiamur. See *H.* I, pp. 119–20.

[20] *De princ.* I, ii, 8.

[21] *H.* I, pp. 119, 187–88 and 302 and *H.* II, p. 11.

[22] Irenaeus, *Haer.* IV, 6, 6; Maximus, *Cent. theol.* II, 71 and 73. See *H.* I, pp. 199 and 302.

invisible and unknowable in his nature (*ousia*), and visible and knowable in his operations (*energeiai*). According to Gregory of Nyssa, even the Incarnation does not reveal God's nature, it simply manifests his goodness to humanity.[23] For Balthasar, on the other hand, the fact that the Incarnation guarantees ever open access to the Father, means that we cannot, as some of the Fathers have intimated, understand the Son to be a sign pointing beyond himself to the groundlessness of the Father.[24] Christ is not a means to an end, but a 'legible' form: the content is within the form not behind it.[25] Although the Council of Nicea had definitively established the consubstantiality of the persons of the Trinity, there is still a lingering hint, especially in the more apophatic Fathers, that Christ is not the final goal of the soul's contemplation. Although pre-Nicean subordinationism had been rooted out in dogmatic terms, it still found an echo with respect to the apophatic ascent of the soul. It is precisely this notion that Balthasar does not accept. In the incarnation, the *Theos agnōstos* of the Areopagus is fully revealed.[26] The incarnation does not point beyond itself to the further mystery of the Godhead, but, as revelation, draws back the veil from the mystery of eternal love.

> Nothing can be understood of the humanity of the Son if it is not from the beginning experienced, believed and adored as the humanity of the Son of the Father.[27]

The central paradox of Christianity – the visibility of the invisible, the form of the formless – for Balthasar involves a stress upon the first word rather than upon the second.[28] He very firmly dismisses the notion that somehow the incarnation of the Son, as the manifestation of the Father, belongs to the realm of *oikonomia* rather than to the realm of *theologia*. But what about the invisibility

---

[23]   *Hom. in beat.* VI, 1269A.

[24]   *H.* I, pp. 251–52 and 437.

[25]   *H.* I, pp. 439 and 150–53.

[26]   *Das Herz der Welt*, Zurich 1954; English translation, *Heart of the World*, San Francisco 1979, p. 50. (Hereafter abbreviated as *HOW*).

[27]   *SRC*, p. 99; see also *HOW*, p. 112.

[28]   See *H.* I, p. 302.

and formlessness of God, that other part of the dialectical opposition so dear to the hearts of the Cappadocian Fathers? In what way
does Balthasar understand it and express it? At first it would appear
that he is in agreement with them, for we find him saying that the
incarnation is the most extreme manifestness within the deepest
concealment. However, this concealment, rather than indicating
something of the Father that the Son does not reveal, or the
Cappadocian notion that unknowability, as an 'attribute' of the
Father, is applicable also to the Son, is understood in terms of
kenosis, as concealment within the ordinariness of human nature,
for kenosis takes us into the 'utter hiddenness of God'.[29]

> But it is concealment because (it is) the translation of God's
> absolutely unique, absolute and infinite Being into the ever
> more dissimilar, almost arbitrary and hopelessly relativised
> reality of one individual man.[30]

It is in this sense that the incarnation becomes an incomprehensible
sign in the midst of the world, for its very fact is incomprehensible.[31]
Thus, Balthasar rejects the earlier Greek Patristic conception of the
'unknowable' Father and the 'knowable' Son; for him the two
concepts, manifestation and hiddenness, are brought together in the
incarnation of God himself.

KENOSIS AND THEOSIS

It is precisely because the Father is fully revealed in the *katabasis* of
the Son that Balthasar stresses time and time again that humanity
cannot come to God by bypassing Christ, a theme that is prominent
in Maximus: 'The *Logos* came down out of love for us. Let us not
keep him down permanently but let us go up with him to the
Father... . For without the *Logos* it is impossible to approach the
Father of the *Logos*.'[32] We can attain to the living God only through

---

[29]   *H.* IV, p. 37 and I p. 457.
[30]   *H.* I, p. 457.
[31]   *H.* I, p. 457 and *HOW*, p. 49; Balthasar uses the Pseudo-Dionysius (*Ep.* III
1069B) in support of this notion, see *H.* II, p. 193.
[32]   *Cent. theol.* II, 47; see *H.* I, pp. 124, 154, and 301 and HOW, p. 179.

the humanity of the Son, anything less would not be true to the witness of the Trinity. The 'formlessness' of the Father is not the terminus of all the world's ways in the sense that after reaching Him, the 'formed' Son has been surpassed; to think of the Father's 'more profound groundlessness' is a delusion.[33] Here again, we find an implicit criticism of the Cappadocian and Dionysian approach which demonstrates a tendency still to move beyond the 'economic' aspect of the incarnation to theology which is proper to the Trinity alone. Therefore, having established that the incarnation itself, the kenosis of the Son is the incomprehensibility of God, we must then ask how Balthasar interprets the traditional Patristic conception of the soul as an ascent to the Father through theosis. For an understanding of this theme, which is ultimately turned on its head in Balthasar's theology, we must look at his conception of incarnation in its eschatological dimensions. *Katabasis* and *anabasis* are not any longer to be understood sequentially, but as eternally in the now, and it is in this way that Balthasar effectively does away with the Patristic concept of ascent as theosis.

The key to Balthasar's thought here is in his 'telescoping' of the two worlds, once again a very definite movement away from a dualistic Platonic or Neoplatonic conception. The great Plotinian theme, expressed in terms of the 'Here' and the 'There' becomes for Balthasar, the 'there' which becomes 'here' in the now: heavenly reality is translated into earthly language.[34] The understanding of the beatific vision, which had been developed at length by Gregory of Nyssa as the eternal seeking for more (what Daniélou called his notion of *epectasis*)[35] in the dark presence of the excessive light of God, is for Balthasar nothing other than what we see now before veiled eyes.[36]

The 'alreadyness' of the vision is not as it was for Gregory, as yearning for something more, something always different that will ultimately be bestowed, but the 'always more' which resides in what has already been bestowed. The consequences of emphasising the notion that the Father is fully revealed in the Son, means that Balthasar cannot give expression to a further, different eschatological

---

[33] *H*. I, p. 252 and *HOW*, p. 207.

[34] *HOW*, p. 50. Dualism is 'the contradiction of all Platonism', *H*. II, p. 123.

[35] *Platonisme et théologie mystique*, Paris 1944, pp. 309–33.

[36] *H*. I, p. 399.

revelation in the beatific vision. It is in this sense that he transforms the Patristic concept of eschatological deification in the beatific vision, for it is not any longer something to be bestowed in the future or a transformation of human nature into divine nature, but a re-seeing in the now, an awakening to a new way of seeing. Here we come to the most important divergence between the earlier Fathers and their twentieth-century reader: God does not become man so that man might become God.[37] Balthasar's understanding of the concept of deification is closer to that of Maximus the Confessor: it is the reaffirmation and restoration of created humanity in its proper and God-established integrity.[38] The fulfilment of humanity is the concept emphasised here, not the absorption into divinity, or the restoration of a fallen image. According to Balthasar, human nature cannot be altered by God, or indeed become God: creatureliness is defined as the 'proper ontological and cognitive distance from the Creator'.[39] The nature of humanity is that it is not God, and it cannot become God:

> This is a new mystery, inconceivable to mere creatures: that even distance from God and the coolness of reverence are an image and a likeness of God and of divine life. What is most incomprehensible is, in fact, the truest reality: precisely by not being God do you resemble God. And precisely by being outside of God are you in God. For to be over against God is itself a divine thing.[40]

A Patristic thematic indeed discernible at the foundation of this expression of not being God, but Balthasar extends it so that it stands in direct opposition to the concept of deification. He is uncompromising in his expression of the boundaries that exist between creator and created:

> We are not God. The silence at this boundary is not to be penetrated. To be bounded is our very form.... We may not shatter our shape.... Love is found only in distance, unity only in difference.[41]

[37] *H.* I, p. 277.
[38] See J. Meyendorff, 'Christ as Saviour in the East', in *Christian Spirituality: Origins to the Twentieth Century* (eds), B. McGinn and J. Meyendorff, New York 1988, p. 241.
[39] *H.* I, pp. 327 and 227.
[40] *HOW,* pp. 35, see p. 32 and *SRC,* p. 110.
[41] *HOW,* pp. 216–17.

Once again it is the concept of kenosis which shapes Balthasar's thought at this point, for in that ultimate self-emptying into dissimilarity, in being outside of God, the Son knew how to be in God. In this sense, precisely by not being God, humanity reflects the life of the Trinity.[42] It is also the concept of kenosis which determines his understanding of the return of the soul. Man wants to soar up to God, just as the Word wants to descend to man; the result will be a crossing of swords and a clashing of purposes. Therefore, instead of endorsing the Patristic concept of the ascent of the soul to deification as *anabasis*, instead of going past God's word in its descent and pursuing a rash ascent to the Father (surely a reference to the rashness of Sophia in attempting to know the incomprehensibility of the Father),[43] we are admonished to turn around and go back down with the Word, to find God on the road to the world. It is here that Balthasar finds humanity's likeness to God; it is not something which can be discovered in the depths of one's soul in private, polished up and used to see the reflection of God's glory, a theme which is given majestic expression in Gregory of Nyssa.[44] It is, rather, a likeness which is constituted in action: being like the Son in his descent from the Father, being sent out (*Sendung*) by the Father with the Son. It is in this sense that Balthasar says that any attempt on the part of the soul to rise up to God will attain only nothingness and empty air: the ladders of certain religious practices ultimately go nowhere, for the only means of return to the Father is a going out and back with the Son.[45]

> And perhaps the going forth from God is still more divine than the return home to God, since the greatest thing is not for us to know God and reflect this knowledge back to him as if we were gleaming mirrors, but for us to proclaim God.[46]

Here again we find a very deliberate reversal of the traditional Neoplatonic outlook of the Cappadocian Fathers, for whom the

---

[42] Ibid., p. 180.
[43] See Irenaeus, *Haer*, I, 2, 2 and Balthasar's reflections on this gnostic myth in *H*. II, pp. 34–35.
[44] *Hom. in cant*. II, 68, III, 90 and *Hom. in beat*. VI, 1270C.
[45] *HOW*, pp. 73, 160, 176 and 213.
[46] Ibid., pp. 33–34.

return to God was always more divine, more important than the going forth.

If then, the return of the soul is understood as a going out with the Son and a returning to the Father with him – surely indicative of a theology of action – where in Balthasar's thought is the place for the Patristic concept of the transcendence of God?

TRANSCENDENCE AND INCOMPREHENSIBILITY

In *Science, Religion and Christianity*, Balthasar asks this most pertinent question: what has happened to the Patristic (and more specifically Cappadocian) emphasis on the idea of the transcendent unknowability of God?[47] The subsequent discussion of transcendence is extremely revealing, for it pinpoints quite clearly this Patristic scholar's understanding of transcendence and indeed of negative theology.[48]

At first it would appear that Balthasar's strict insistence upon the fundamental assertion of the full revelation of the Father in the Son leaves little room for an understanding of divine incomprehensibility. And yet this is not, nor indeed can it be the full story, for Balthasar could not have been other than influenced by this most Patristic of themes. However, once again his understanding of it is manifestly different from that of Gregory of Nyssa, for it reveals Balthasar's basic affiliation to a more 'positive', kataphatic kind of theology, and a reliance upon Irenaeus, Origen, Augustine and their theological successors. Balthasar's theology is based upon a 'mysticism of light'; it is light and vision-dominated, for quite simply 'theology begins by seeing what is'.[49]

Balthasar suggests that contemporary atheism can be understood as an experience of the transcendence and absence of God and remarks that at the beginning of Christianity there was a similar 'disappearance of God into an inaccessible transcendence', although he does not suggest that the two are entirely similar.[50]

---

[47] See p. 100ff.
[48] My observations here are dependent chiefly on three texts in Balthasar's writings: *SRC*, p. 92ff., *Eluc.*, p. 18ff. and *H*. I, p. 451ff.
[49] *H*. II, p. 45.
[50] *SRC*, p. 100.

Generally speaking, contemporary theology, especially dogmatics, has forgotten the transcendence of God, the consequence being that most people stop short at the visible Son. The iconostasis is, for Balthasar, symbolic of the banishment and forgetfulness of transcendence, although in the same measure he expresses the tendency to prevent the transcendent God from becoming immanent, once again signified by the iconostasis.[51] We should not be tempted to regard the Patristic and indeed medieval understanding of transcendence and unknowability as something which can be taken out of a cupboard, dusted off and used in dialogue with the likes of Buber, Jaspers and Heidegger.[52]

The lengthy passage Balthasar quotes from Novatian on the unknowability and ineffability of God[53] – it is interesting that he should use a Latin source in this instance – is explained in terms of the distinction traditional among the Greek Fathers of the fourth century between theologia and oikonomia. *Theologia*, he says, refers to God in himself, exalted above all things, and *oikonomia* denotes God for us, condescending by grace (*synkatabasis*). According to Balthasar, economy can only be measured as grace if it is clear who it is that is descending: God himself, the object of theology. Now this distinction in the Greek Fathers of the fourth century, even after consubstantiality had been affirmed by Nicea in 325, implied a desire to 'go beyond' the economic aspect of the divine nature, a desire to see the Trinity extricated from cosmological implications, as Vladimir Lossky puts it, a concept which reaches its zenith in the Dionysian desire to see the One behind even the Three.[54] However, at the beginning of Christian theology we find Origen's understanding of *theologia* as *gnosis*, and specifically *gnosis* of God in the *Logos* and it is with Origen that Balthasar's thought finds its deepest resonances. Although for Balthasar there is no half-hidden Father 'behind' the Son, the Abyss beyond the manifestation, at the same time he cannot simply ignore the concept of transcendence which was developed at length by the Greek Fathers of the fourth century.

What place then does Balthasar give to transcendence and unknowability in his own writings? One would expect that the

---

[51] *HOW*, p. 129.
[52] *SCR*, p. 100.
[53] *Liber de Trinitate, PL.* 3, 889–91.
[54] See *In the Image and Likeness of God*, London and Oxford, 1974, p. 15ff.

concept of transcendence would be given focus by his Patristic sources, but it is to a modern writer that Balthasar turns in his answer to the age-old question: does the incarnation of the Son mean that the Father comes within the reach of humanity? In answer to this most central question Balthasar draws upon Erich Pryzwara's elucidations of the Fourth Lateran formula: ... *quia inter creatorem et creaturam non potest similitudo notari, quin inter eos maior sit dissimilitudo notanda* (however great the similarity between creator and creature, the dissimilarity is always greater).[55] According to Balthasar, conciliar formulations – which we must from time to time recognise as insufficient – are an attempt to protect the mystery against rationalisation, but he acknowledges the dangers inherent in so doing: the approach can be made too difficult (either by a literal or figurative iconostasis), or the impression can be given that the unknown God has been captured and made known.[56] He suggests that similarity and dissimilarity should be understood together in a dialectical fashion: God is dissimilar and Wholly Other in himself, although he became man, became Not Other.[57] However, Balthasar also expresses this dialectical truth in a most Patristic fashion (recalling Augustine's proclamation of the twofold truth of *secretissime* and *praesentissime: tu autem eras interior intimo meo et superior summo meo*):[58] 'the nearness of God who is nearer to man than man is to himself, is as overwhelming as his distance which cannot be bridged'.[59]

However, as we have seen, the difference and dissimilarity between God and humanity is not something with which Balthasar has any problems: what is interesting is that similarity pertains also to the begotten Word as well as to the image of God after which human nature has been made. It is because God is at the same time Wholly Other, dissimilar, that Balthasar explains that it is only analogously that we can speak of 'persons', 'begetting' and indeed of 'three' in God: for what 'three' means in relation to the absolute,

[55] H. Denzinger, A. Schönmetzer, *Enchiridion Symbolorum*, 34th edn., Rome 1967, 806 (432).

[56] *Eluc.*, pp. 21–24.

[57] On the dialectic between Wholly Other and Not Other, see *H.* I, p. 459, *LA*, pp. 47ff. and 122 and *SRC*, p. 114.

[58] *Conf.* VIII, 11.

[59] *SRC*, pp. 102 and 117.

'is in any case something quite other than the inner-worldly 'three' of a sequence of numbers'.[60] Given then the analogous nature of speech and the fact that God remains always incomprehensible even when he reveals himself, Balthasar asks if we have found a mandate to abandon speech and thought (presumably in the Nyssean and Dionysian senses). His reply to this most central of questions is that even though the similarity is always overruled by the ever greater dissimilarity, we do not have the authority to abandon speech and thought, for the fact remains that God did reveal himself. 'Visible form not only "points" to an invisible, unfathomable mystery and reveals it while, naturally at the same time protecting and veiling it.'[61] Can we take this to mean that there is something hidden in the divine nature that we cannot know? According to Balthasar, if God is to become manifest in his nature as God, then a necessary part of that revelation is the manifestation of his eternal incomprehensibility. Balthasar actually qualifies the notion of incomprehensibility here, saying that it is not to be understood as a negative determination of what we do not know (and this subjective sense was always one aspect of unknowability in the Cappadocian sense), but 'a positive and almost "seen" and understood property of him whom one knows'.[62] Does this mean that we can actually know God's unknowability? In one sense we can, for the incarnation itself is 'the ungraspability of God, which becomes graspable because it is grasped'.[63] The 'dazzling darkness' of divine beauty is not that which remains inaccessible to human understanding, but the splendour of the love of God 'which gives itself without remainder'.[64] What is incomprehensible is really found in what is comprehensible.

Can we then definitively say that Balthasar rejects any approach to God through a systematic application of the *via negativa*? Some comments at the end of *Heart of the World* are conclusive in respect of this question.[65] The 'way of the Yes', positive theology, sees God in all creatures since they are a reflected ray of his glory; the 'way of the No', apophatic theology, abandons all creatures since they

[60] *Eluc.*, pp. 23–24.
[61] *H.* I, p. 151.
[62] *H.* I, p. 186.
[63] *H.* I, pp. 461 and 609–10.
[64] *H.* II, p. 11.
[65] *H.* I, pp. 205ff.

cannot contain the infinite; the 'way of the ultimate beyond', presumably the way of 'unknowing knowing', smashes and dilates the measured into the measureless. The first, says Balthasar, is a dictum, the second a contradictum and both lead to the abyss – but not to the abyss of God; the third way is simply impossible. The only true way is the Son himself, and even though we cannot grasp God's wisdom fully, we are advised to be like a bowl under a fountain, to grasp what we can. Balthasar's understanding of the three ways here (and elsewhere) appears to be more Neoplatonic than Christian, and he often opposes a 'philosophical negative theology' (where God's being remains hidden over and beyond all analogous utterances) to negative theology understood from within the theological perspective, in which God appears unreservedly in the form of his 'ever-greater incomprehensibility'.[66] For Balthasar, incomprehensibility is not any longer a mere deficiency of knowledge, it does not include the subjective aspect it very definitely had in the Cappadocian Fathers; it is 'the positive manner in which God determines the knowledge of faith'. Negative theology is meaningless without the revelation of love; it drifts into atheism, agnosticism or a philosophy of identity. For Batlhasar, the Christ event raises theology above the level of philosophical *apophasis*.[67]

Although Balthasar's expression of the eschatological dimensions of divine incomprehensibility have much in common with Gregory of Nyssa's understanding of *epectasis*, where the 'vision' of God consists in never being satisfied in the desire to see him,[68] for Balthasar, it is because incomprehensibility is solely objective and not subjective that it extends into the *visio facialis* of the beatific vision. Then God's ever-greater incomprehensibility will constitute the 'content' of the vision, despite the real grasp of God which will be bestowed.[69] The Fathers were right, he says, to reject the notion that the vision of God 'face to face' would reveal the whole of the mystery of god, for *si comprehendis, non est Deus* – an expression

---

[66] *H.* I, p. 461; see also p. 448 where Balthasar says that positive theology must lead to a comprehensive negative theology, although he does not elaborate the point.

[67] See *LA*, p. 48 and *Eluc.*, p. 23.

[68] *Vita Mos.* II, 239.

[69] *H.* I, p. 461; 'we will see that God is forever the greater': *H.* I, p. 186.

which Balthasar repeats time and time again.[70] Divine incomprehensibility means that we shall never exhaust or encompass God's essential mystery, even in its eschatological dimension; only there, in heaven, it will be transformed from *spes* into *res*.[71]

CONCLUSION

Balthasar always upholds the central truth of the transcendence and immanence of Christianity: if we push God into inaccessibility, the result is indifference; if we draw him into the historicity of the world, God will fall prey to human *gnosis*. However, unlike the Cappadocian Fathers, Balthasar's stress falls upon immanence rather than upon transcendence, on the spoken word rather than on the unspoken word, for ultimately, the contours of the form of revelation are comprehensible.

His muted objections to the Nyssean and Dionysian expression of the supra-experiential theology of *apophasis* can be understood in two ways. Firstly, Balthasar's basic adherence is to a theology of experience, as expressed by Diodochus of Photice and Origen where faith is understood as realised experience,[72] although he does say that all senses, thoughts and images die, descend to the underworld and rise to the Father in an ineffable manner which is both sensory and non-sensory.[73] When Balthasar is describing Maximus' understanding of mystical experience as a coming-into-consciousness of the transcendence of spirit which casts itself unknowingly at the unknown God, he offers no commentary; he simply says: 'this is an Areopagitic trait'. His choice of word is significant here: it is a trait, not the fullest expression of an 'experience' of God. Although Balthasar endorses Dionysian mysticism as Christian and indeed ecclesial (in that it does not degenerate towards the frontiers of Buddhism), nevertheless he is suspicious of all mystical experience that is not expropriated into ecclesial mysticism.[74] The *ekstasis* which is a prominent feature of the ascent of the soul in so many of

---

[70]   *SRC*, p. 113; see also *H.* I, pp. 186, 450 and 461–62.
[71]   *See H.* I, pp. 462 and 186ff.
[72]   *H.* I, p. 284ff.
[73]   *H.* I, p. 425.
[74]   *H.* I, pp. 414–15.

the Fathers, is absent in Balthasar as it is in Origen. There is not any longer a casting of oneself at the unknowability of God, but an openness to the advances of God.

Secondly, I think we can see his objection to an apophatic ascent in the light of his Johannine and Origenist affiliation to a theology of sight and vision, where *theoria* is always superior to *gnophos*, rather than to the Nyssean and Dionysian theology of darkness and presence. The basic fact for Balthasar is that there is something to be seen and grasped, something offered.[75] The very objective of *Herrlichkeit* as a theological aesthetics determines his fundamental position that *gnosis* is *theoria*: it is knowledge of the radiance of God's glory penetrating the darkness of the world. It is perhaps in the light of these two basic positions that we can understand Balthasar's attraction to Origen. Where Balthasar is very definitely anti-Origenist, and indeed anti-Cappadocian, is in his refusal to submit the revelation of the Son to the Patristic distinction pertaining between *ousia* and *energeiai*.

Ultimately for Balthasar, what sets Christianity apart from Neoplatonism and indeed other religions, is not the paradoxes with which the Fathers felt so much at home, but the fact that the One who is Wholly Other and Not Other became man. Even though the notion of divine incomprehensibility was developed by the Cappadocian Fathers as theological reflection upon the central message of the New Testament, Balthasar appears to find some difficulty as to how transcendent unknowability can find a place within the context of revelation.

Therefore, although Balthasar was indeed influenced by his reading of Irenaeus, Origen, Augustine, Gregory of Nyssa, Maximus and others, his own thought is very much a response to the theological problems of today. In contemporary theology we are far removed from the raging controversies between Arius and Athanasius, Eunomius and the Cappadocians. Their theological reflections were developed against a different background and with a different perspective and aim. Balthasar's emphasis on the revelation of the Son can be understood largely in the context of contemporary secularisation and atheism: the concept of *Sendung* once more assumes a central position as a means of combatting such develop-

---

[75] *H.* I, pp. 121, 125–26, 148 and 551.

ments. The solitary mystic so familiar in the world of the Fathers is no longer commonplace, for the emphasis is on community rather than on individualism. However, Batlhasar's attempt to focus upon the Patristic theme of the transcendence of God, while admittedly not occupying a central place in his thought, is something that contemporary theologians could reflect upon and perhaps develop, for Balthasar's vision and the vibrancy of his approach to theology does indeed reflect something of the fresh vision of the Fathers: to those with eyes to see, the Spirit has always been brooding over this bent world with bright wings.

5

THEOLOGICAL DRAMATICS

Gerard O'Hanlon, S.J.

The late John Hyde used a telling, if inelegant, simile to convey his sense of difficulty in introducing people to the work of Balthasar. It's a bit like a fly, he used to say, trying to show an elephant to visitors to the zoo – the fly keeps getting whisked off the immense corpus. The trouble is of course that Balthasar, due to his imposing theological stature, can end up being admired uncritically, or at a distance, rather than being engaged in a dialogue which might have real implications for theology and life. To try to obviate this danger I propose in what follows first to give a brief outline of theological dramatics in Balthasar, but then to bring this outline into dialogue with the attempt to create a social theology within our Irish context. After all, as Balthasar himself often intimated it is the deed which is decisive[1] – might we not expect then that his theological dramatics would shed light on the critical debate concerning the nature and operation of Irish society?

I. BALTHASAR'S THEOLOGICAL DRAMATICS

INTRODUCTION

Balthasar himself is very clear that to speak of the theological aesthetics as the masterpiece, the work of his life, is to misunderstand his fundamental intention.[2] In his own mind the trilogy has

[1] See *In Retrospect*, pp. 217–218 (pp. 194–221: original in 1965) in John Riches (ed.), *The Analogy of Beauty*, Edinburgh: T&T Clark 1986.
[2] See John Riches, op. cit., pp. 224–5 (pp. 222–33); and for what follows, ibid., pp. 217, 218, 222–33; *Theodramatik* I, Einsiedeln: Johannes 1973, pp. 9–

to be taken as a whole. The aesthetics, the manifestation of God in the manner of a fundamental theology from the formal viewpoint of the beautiful, is a theophany in created form which is only the prelude to the central event: the encounter, in creation and history, between infinite divine freedom, the self-emptying love of God, and finite human freedom. This approach from the formal viewpoint of the good is then completed by a reflection on the way in which the dramatic event can be transposed into human words and concepts. This is intended to be a methodical, *a posteriori* reflection from the viewpoint of the true on what has been done in the first and second parts. Drama then mediates between aesthetic and logic: it puts the event into an image or form which is then capable of being spoken about.[3]

It is worth pausing for a moment to ponder on the significance of this threefold approach. First, in his return to the High Scholastic and classical preoccupation with Being and the transcendentals true, good and beautiful, Balthasar is deliberately countering the so-called *anthropologische Wende* in modern theology in which the human subject is the starting-point of theological reflection.[4] Of course the notion of Being and its transcendentals are situated within an understanding of the 'ever-greater dissimilarity' of the analogy of Being which allows for the primacy of God at the centre of the theological enterprise. Secondly, the original use of the good and the beautiful as formal approaches makes clear Balthasar's abhorrence of any rationalising tendencies in theology – the word issues from the perception of a form (*Gestalt*) which itself turns out to be an event.

The contemplative theology of the aesthetics then turns into the combative, passionate theology of the dramatics.[5] The reality of

---

10, 15–22, 116–18 (=TD, I); M. Kehl, 'Hans Urs von Balthasar: A Portrait', in M. Kehl, W. Löser (eds.), *The von Balthasar Reader*, Edinburgh: T&T Clark 1982, pp. 46–50 (pp. 3–54); John Riches, 'Afterword', in John Riches (ed.), *The Analogy of Beauty*, pp. 180–81 (pp. 180–93); L. Roberts, *The Theological Aesthetics of Hans Urs von Balthasar*, Washington: Catholic University of America Press 1987, 203–31; G. O'Hanlon, *The Theological Metaphysics of Hans Urs von Balthasar*, Unpublished STL dissertation 1980, pp. 15–19.

[3]   Hans Urs von Balthasar, TD I, p. 17.

[4]   See Gerard O'Hanlon, 'The Jesuits and Modern Theology', *ITQ* 58 (1992), p. 25 (pp. 25–45) and 'The Legacy of Hans Urs von Balthasar', *Doctrine and Life* 41 (1991), pp. 401–10 (pp. 401–07).

[5]   See J. McDade, 'Reading von Balthasar', *The Month* 20 (1987), p. 139 (pp. 136–43); B. McNeil, 'The Exegete as Iconographer: Balthasar and the Gospels', in John Riches, op. cit., p. 144 (pp. 134–46).

Being and its tendency towards concrete form is illustrated best of all in the universal concrete form that is Jesus Christ. Already within the aesthetics there was implicit in the enrapturement that accompanied the perception of the form an opening to the truth shown in Jesus that the deed of love in freedom is what is at the centre of reality, divine and human. We are asked not simply to contemplate Jesus but with Christian *eros* to follow him, be disciples, giving witness even to the point of death to what we have seen in him. Jesus reveals to us that God is love, and by his cross in particular he shows us that the human response to God's love has to take account of the reality of evil. If God is love, and if, in particular, this love is in dialogue with our freedom and with evil, are we not in the midst of a drama which involves both God and ourselves?

Before looking at this drama more closely some mediating observations are in order. First, drama involves action between characters: it is no accident that running right through Balthasar's theology is his use of the analogy of inter-subjectivity to speak about God, us, and the relationship between us and God. In this respect he differs from the tradition of German Idealism, taken up by Rahner and the Transcendental Thomists with their focus on the human subject him/herself. The dialogical relationship between mother and child, between lovers, is a better pointer to what goes on in reality, divine and human. Secondly, there is of course a very difficult problem to be faced in any talk of God's dramatic engagement with our world.[6] Balthasar is aware that both the mythical alternative of a God who becomes enmeshed in our world like an ancient hero or the philosophical alternative of the Absolute and impersonal One are inadequate answers to our real questions about our place in the world and to the Christian revelation.[7] In a way that will emerge later he is confident that the trinitarian God preserves the two poles of transcendence and immanence. Thirdly, he notes how the notion of a theological dramatics is capable of integrating many of the tendencies of contemporary theology such as its focus on the event, the historical, orthopraxis, the dialogical, the political,

---

[6] See *Engagement with God*. London: SPCK 1975 (original in 1971).
[7] See *Theodramatik, II/1*, (= *TD*, II/1), Einsiedeln: Johannes 1976, pp. 38–46.

the future, the functional, the role, freedom and evil.[8] This is important because it means Balthasar sees himself as engaged with the kind of issues which are relevant to a social theology. Fourthly, it is interesting to note the influence on Balthasar's life from Greek tragedy and from moderns such as Schneider, Claudel, Brecht and others.[9] Again, within the perspective of *Herrlichkeit*, this is sometimes forgotten – more stress is laid on his undoubted debt to the Patristic tradition, in particular to Platonic thought.

We turn now to a more detailed outline of Balthasar's *Theo-dramatics*. We are not neutral observers; we are all involved in God's play, ours is a play within a play, or rather the one divine drama includes both God and ourselves in a differentiated way.[10] How does Balthasar use this formal approach from drama to convey involvement without loss of critical objectivity?

THE THEO-DRAMATICS

An overview of Balthasar's *Theo-dramatics* indicates the structure of his thought.[11] The first volume, the *Prolegomenon*, is introductory. In it the possibility of using the categories of drama as an instrument for theological reflection are explored. The notion of the world being a theatre ('all the world's a stage …') is evoked, with careful acknowledgment of the fact that God and ourselves are not simply equal co-players on the stage. But within the requisite distance provided by analogy one can begin to fashion a theology of history with the help of dramatic categories such as author, actor, director, role and representation, time and space, the struggle against evil and for good. This dramatic structure is explicitly trinitarian: the author is the Father, the chief actor the Son, the director is the Holy Spirit.

---

[8]   *TD*, I, Einsiedeln: Johannes 1973, pp. 23–46.
[9]   *In Retrospect*, pp. 209–10; D. MacKinnon, 'Some Reflections on Hans Urs von Balthasar's Christology with Special Reference to Theo-dramatik II/2 and III', in John Riches, op. cit. pp. 170–72 (pp. 164–179); John Riches, op. cit., p. 191.
[10]   See *TD* I, p. 18; *Another Ten Years*, pp. 224–26.
[11]   *TD*, II/1, pp. 11, 17: *Theodramatik*, III, (= *TD*, III), Einsiedeln: Johannes, 1980, pp. 11–12; *Theo-dramatik*, IV, (= *TD*, IV), Einsiedeln: Johannes 1983, pp. 11–12; Gerard O'Hanlon, *The Immutability of God in the Theology of Hans Urs von Balthasar*, Cambridge University Press 1990, passim, especially pp. 79–87, 110–36.

The dramatic notion of role becomes identified with the theological notion of mission – we as human beings have a role within the divine drama by becoming persons, which we do in answering our mission as beings called and sent by God. The notion of representation is used in a twofold way to describe first the way in which as actors we present the divine drama, and then secondly to indicate how crucial is that representative action by which we act on behalf of one another (the chief referent here of course being the representative action of Jesus Christ on our behalf).

After this introduction the second volume introduces us to the characters of the play. It now becomes clear that freedom is the key concept which structures the action of this divine-human drama. There is an analogy of freedom between the infinite divine and the finite human freedom which makes a common history and drama possible.[12] As creatures then we are 'human beings in God' in the sense that, as the first subvolume (II/1) makes clear, we owe our freedom to God's prior, creative act of freedom, and it is within this paradoxical space of owed freedom that we operate. More precisely, as the second subvolume clarifies (II/2), we develop from the status of human being to that of true personhood by our association with the person Jesus Christ – we are 'persons in Christ'. It is within this graced context that it becomes even clearer how the created paradox of owed freedom is by no means a contradiction – by being related particularly to Jesus Christ we are drawn into the event of infinite freedom and love which is the relationship between the Father and the Son in a way which reinforces our own freedom and the openness of our history.

Balthasar is conscious that up to now, due to the necessary setting of the stage for the drama, he is open to the charge of being quite formal in his approach. In particular he has offered an extended treatment of classical Christology in his account of the person of Christ and has clarified the parameters of the action without much attention to its inner rhythm. All this is remedied in the third volume. This is soteriology and focuses on the action involving Jesus Christ, the whole Trinity, and ourselves, as God finds a way to deal with evil and the abuse of finite freedom. Already at the beginning

---

[12] See M. Kehl in M. Kehl and W. Löser (eds.), *The von Balthasar Reader*, Edinburgh: T&T Clark 1982, pp. 48–49.

of this volume the dramatic scene is set by placing it under the sign of the Apocalypse. The power of evil in all its dimensions, personal, social and cosmic, is adverted to, as is its increase in direct proportion to the definitive offer of God's love in Jesus Christ. There is then proposed a dramatic soteriology in which the cross, descent into hell and resurrection constitute a Paschal Mystery which affects not just the human struggle with evil but also the very inner life of God.

The *Triduum Mortis* has at least four main points which require brief comment. First, the cross is a trinitarian event through which the justice and love of God are seen to be one, in the course of a drama between Father and Son which is directed by the Holy Spirit in a way which allows for the unity-in-diversity of the Trinity to embrace a unity-in-difference or opposition. The opposition is due to God's loving plan to have the Son enter into solidarity with human death and sin, sin being the object of God's anger and abhorrence. This is something like a trinitarian re-reading and rehabilitation of Anselm – God, all three persons, is first and last a God of love: but in the triumph of costly grace the Father's loving anger is borne by the Son whose loving obedience brings about the reconciliation which we call redemption. Secondly, this is radicalised in the motif of the descent into hell.[13] Balthasar, deeply conscious of the power of evil, not least in its manifestations in our own century, describes the ultimate solidarity of the Son with the consequences of the second death that is human sin and hell is re-interpreted not as an active, triumphant leading back of the waiting just but rather as the entirely passive accompaniment by Jesus Christ of those who have thought to say a definitive 'no' to God. Once again it is the Holy Spirit whose role it is to ensure that the love between Father and the Son can bridge even this ultimate hiatus and lead to the dramatic vindication that the resurrection brings. Thirdly, this dramatic interaction between ourselves and God, and, in particular, between Jesus and his Father, affects God very deeply. The drama is an inner-divine one as well, indeed principally. This is so even with Balthasar's very careful and confident acceptance of

---

[13] *Theologie der Drei Tage*, Einsiedeln: Johannes, 1969; *Epilog*, Einsiedeln: Johannes 1987, 49–58; J. Riches, op. cit., pp. 190–93; J. McDade, op. cit., pp. 140–42; D. MacKinnon, op. cit., passim, especially pp. 166, 169, 179; John O'Donnell, 'Hans Urs von Balthasar: The Form of his Theology', *Communio* 3 (1989), pp. 465–68 (pp. 458–74).

the distinction between economic and immanent Trinity. Already it is a step beyond the tradition to speak of the economic Trinity being affected: but can the Father remain impervious to the Son's suffering, can the Son's suffering really be in his human nature only if we are to take seriously the unity of person stated in Chalcedon and the analogy between the divine and human natures suggested by the neo-Chalcedonian movement? And so Balthasar moves to a notion of a very mysterious but real 'supra-suffering' in God, which he specifies more clearly in the next volume as a victorious acceptance of seizing or overcoming of pain by God, freely embraced, compatible with joy and only very faintly analogous to human suffering.[14] There is then an analogous 'pre-sacrifice' within divine love, a renunciatory character which is ready to pay for human freedom and its terrible abuses. This means that the historical sufferings of Jesus, the transfigured wounds which remain in the resurrected Christ, and the Slain Lamb of the Apocalypse are not by any means foreign to God but are all very real modalities of divine love which is revealed as dramatically trinitarian.[15] Fourthly, we are not mere spectators of this divine drama. We are co-players, actors, even if our roles are characterised most centrally by that 'letting-be' of God which is rooted in the form of Christ and which results in the normative *fiat* of Mary and the Church.[16] We are challenged then to appropriate subjectively the victory over evil won for us by Christ. We are invited indeed to become co-redeemers with him (*Colossians* 1: 20). We too then are at the heart of this drama, with a mission to combat evil and become part of God's inner life made possible by the elective power of trinitarian love.

The last volume (IV) tells of the conclusion of the drama and is devoted to eschatology. Here, while careful not to flatten everything

---

[14] For a more extended and exact treatment of this see G. O'Hanlon, 1990, chapters 2 and 4.

[15] *TD*, III, p. 302: 'That God (as Father) can give away his divinity to such an extent that God (as Son) does not merely receive it as something borrowed, but possesses it in the equality of essence, implies such an unspeakable and unsurpassable "separation" of God from himself that every other separation (made possible by it!), even the most dark and bitter, can only occur within this first separation.' Also: *TD*, IV, pp. 467–476; John O'Donnell, op. cit., 465–68.

[16] *Engagement with God*, pp. 52–53; D. L. Schindler, 'The Church's "Worldly" Mission', *Communio* 3 (1991), pp. 367–72 (pp. 365–97).

into some surveyable undramatic *apocatastasis* system, Balthasar does use the descent into hell motif of the *Triduum Mortis* as the basis of a very firm hope for the salvation of all. What is of great interest here is a reaffirmation and indeed radicalising of the trinitarian nature of this drama. God's engagement in the battlefield of the world justifies the question of what the world means for God and, in particular, challenges the traditional notion of divine equanimity in the face of human damnation. It is the trinitarian mystery of unity in diversity which is the condition of the possibility for the free existence and creation of the world ('the world from God') in the first place. Already, with the Son, there is otherness within God without threat to the unity of divine love – the world is a free extension of this otherness into the realm of creation. Similarly, due to the same interplay of unity and otherness in love, the Trinity is the *a posteriori* revealed condition for the possibility of human freedom, and for the transcendent and yet immanent involvement of God in tackling the abuse of freedom. Above all it is by means of the Trinity that Balthasar is able to speak of the pain and hope of God in the context of God's desire that this world may return to God ('the world in God') at the end in its entirety for the celebration of the feast of the bride. This is because within the event of trinitarian love Balthasar can speak of an analogous receptivity, suffering, and indeed surprise and ever-more. The love that Father and Son have for one another, personified in the exuberant and ecstatic character of the Holy Spirit, is always greater not just than we can ever know but also greater than Father and Son themselves realise. There is a surplus of love over knowledge in the divine interaction, due to the infinite divine freedom. This is not to say that God changes in any univocal sense. Rather, within a notion of the eternity of God which is a supra-time analogous to our temporal experiences of intensity,[17] Balthasar will posit an analogous, divine supra-mutability which allows him to speak in terms of the world as God's gift to God within the trinitarian life. In this context clearly the world matters, and its final destiny is of great concern to God.

There are two final comments arising from this finale to the drama before I offer a concluding summary to take us into dialogue

---

[17] See Gerard O'Hanlon, 1990, chapter 3; and D. L. Schindler, 'Time in eternity, eternity in time', *Communio* 1 (1991), pp. 52–68.

with the Irish context in the second part of this paper. First, Balthasar speaks of divine drama even when there is no question of conflict. There is drama then in heaven, due to the eternal liveliness of the trinitarian interaction, and in particular to that element of surprise which is a perfection of love.[18] This alerts us to the suggestion that action and surprise are more fundamental to drama than conflict – though we do need to note that the original image of conflict, at least as a condition of possibility, is in God always, and, arguably, a transfigured suffering that is compatible with the joy of heaven. Secondly, it should not be inferred from the frequent use of the prefix 'supra' to describe aspects of the divine life that Balthasar is being 'merely' poetic. Rather, as MacKinnon says in a different context, Balthasar uses words in a way which 'presses beyond poetry into ontology'.[19] In this respect Balthasar is in fact arguing for the place of metaphor and poetry within a properly ontological and theological discourse.[20]

THEO-DRAMATICS: CONCLUDING SUMMARY

Balthasar's *Theo-dramatics* involves an exciting combination of anthropology (vol. I), Christology (vol. II), soteriology (vol. III) and eschatology (vol. IV). Its overall aim is to outline a theology of history, a theopraxis, which takes full account, 'through a remorseless emphasis on the concrete', (MacKinnon),[21] of the ambivalence of worldly progress. There are particular aspects of this theology which are problematic – for example, how does one reconcile the theology of Holy Saturday with the definitive nature of the human 'yes' or 'no' to God within time? Is not the conflict between justice and love within God in the soteriology inclined to leave us back with an angry Father-God, unless one introduces the notion of solidarity between this Father and the victims of sin and oppression in our world? But rather than engage in critical point-scoring over particular details I want instead to explore the strengths and weaknesses of Balthasar's overall approach in dialogue with the urgent need to

---

[18] See *TD*, II, pp. 184–5; *TD*, IV, pp. 68–69. For the more usual, conflictual notion of drama, see *TD*, I, p. 17.

[19] See D. MacKinnon, op. cit., p. 168.

[20] See O'Hanlon, 1990, pp. 137–44.

[21] See D. MacKinnon, op. cit., p. 167.

create an Irish social theology. Is this approach in touch with concrete reality as is promised, or is it in the end overly speculative and ahistorical?[22] What is Balthasar saying implicitly about the drama between God and humanity which is being acted out in most concrete terms on the Irish part of the world stage in the 1990s?

II. THEO-DRAMATICS AND AN IRISH SOCIAL THEOLOGY

Rose lives in a new Corporation housing estate on the outskirts of Dublin. She does part-time work cleaning in a hospital. Her husband Paul is unemployed, but does the odd 'nixer'. They have five children. The two eldest have left school, are unemployed, and one of them is serving a jail sentence for stealing a video. The other children are still at school but they will leave early. There are no prospects of permanent work for any of them. Rose worries a lot about her teenage children – there is a big drug problem in the area, joy-riding is common, the youth are restless and occasionally violent with little to do with their time. There is a lot of fear in the air. She worries about not having enough money – the two youngest children have to be looked after for Communion and Confirmation, Christmas and Easter are pressure points, and meanwhile the day to day bills have to be paid. She is afraid of falling back into the hands of the moneylender, which happened recently unknown to her husband who would only get depressed if he found out. She wishes there were more facilities in the area, that it didn't look so run-down, but nothing can be done about it – people have tried before, have failed, and only got abuse for their trouble. Paul is depressed a lot of the time. He gets up late, goes out to the bookie now and then for a bet, goes for a drink and a game of darts once a week. Mostly he feels out of things, apathetic, has very little to contribute. Rose is tired, and gets a bit of peace from going to Mass. Her youngest daughter is an altar server but was forbidden to serve Mass on a recent episcopal visit – this upset Rose. She has joined a women's group recently and has begun to get angry at her situation. Paul believes in God but feels out of place in Church. They both feel

---

[22] See Gerard O'Hanlon, 1990, p. 170 and 'The Legacy of Hans Urs von Balthasar', op. cit., pp. 405–06.

they have little in common with people elsewhere in Dublin and Ireland: they know that others look down on them for living where they do, and they have a sense of not belonging to the wider Ireland. They have some good neighbours though, and they really enjoy a good celebration. Spirits were great in the whole family when the Irish soccer team was playing in the World Cup, and there was a mighty street party to celebrate the Dublin Millennium. They would both be in favour of a United Ireland, but they have never visited the North and have little interest in the whole issue.

We have enough reports from the ESRI and other reputable bodies, as well as our own experience, to know that many people in Ireland at the moment, whether in urban or rural areas, lead lives of quiet desperation. There are both personal and structural reasons for this. Does a social theology have something to say to this reality? I use the term social theology as shorthand for a theology which would reflect on our situation in the light of the gospel, and would attend to the social, economic, political and cultural, as well as the personal, dimensions of that situation. It would, most crucially, see itself as part of a process to bring about change – it will not do to be intellectually excited in protest against apartheid in South Africa and fail to engage in any committed way with the development of the housing and concomitant social apartheid which we have all been party to over the past thirty years in a city like Dublin. Such a social theology is already under way in Ireland, calling for a new solidarity among Irish people, in particular exploring ways in which Christian faith fosters and energises this solidarity.[23] In what way might Balthasar's theological dramatics contribute to this enterprise?

Balthasar's contribution is an extremely nuanced one. It emerges in the context of a debate with Liberation Theology,[24] with Moltmann

---

[23] Tim Hamilton, Brian Lennon, Gerry O'Hanlon, Frank Sammon, *Solidarity: The Missing Link in Irish Society*, Dublin 1991. See also the writings in this area of Enda McDonagh, Donal Dorr, Patrick Hannon, Katherine Zappone, Mary Condron. The Inter-Church Group on Faith and Politics, Michael Casey. Proceedings of the Irish Theological Association, and many others, including articles in Irish theological journals.

[24] For this, and what follows, see 'Liberation Theology in the Light of Salvation History', in J. V. Schall, *Liberation Theology*, San Francisco: Ignatius Press 1982, pp. 131–46 (translation of original in 1977); *TD*, III, pp. 449–54; *TD*, IV, p. 159, note 16.

and the theology of hope,[25] as well as in his own positive exposition of the implications of his *Theo-dramatics*.[26] First, there are many features of his approach which encourage in an obvious way the notion of social theology as described above. Discipleship involves mission, and mission involves the ethic of justice and love that Jesus preached and lived. Jesus does take the side of the poor, and the text in *Matthew* 25 indicates the crucial and normative nature of this engagement. In circumstances of extreme social deprivation there may well be a need to tackle these conditions first, before one can hope to move to the deeper dimensions of our mission as disciples which is our saying 'yes', our *fiat*, to the call of God. There is a primacy to be accorded to personal conversion, but there is also need of a conversion of structures. Lay Christians in particular are urged to become competent in the social, economic and political sectors of society in order to facilitate this conversion. We ought as Christians to lead lives of simplicity and not luxury, and educate ourselves to acknowledge the often unrealised guilt we may share due to our participation in a social system that sanctions an unjust distribution of goods. In particular the Church has an opportunity to mirror a more just society, unhindered as it can be by some of the coercive dimensions necessary to civil society. Finally, and most characteristic of Balthasar, our modern technological society has lost touch with its roots in God. The modern *anima technica vacua*[27] needs to root its autonomy in the infinite freedom of God, and out of this will follow the kind of 'dramatic collaboration' which may effect that change, including the conversion of structures, which is so complex and to which we are so resistant.

Secondly, there is another, more dominant, strand to Balthasar's thought which qualifies these first remarks both in a way which is enriching and in a way which is arguably emasculating and theologically more questionable. Here he is at pains to caution against a

[25] For this and what follows see *TD*, IV, pp. 148–59; Gerard O'Hanlon, 'May Christians Hope for a Better World?' *ITQ* 54 (1988), pp. 175–89.

[26] For this, and what follows, see *Engagement with God*, op. cit.; *TD*. III, pp. 449–54; *TD*, IV, pp. 447–449; *Homo Creatus Est* (=*HC*), Einsiedeln: Johannes, 1986, p. 354ff.; *Theologik*, III, (= *TL*, III), pp. 13–20, 234–52, 360ff., 374ff., 391–95, 402.

[27] See D. L. Schindler, 'The Church's "Worldly" Mission', op. cit., pp. 371–72.

utopian approach to hope for a better world that has more in common with Marx and Hegel than with the Christian gospel. A monistic view of the relationship between religion and politics, the kingdom of God and civil society, has always been disastrous for Christianity, as instances like the Constantinian era, the Crusades, the Inquisition, the Jesuits in Paraguay, caesaro-papism all show. Liberation is primarily from sin and death, to a sharing in the life of God – it includes the past, those who have died, it has already been won definitively in principle with the paschal mystery of Christ, and it does not depend solely on what progress is made in the future. The tendency in *Gaudium et Spes* to speak of a convergence between the kingdom of God and earthly progress is over optimistic – the world is ambivalent, it is not simply a reflection of the kingdom of God, the 'eschatological proviso' of the kingdom signals discontinuity as well as continuity in the relationship between the two. There is no complete system possible which would order world affairs in a just way. If one tries for such a system one ends up with 'the entanglement of the individual in the mesh of "just" socialistic systems of distribution'.[28] In particular there are no theological grounds for hope in a better world. Rather one may at best speak of a natural, human hope for progress – theologically one can simply speak of the mission of all Christians which will indeed involve the search for a better world. This distinction between hope and mission is not a mere semantic quibble without any substantive significance. Rather it alerts us to the reality that 'the form of this world is passing away' (1 *Corinthians* 7: 31), that there is a fundamental provisionality about our world order with its characteristic master/slave relationship, that structures will always be unjust, that the disciple of Christ is promised not success but persecution and death as s/he takes up the daily cross, that life is carried on under the sign of the Apocalypse by which evil grows in proportion to good. Christian hope is at its best primarily in situations which are by definition hopeless – for example in care of the terminally ill. Within this whole context the Church must be aware that it has no blueprint for social progress, it is not another political party. In particular lay Christians, who more properly engage in the project for social betterment, need to discern carefully how to go about their mission with its difficult dimension of tackling the deep issue of the use and abuse of power.

---

[28] See Hans urs von Balthasar in Schall, op. cit., pp. 142–43.

Power tends to absolutise itself and become removed from love even when the intention is to use it for the good. They need to face the possibility that, as Péguy remarked, proverty may be the normal state of a Christian – it is only misery, abject destitution which needs urgent attention. After all, while Jesus did indeed side with the poor, his call is universal and for the conversion of all. Above all they will be realistic, recognising that politics is the art of the possible, that structures are complex and difficult to change, that compromise is ultimately more likely to succeed than violent revolution or simple global denunciations of capitalism, and that even non violence is not the only Christian option. In particular, *pace* Ghandi and Martin Luther King, they will be wary of using the cross as a tactic of non-resistance and powerlessness – the cross is not to be reduced to a political tactic, and, moreover, a political leader may ask the ultimate renunciation more easily of him/herself than of the whole group, as the increasing aloneness of someone like Ghandi shows. All Christians then need to be cautioned against the reduction of religion to an ethic of social engagement, not least several major religious orders in their post-Vatican II attempts at renewal. And finally, theology itself needs to recognise its own lack of competence in the area of structural change.

I think the positive side of these qualifying positions of Balthasar is indeed very helpful. It cautions against an irresponsible, facile optimism with regard to social change, an optimism which is as condescending and unreal to the victims of oppression as it is untrue to the gospel message. There is a natural intractability about structural reform, compounded by the resistances of sin. Balthasar does well to alert us to the fundamental realities of our personhood in God which are deeper than poverty and social status, and which are of great importance to the poor and socially deprived. He notes the human tendency to greed when the plight of the poor begins to be remedied. He rightly brings to mind the complexity of social reality and the limited power of politicians. As Vaclav Havel remarked recently: 'Politicians who offer people a complete recipe for human happiness ... deceive people. Politics can offer only a limited number of things. It can provide and develop conditions under which people can lead a more dignified life: it can guarantee certain liberties. However, it cannot guarantee an earthly paradise ... our society should and must have certain ideals but cannot and must not substitute another utopia for the communist one.'[29] We are well cautioned against a Marxist utopian view especially in so far as it involves an anthropology which sacrifices the individual to the group project. It is good to be reminded that there is a discontinuity between history and what God has prepared for us at the end, that, as the cross of Christ indicates, and as Martin Luther King said with such conviction, 'unearned suffering is redemptive'. What is more questionable however is the dichotomy between human and theological hope, based on the primacy of the spiritual, the kingdom of God, over the material, the Earthly City.[30] Balthasar's Augustinian stress on the discontinuity between the two cities would seem to put arbitrary limits to what must be striven for and what may be achieved, limits which might daunt even the realism of Havel. Who knows what might not be achieved by God working through good women and men to transform our world, given that this is an incarnate God who wants to bring us life to the full and whose preferential measurement of success is how the poorest are treated? With all our need to stress the primacy of God, of the spiritual, indeed of personal conversion, are not all these primacies relativised by God himself in the pairing together of the two great commandments, in the emptying of self to take on human flesh in Jesus of Nazareth, and in the inevitable social implications of personal conversion (now available to human consciousness in a hitherto unprecedentedly differentiated way)? Is there not also a continuity between history and the kingdom of God, so that already we may hope for partial, anticipatory realisations of this kingdom right in the midst of human history in all its dimensions? Are not the spiritual and personal expressed precisely in the material and social? Is not this dichotomy an emasculation in the Balthasarian sense of the male and female stereotype: our theatre of action is being limited, our receptivity is directed away from certain no-go areas?

CONCLUDING ASSESSMENT

In a recent article in *The Way*[31] Simon Barrow characterised

---

[29] Irish Times, Thursday, 16 April 1992: interview with Richard Kearney.
[30] See Gerard O'Hanlon, 1988, for a more detailed critique.
[31] S. Barrow, 'Mystique and Politique: Spirituality Left or Right', *The Way*, 32, 1992, pp. 43–53.

spritiualities of the political right by their stress on the sinfulness of humanity, the dignity of the individual, the separation of the realms of God and of the state in the manner of Augustine's two cities or Luther's two Kingdoms, the conjunction between natural and divine order, and the limited possibility of change in this life except for the area of personal conversion. The tendency is dualistic. Spiritualities of the left take a more transformatory approach, sanguine about the possibility of radical social justice, based on the notion of the reign of God, focusing on equality rather than freedom, and being somewhat weak on suggestions for practical implementation. One is reminded of John Courtney Murray's earlier classification distinguishing a more eschatological from a more incarnational world view.[32] Clearly both views have their strong and weak points, their theological legitimacy, and Balthasar in his tendency to espouse the more right-wing, eschatological approach is much too balanced and qualified to be anything less than formally orthodox in his position.[33] Yet when one views what he says in the light of our Irish situation as illustrated practically by the Roses and Pauls of contemporary Ireland, one may come to several critical conclusions.

First, and very tellingly given our topic, while Balthasar may indeed be formally correct in his position one misses any great sense of drama, of passionate engagement in the project for a new world order. If, again to quote Péguy, it 'is the mystic who nourishes politics',[34] might not someone imbued with the passionate spirit of the Jesus who sided with the poor be expected to support with might and main those 'for whom *mystique* usually means the mystification of suffering and *politique* the postponement of hope?'[35] The real drama in Balthasar occurs in the heart of the individual and, above

---

[32] See J. Courtney Murray, *We Hold These Truths*, London: Sheed and Ward 1960, chapter 8 'Is it Basket Weaving?'

[33] So much so that David Schindler can use Balthasar's position to argue against the neo-conservative movement in the United States of America – see D. L. Schindler, 'The Church's "Worldly" Mission', op. cit., *passim*. In particular, pp. 367–72, Schindler notes the immanent as well as transcendent dimension of the Eucharist in Balthasar's thought. Our criticism is not that Balthasar lacks this dimension but rather that it is incorrectly weighted and its implications are not fully developed.

[34] See S. Barrow, op. cit., p. 43.

[35] Ibid., p. 52.

all, in the life of God. But might not this indicate some justification to critics who charge him with being a-historical? Is there not a danger of being overcentred on the eternal Trinity to the relative neglect of the historical Jesus? That 'remorselessness emphasis on the concrete' which MacKinnon spoke about in Balthasar needs to be qualified by what a recent study by Hilary Mooney diagnoses as his downgrading of existential, subjective contexts.[36] I think it may be ingenuous of Balthasar to criticise Liberation Theology for its nationalism: when Sobrino speaks of the role of theology in terms of telling the story of his country it is clear that this story is indeed related to that of the *catholica*, as indeed must any Irish social theology.[37] With McDade I think it is much more likely that Balthasar's distance from the socio-economic and political is much more a matter of personal sensibility than theological judgment.[38] In this sense he is very much, as all of us to a certain extent, a creature of his own milieu, a point well made again by Hilary Mooney in noting the influence of the highly cultivated, educated Swiss milieu on his thought.[39] One wonders, for example, about the difference it might have made to someone like Balthasar to meet the Roses and Pauls of this world on a daily basis. Might there not be some clue here as to the epistemological significance of that learning from the poor which is so central to Liberation Theology and so missing in Balthasar?

Secondly, there is almost a detached, neutral stance taken by Balthasar to structures such as capitalism and patriarchy which is naive rather than merely politically innocent. From one who is so

[36] See H. Mooney, *The Liberation of Consciousness*, Bernard Lonergan's Theological Foundations in Dialogue with the Theological Aesthetics of Hans Urs von Balthasar, Frankfurt: Knecht 1992, pp. 246–48. More fundamentally Mooney, op. cit., pp. 243–44, diagnoses the lack of a critical reflection, found in Lonergan's use of the notion of judgment, to ground Balthasar's identification of what is true, good and beautiful. This lack may explain the unease of many critics with Balthasar's use of symbolism, in particular, for example, with reference to male and female identities and roles.

[37] See Schall, op. cit., pp. 132–33. For Sobrino see D. Carroll, *Towards a Story of the Earth*, Dublin: Dominican 1987, p. 191. For a discussion of the respective approaches of Balthasar and Sobrino see Paul E. Ritt, 'The Lordship of Jesus Christ: Balthasar and Sobrino', *TS* 49 (1988), pp. 709–29.

[38] See J. McDade, op. cit., p. 140.

[39] See H. Mooney, op. cit., pp. 251–52.

conscious of the reality of evil there is a curious lack of engagement with the great modern structural evils. Granted every primacy to individual conversion, can we really afford to be so lacking in a hermeneutic of suspicion with regard to social evils? Can we, precisely from the Christian perspective, avoid sharing the anger of those oppressed by unjust structures, and, with every respect for realism and complexity, avoid joining in the search for more just replacements? Can we view in-built, systematic, grave disparities in economic and social status with anything less than urgent attention? In this sense, while accepting Balthasar's caution that theology is not competent to change structures, one regrets any serious attempt in his work to engage in the kind of social analysis in an inter disciplinary way which would allow theology to contribute in this area. After all if art, music, drama, philosophy and so on may be dialogue partners for theology, why not economics and politics? And might not the very Christian engagement in economics and politics lead precisely to that lesson of suffering and the cross which Balthasar fears will be lost in a search for a better world – after all, is not the greater danger a too quick accommodation with the *status quo*, a failure to risk both the failure of the cross and the unexpected anticipations of the resurrection that will surely come if we respond to the call of Christ in all the areas of human living? Certainly the 'masters of the universe' are more likely to be left to enjoy their bonfire of vanities by a theology which pronounced with passion on eternal verities but which neglects to bring these pronouncements out of the armchair – or even the kneeler! – into the marketplace. And all this by a theologian living in Switzerland where it is said in the local idiom that Zurich stands on money while Basle, where Balthasar lived, sits on it! In Ireland is it not precisely the way of the Paschal Mystery to try by social analysis, theological reflection and action to forge real solidarity between rich and poor, women and men, clergy and laity, travellers and settled? Is not this a sure way to a discipleship of the cross, lived out in hope of the resurrection? Once again I suspect a very understandable temperamental limitation in Balthasar here, perhaps hinted at in his own admission of dissatisfaction with an earlier attempt to tackle contemporary issues.[40] Whatever the reason the consequences are clear: his mag-

---

[40] See *In Retrospect*, op. cit., p. 212 referring to the 1956 work *Science, Religion and Christianity*.

nificent theological drama can more easily be hijacked to support an unjust *status quo*. His encouragement to the *Communione e Liberazione* movement in Italy does little to allay this fear.

Thirdly, this naiveté is illustrated in particular by his remarks on the Church and structural change. While rightly cautioning a non-party political role for the Church in civil society he assigns this kind of activity to Christian lay people without really adverting to the problem that they too are Church, indeed are in a real sense normatively Church. This is a complex issue which Balthasar seems to neglect. Furthermore there is arguably a rather over-sanguine view taken of the ability of the Church to mirror more closely than civil society the Kingdom of God in her own conduct and structures. One has only to look at the question of the equal treatment of women within the Church to be aware that the rightful constraints of orthodoxy and fidelity to a long tradition can often mean that, despite its apparent advantage in being a free association of the faithful bound together by love, the Church in fact can arrive a little breathless and late at a point of justice long since attained by her secular cousins. Here one might wish for a hermeneutic of greater generosity with respect to civil society, despite all its real evil.

Finally, to end on what I regard as the more dominant positive note. It seems to me that with all these qualifying, critical remarks Balthasar nonetheless has an important and indeed unique contribution to make to the notion of an Irish social theology. That contribution as outlined in this second part of my paper, is, I suggest, relatively unremarkable. It is correct, useful, but not too inspiring. It has the brake on, it is undramatic. What needs to happen is a more sustained bringing together of the first and second parts of this paper – in other words a development of Balthasar beyond himself, using his magnificent trilogy, and in particular the Theo-drama, to articulate a more historical engagement of God with human reality.[41] I have argued elsewhere that this need not be seen as contradicting Balthasar's own thought, and I have indicated some of the main lines of the development in question.[42] Suppose

[41] See Gerard O'Hanlon, 'Does God Change?', *ITQ* 53 (1987), p. 179 (pp. 161–79).

[42] See Gerard O'Hanlon, 1992 and 'The Trinitarian God: Towards a New Ireland', *ITQ* 55 (1989), pp. 99–114. Also, *Solidarity*, op. cit.

one saw the dramatic, eventful trinitarian God of Jesus, who loves all and who identifies in particular with the outcasts, as inviting us now to mirror in partial anticipation the divine society in our human world? Suppose the drama between God and us, affecting God while preserving divine transcendence, called to transfiguration all the areas of human living, including the social, economic, political and cultural dimensions? And suppose in the conflict to bring this about God himself is in the eschatological vanguard, and through the cross and resurrection of Jesus we could experience ourselves as graced collaborators in the new creation which begins already and whose final form, beyond human imagining, will come at the end? This is to transpose the main motifs of Balthasar's theology into a key which is arguably in harmony with his own desire in the 1930s and 1940s to overcome the dualism of neo-Scholasticism.[43] Think of the urgency and the excitement which this vision of God might inspire in us, as we take Jesus at his word! Dare we hope for this? Are we allowed by God to hope for this?

---

[43] See O'Hanlon, 1992, op. cit.

6

MARIAN LIGHT ON OUR HUMAN MYSTERY[1]

Johann Roten, S.M.

In the introduction to *Epilog*,[2] meant as *envoi* (*envoi* as in old French ballads) to his fifteen-volume theological synthesis, Hans Urs von Balthasar strikes a somewhat sad and self-deprecating note. Will this monument do any good? he muses, and how many of his contem-

---

[1]   This presentation is an attempt at bringing together the major articulations of Balthasar's anthropology in the light – as stated in the title – of his Marian thinking. Mirroring the anthropological in the Marian, and vice versa, I had to concentrate on constitutive characteristics only, which means that this article lacks detailed analysis of specific aspects such as, for example, the interaction of divine and human freedom.

I have tried to combine in the present assessment both early and more recent literature, minor writings as well as major works, in order to stress the continuity in Balthasar's thinking and to highlight the all-pervasiveness of some of his key thought patterns.

Only important passages are quoted explicitly, even though most of the affirmations made could have been readily substantiated from Balthasar's own writings. Given the quantitative constraints of this article, no critical account was intended. It should also be mentioned that a certain amount of personal interpretation of Balthasarian concepts went into this presentation, not to curb their meaning but to point to the vast range of their applicability.

Balthasar's anthropology is literally pre-programmed in his own biography. It rests on the simple word *yes*, in its complex and comprehensive meaning ranging from acceptance (*Bejahung*) to fruitfulness, and is discursively articulated in Balthasar's *Theologic*. The Balthasarian yes, as constitutive anthropological act, is made still more explicit in the configurations of *ecstasis* and *kenosis*, as articulated in his *Theoaesthetics* and *Theo-dramatics*. Balthasar is eager to point out how these constitutive anthropological articulations impact the history of ideas in the past and in the present. These are some of the guiding principles I have used to explore Balthasar's anthropology in the light of his Marian thinking.

[2]   *Epilog*, Johannes Verlag, Einsiedeln 1987, pp. 7–8.

poraries – all of them potential victims of a disease called *anima technica vacua* – will venture to cross the threshold of this theological Versailles for more than a casual tourist's visit? In some ways, the introduction to *Epilog* reads like the tired and repeatedly performed gesture of throwing still another bottle into the sea, in the hope that some day it will wash up on a distant shore, to be unsealed and avidly deciphered by people starving for what seems dearest to Balthasar's mind and heart: the whole of the Christian mysteries.

PERSONAL APPROXIMATIONS

Yet, this seemingly tired gesture somehow strikes a familiar cord. It is indeed a recurrent theme in Balthasar's biography. Early on, at the time of *Das Weizenkorn*,[3] he already shows a realistic inkling of what life has in store for those who go against the grain because mandated to do so:

> Things will never change. One day somebody wakes up among the mass of people; he outgrows them, intuits his vocation and speaks out. Yet as he grows and his soul expands and is filled, he gradually becomes a stranger and a riddle for the people around him and is no longer listened to. Finally, he dies, drowned in his own abundance. In the end, when everything is over, they will, of course, put up a monument for him.[4]

Tragic as this may sound, Balthasar's foreboding is part, an important part, of his constant self-understanding, as he expressed already in the early forties: 'It does not matter whether the vase breaks or simply overflows; one thing only is important: to pass on the message.'[5]

THE BALTHASARIAN CONSTELLATIONS

Between *Weizenkorn* (1944) – and even before it – and *Epilog* (1987), between the beginning and the termination of his work as

---

[3]   *Das Weizenkorn, Aphorismen.* Räber, Luzern 1944 (Johannes Verlag, Einsiedeln 1953[2] and 1989[3]) (=Wz).

[4]   Wz, 63 – quotes are from the first edition; their translation is the work of the author and is so throughout this article unless otherwise indicated.

[5]   Wz, p. 156.

a theologian and writer, there flows a steady stream of missionary consciousness. It may be captured and capsulised in a sentence by which Balthasar lived and acted, a sentence that could serve as the motto of his life and which represents one of the cornerstones of both his anthropology and mariology: 'More than anything else' – he says in one of his theological progress reports – 'it is the fact to have been commissioned and to serve which constitutes authentic Christian identity'.[6]

Although they seem at first sight only colourful patchwork, the various episodes and quotes so far mentioned form a tightly knit fabric of beliefs and convictions by which Balthasar structured and oriented his existence. They are the 'constellations representing my thought and my action'.[7] The most visible of these constellations which constitute Balthasar's understanding of himself is the task or commission to pass on the message once received. This is a truly noble task, a task that is diametrically opposed to the bourgeois ideal of seeking personal perfection for itself. This accounts for Balthasar's strongly felt urge to disappear behind or within all that is important to him: the community of St John, his publishing house, even his own theological work.[8] Yet, the importance of the work to be accomplished and the message to be passed on are not the result of any personal scheming plotted in ivory-tower seclusion and implemented with an iron fist. As Balthasar once said: 'In the beginning we are objects and not self-sustained subjects, and so we need the humility to receive before we can even start thinking about how to give.'[9]

OBJECTIVE INTERIORITY

The complementarity of receiving and giving constitutes 'objective interiority', the one solid point of reference in the human person that cannot be dissolved in subjectivity and thus escapes the

---

[6] 'Kleiner Lageplan zu meinen Büchern', in: *Schweizer Rundschau* 55 (1955), p. 213 (= KL).

[7] Wz, p. 43.

[8] Zeugen des Jahrhunderts. Manuskript-Text der Sendung von Erwin Koller im Schweizer Fernsehen am Karfreitagabend, 20. April 1984. p. 35. (Manuscript of a Balthasar feature on Swiss television presented on Good Friday, [20.4] 1984.)

[9] Wz, p. 19.

deconstructivist tendencies of psychology and sociology. 'Objective interiority', according to Balthasar, is both the source of personal action and the river of God's loving call which flows through out very heart and thus carries and feeds the source of our personal response and endeavour. In mapping out his spiritual territory, and by defining it as the space between John and Ignatius,[10] Balthasar again refers to 'objective interiority' as the true hallmark of both these saints. John stands for the free and loving self-communication of God, whereas Ignatius is the ever present figurehead of free call, free election and mission. Similarly, 'objective interiority' represents the genetic code of Balthasar's 'great individual', that is the human person who towers over the masses, not of his or her own volition or merit, but because such a person's soul is filled with and expands under the onrush of his/her mission's grandeur and force. The ensuing and inevitable loneliness and rejection – as expressed in *Epilog* and *Weizenkorn* – are not, in Balthasar's mind, a senseless tragedy, but an integral part of authentic Christian identity.

THEOLOGICAL BIOGRAPHY

Balthasar's theology is the grandiose attempt to overcome the centuries-old and tragic split between 'sitting- and-kneeling-theology', the schism of doxography and biography. We detect in Balthasar's work what he himself remarked about Maximus Confessor: the beautiful and loving unity between objective and real values and those which are dear and indispensable to our own heart.[11] In this way, Balthasar's theology is eminently theological biography. Universalist in its construction, leaving out nothing, taking into account all of Scripture and tradition – it has the ring not so much of the professor's but of the confessor's voice.[12] Sovereign in its approach and promethean in its dimension, Balthasar's theology is so obviously received and candidly owed that the reader feels himself become a part of something greater than the master's work. He or she who transmits has to *personalise*, Balthasar reminds us, meaning

---

[10] KL, p. 213.
[11] *Kosmische Liturgie. Das Weltbild Maximus des Bekenners*, Johannes Verlag, Einsiedeln 1961², p. 20.
[12] *Cordula oder der Ernstfall*, Johannes Verlag, Einsiedeln 1966, p. 6.

that theological biography occurs only in the original act of *tradere*, which is impossible without the double gesture of receiving and passing on.

These attitudes are so genuinely Marian. The whole of Balthasar's theological existence and work is thus centred around the realities of vocation and mission. Because of it, his theological biography is unmistakably impregnated with the Marian watermark. And, since true Christian identity is likewise centred on vocation and mission, Balthasar's theological anthropology – for him the only real anthropology – also bears the Marian hallmark.

THE CONSTITUTIVE ANTHROPOLOGICAL ACT (ANTHROPOLOGY *IN ACTU*)

The methodological key to Balthasar's anthropology, it would seem, lies in the German *Bejahung*, meaning a positive attitude which conveys both the intellectual habitus of affirmation and the more existentially oriented habit of acceptance. Balthasar refrains from systematising, since truth does not suffer violence. Intellectual discourse is circular, i.e., affirmative and interpretative at the same time. Most of Balthasar's writings are – in his own mind – sketches and fragments, the ever-new attempt to affirm and confirm more thoroughly and more extensively. Philosophy as controversy is a waste of time; what matters, counts and will last is affirmative truth.[13] In 1927 already, he coins the lapidary sentence: 'He who affirms more and better is and will be right.'[14]

More recently, Balthasar points to Mary as the archetype of countless possibilities to say yes (affirmation/acceptance): 'Mary opens up countless possibilities of saying "Yes" for all who come after her. All of them are personal, all of them are original; according to God's commission, all of them are new and have never existed before; yet they are all related to one another in their positive aspects [*Positivität*, J.R.]. For the Christian, above all else, is a man who says

---

[13] *Apokalypse der deutschen Seele. Studien zu einer Lehre von den letzten Haltungen.* Bd. 2: *Im Zeichen Nietzsches.* A. Pustet, Salzburg 1939, p. 20.
[14] 'Kunst und Religion', in *Volkswohl* (Wien) 18 (1927), p. 354.

"Yes".[15] Christianity is, for Balthasar, the only *Weltanschauung* truly to say yes to the world and to the present.[16]

IN PRAISE OF FINITENESS

Affirmation is the central motif of the Balthasarian intellectual discourse takes on three different and complementary expressions. The first and most immediate one, which we would like to call 'praise of finiteness', mainly results from Balthasar's spiritual encounter with great figures of German and French literature and philosophy. He has, for example, a special liking for Goethe's truthfulness and trustworthiness of reality[17] and frequently refers to Claudel's idea of perfection of finite reality – as, for example, expressed in these words: 'Soyez béni, mon Dieu, qui ne laissez pas vos oeuvres inachevées / Et qui avez fait de moi un être fini à l'image de votre perfection.'[18] Creation, indeed, has its own contours and consistency; its finiteness must be praiseworthy finiteness; for if it were only the shadow of infinity, Incarnation would be reduced to a purely gnostic or cosmological event.[19] Praise of finiteness has also the meaning of delving courageously into the river of truth, instead of standing doubtfully on its bank, debating the question whether the river exists or not.[20]

Finiteness is praiseworthy and should be wholeheartedly affirmed in its finiteness, because it is not closed upon itself. Finiteness means openness calling upon infinity for completion and perfection, just as the immense openness of Greek temples was brought to completion in and by the keystone of Gothic cathedrals.[21] Thus, to say yes to finite reality – the joyful affirmation of things and persons,

[15] *You Crown the Year with Your Goodness: Sermons through the Liturgical Year*, Ignatius Press, San Francisco 1989, p. 24 (translated by Graham Harrison).

[16] 'Geist und Feuer, Michael Albus: Ein Gespräch mit Hans Urs von Balthasar', in *Herder-Korrespondenz* 30 (1976), p. 77.

[17] *Apokalypse der deutschen Seele. Studien zu einer Lehre von den letzten Haltungen*. Bd. 1: *Der deutsche Idealismus*. A. Pustet, Salzburg 1937, p. 409.

[18] 'Philosophie und Theologie des Lebens', in *Das Problem des Lebens in der Forschung, Schweizerische Hochschulzeitung* 1 (1938), p. 47.

[19] *Theologie der Geschichte*, Johannes Verlag, Einsiedeln 1959³, p. 86.

[20] *Wahrheit*, Bd. 1: *Wahrheit der Welt*, Benziger, Einsiedeln 1947, p. 13.

[21] *Apokalypse der deutschen Seele. Studien zu einer Lehre von den letzten Haltungen*, Bd. 3: *Die Vergöttlichung des Todes*, A. Pustet, Salzburg 1939, p. 237.

the works of nature and of human ingenuity – has a deeper and twofold meaning: it is truly praise of finiteness, yes, but as such it becomes praise of infinity present in the figure of finiteness.

HOLY OBSESSION WITH THE CONCRETE

The praise of finiteness is intimately linked with Balthasar's holy obsession with the concrete character of truth. He puts up his gnoseological tent between the positions of positivism and the multifaceted expressions of Platonism and idealism. Concreteness is uniqueness and bodiliness since it results from fusion, concretion, and interconnectedness.[22] In Balthasar's world of intellectual figures it specifically indicates the bodiliness of the Spirit and the spiritualisation of the body. The collective memory of western civilisation will always remember, according to Balthasar, that the ultimate goal of intellectual abstraction is heightened concreteness, the ever greater and more radical bodiliness of the Spirit.[23] The idea of the apple is best intuited by the eye that sees and the tongue that tastes the apple. Ideas are without consistency; ideas do not have binding character.[24] Individuation alone has the power to deliver and redeem the intellect/spirit from abstraction. In humility, every being is bound to learn how to be *this* individual being only.[25] Bodiliness is the actual and visible criteria of performance; body is the spirit's 'liberating barrier or boundary' and thus constitutes the concrete criteria of love, the measure of accomplishment versus futile promise.

Balthasar's holy obsession with the concrete character of reality points to biblical roots. For him, there is no theological anthropology without biblical foundations – a concern he shares with confrères such as Karl Barth, Romano Guardini, Gustav Siewerth and, again, Paul Claudel.[26] Human experience of God and world is

---

[22] *Das Weltbild Hans Stockers*, in, Hans Stocker. *Sakrale Kunst*, Bd. 8. Hrsg. von der Schweiz. Lukasgesellschaft, NZN Buchverlag, Zürich 1957, p. 130.

[23] *Das Weltbild Hans Stockers*, loc. cit., p. 131; see also: 'Christlicher Humanismus', in *Gloria Dei* (Seckau) 4 (1949), pp. 37–38.

[24] 'Christlicher Humanismus', loc. cit., p. 44.

[25] Ibid.

[26] See *Herrlichkeit. Eine theologische Aesthetik*, Bd. I: *Schau der Gestalt*, Johannes Verlag, Einsiedeln 1961, pp. 367–93.

wholistic, involving both body and spirit; ultimate reality – the real real! – is the person as *Thou*, that is, God and fellow human beings. The encounter between God and humanity occurs in the realm of the senses, where flesh speaks to flesh.

The true *exinanitio Dei*, therefore, is embodied in the Word made flesh, the one and only, whom Balthasar calls *concretissimum ens*. Jesus Christ is the quintessence of concretion and concreteness; through him and for him all things in nature and history are concrete.[27] In the person of Jesus Christ the schism and chasm between the particular and the general are abolished: being God, he is the *universale concretum*, the true *phoenix Christus*. Being the ultimate norm and true subject of history, Jesus Christ, the particular and contingent being, also 'embodies' and represents the general and the necessary.[28]

THE AFFIRMATION OF BEING

The apprenticeship of affirmation and acceptance then – the habitus of saying yes – is steeped in concretion and concreteness. There exists no real yes where there is no concretion of call and response, based on the concrete situation of the concrete caller and responder and the actual concretisation of the yes. Yet, there is in Balthasar a second form or expression of affirmation: the affirmation of being.

Balthasar's thinking is universalist and comprehensive, it is constantly focused on the totality of reality. Affirmation, in turn, has to be full and comprehensive, constantly focused in awe and wonderment on the fullness of Being. What Balthasar suggests and intends is a profession of faith in favour of ontology and metaphysics. The Christian, since he is a person of faith, must also be an adept of philosophy. If he really believes in God's absolute love for the world, then he is bound to read the ontological difference in Being as a manifestation of God's love.[29]

The Christian is and remains the shepherd of that metaphysical wonderment which constitutes the act of philosophising and with-

---

[27] *Das Weltbild Hans Stockers*, loc. cit., p. 132.
[28] See *Verbum Caro*, Johannes Verlag, Einsiedeln 1965², pp. 182–83.
[29] *Herrlichkeit. Eine theologische Aesthetik*, Bd. III/2. *Neuzeit*, Johannes Verlag, Einsiedeln 1975², p. 974.

out which philosophy cannot exist. Balthasar makes a difference between wonderment and admiration. Admiration is a threat to wonderment. It freezes being into an object of aesthetics or science. The chasm between admiration and wonderment can be bridged only by love.[30] Love alone is able to receive being as a gratuitous gift and to give thanks and praise for it. Finally, Christians, the shepherds of metaphysical wonderment, are called to say yes to Being in lieu and in place of humanity at large.

THE WHOLE OF REALITY

Such is, thus, metaphysical affirmation: the loving yes to the ontological difference, meaning the wonderful and, at times, painful experience of complementarity and difference between gift and giver, beauty and glory, the mystery of being and the splendour of the act that posits our existence. Implicitly a theological act, metaphysical affirmation says yes to the whole of reality. Balthasar's circular approach to reality generates a variety of descriptions of totality.

Already in 1925 this approach surfaces as the call for synthesis, the deep-seated conviction that there is in reality – as Clement of Alexandria pointed out – a convergence toward a maximum of meaning and significance.[31] In his lifelong quest and concern for totality, Balthasar frequently fustigates the importance of analysis and the sterility of systematisation.

Central to his quest is the *living figure* or form (the German *Gestalt*),[32] as we find it in the figure of reality or in the figure of revelation. It is compared to the human person and the artwork; it is a many-splendoured thing that opens ever new perspectives and offers countless angles of vision.[33] Figure or form rejoin concreteness; for its ultimate legitimation lies in the *concretissimum ens* of Jesus Christ. Figure can neither be construed[34] nor can it be

---

[30] Loc. cit., p. 975.
[31] 'Die Innsbrucker Herbsttagung des Verbandes der Vereine katholischer Akademiker', in *Schweizer Rundschau*, Einsiedeln 25 (1925), p. 383.
[32] Concerning meaning and translation of the German term *Gestalt*, see, e.g., M. Waldstein, 'An Introduction to von Balthasar's *The Glory of the Lord*', in *Communio: International Catholic Review* (1987), p. 19.
[33] 'Geist und Feuer', loc. cit., p. 76.
[34] *Herrlichkeit*, Bd. I. loc. cit., p. 448.

dissolved, except for its destruction in the cross of Christ (*Ungestalt*) and its 'reconstruction' in his resurrection (*Übergestalt*).[35]

Where Balthasar's pledge to wholeness is couched in metaphors such as 'totality', this does not indicate a sudden nominalist slip of the tongue. Totality means integration, integration of particular viewpoints. Totality is the rule by which the truth is managed; it makes intellectual confrontation meaningful and fruitful.[36] It points to the perspectivist character of truth, where intellectual exchange and comparison will earn legitimation only in reference to totality. And at the heart of totality lives love, for there is authentic passage from partial to total truth only when a mortal human being's partial knowledge becomes, in and because of love, potentially unlimited.[37] There is no proof for totality; there is only the report about it that is a stammered account about the evidence of its splendid and glorious revelation. Totality is announced in love and echoed by the loving restitution of self back into totality. According to Balthasar totality in this world is represented by love, and he therefore established the following denominator of coextensivity: totality-being-love-trinity. No wonder then that Balthasar adopted this method: to see, to ponder, and to recognise totality.[38]

In still another metaphor, the *centre* becomes the vanishing point of totality. The movement of both understanding and faith origi-nates at the centre and returns to it, stressing thereby the importance of the Balthasarian notions of convergence and integration.[39] Inte-gration, as it is articulated, for example, in Balthasar's indefatigable insistence on the Catholic *Et-Et*,[40] is best and maybe most charac-teristically voiced in the unbreakable unity and complementarity of philosophy and theology on the one hand, of theology and spiritu-ality on the other hand.

---

[35] See, e.g., M. Jöhri, 'Descensus Dei. Teologia della croce nell'Opera di Hans urs von Balthasar', *Corona Lateranensis* 30, Roma 1981, pp. 338–67; W. Link, *Gestalt und Gestalglosigkeit der Kirche*, Diss. Pontif. Univ. Gregoriana, Roma 1970.

[36] *Theologik I: Wahrheit der Welt*, Johannes Verlag, Einsiedeln 1985, p. 209.

[37] Loc. cit., p. 139.

[38] *Klarstellungen. Zur Unterscheidung der Geister*, Herder, Freiburg 1978[4], p. 15.

[39] See concerning the meaning of these notions for theology: *Convergences: To the Sources of Christian Mystery*, Ignatius Press, San Francisco 1984.

[40] *The Office of Peter and the Structure of the Church*, Ignatius Press, San Francisco 1989, pp. 301–8 (=OP).

Yet, the most decisive of all the various descriptions of totality and wholeness is what we would like to designate as the comparative dynamic of reality, the Balthasarian *immer mehr* (ever more), the Augustinian and Ignatian expression of *maior*. It lends depths to totality, shapes truth according to the laws of the comparative of being and directs it toward the future. Thus, the discovery of truth leads to the ever greater riches of being,[41] and similarly the disciple is drawn by the God of the Gospel into ever deeper personal involvement and commitment.[42]

THE IGNATIAN ATTITUDE

There is a third and highest form of affirmation in Balthasar's life and work. We would like to call it the Ignatian attitude. Balthasar's sense of existential direction is deeply Ignatian. The Ignatian attitude is based on a high-level meditation about Jesus Christ and characterised – in a nutshell – as 'listening *into* [sic!] the calling of the Word and the freeing of self in the answer expected of us'.[43] Its structural articulation is threefold and patterned according to the stages of election, indifference and obedience.

Balthasar's anthropology leans neither toward Augustine's *cor inquietum* nor toward Thomas' *visio beatifica*. And why so? God cuts through both restlessness (Augustine) and striving (Thomas) to freely elect the human person for his own concern and endeavour. There exists an open and ongoing dialectical movement between human decision or choice and God's election. What we designate as election indicates that the centre of the human person ultimately is made up neither of restlessness nor striving, but that it is constituted as *disposición*. God's elective will cannot be discovered and ascertained – neither in part nor as a whole – in and through human nature. It is rooted in God's personal sovereignty expressed in Jesus Christ and has to be understood as a particular act on behalf of or toward a particular being at a given time. Election stresses the uniqueness and originality of the encounter between God and the

---

[41]   *Theologik I*, loc. cit., p. 227.
[42]   *The God Question and Modern Man*, The Seabury Press, New York 1967[2], p. 142ff.
[43]   *Rechenschaft 1965*, Johannes Verlag, Einsiedeln 1965, p. 8.

human person. This is what Balthasar calls the *analogia electionis*.[44]

The Ignatian attitude of affirmation evolves toward a second stage, characterised as indifference.[45] Indifference amounts to a quasi-ontological disposition; it is a permanent human attitude in and through which we existentially profess the primacy of God's will. In this stage of indifference, we are led by faith, hope and charity to give permanent preference to God's truth, to God's love and to his promise. Indifference represents the human foundation upon which 'election', the divine act by which we are constituted as Christians, can be firmly posited. And there is progression in indifference, too: from humility (the recognition of God's norm in everything), we are led to radical availability (directed in the first place to God personally, not towards his plans for us), and on to christiform indifference (lived and expressed in poverty, trial and the folly of the cross).

The Ignatian attitude culminates in obedience.[46] It is the most specific and comprehensive act of our saying yes to God's will, an act posited, in the present, by a concrete person and on behalf of this concrete person. Patterned on trinitarian obedience as its ultimate model, Christian obedience is not an expression of spiritual isolationism. It connects the person with the entire christological constellation, foremost with the Church.[47] Finally, in obedience we not only reinforce our disposition of receptiveness and self-giving, but obedience also connotes an eminently active orientation prompting implementation and realisation.

BALTHASAR'S EXISTENTIAL YES

Of all three forms of affirmation, the Ignatian attitude is the most explicitly Marian. It is one of the salient features not only of Balthasar's work but also of his life. The Ignatian attitude – prefigured in the archetypal yes of Mary – is mirrored in both

---

[44] See *Theo-drama: Theological Dramatic Theory*, III. *Dramatis Personae: Persons in Christ*, Ignatius Press, San Francisco 1992, pp. 263–71 (=TD).

[45] See 'Drei Formen der Gelassenheit', in *Geist und Leben* 54 (1981), pp. 270–75; A. von Speyr, *Ignatiana*. Johannes Verlag, Einsiedeln 1974, pp. 354–56.

[46] See Speyr, *Ignatiana*, p. 247ff. (Schule des Gehorsams). Balthasar's writings about obedience are legion.

[47] OP, pp. 136–45.

Balthasar's doxography and his biography. Let us recall only two events of his life where the Ignatian attitude bears epochal importance.

First, there is the event which led to Balthasar's existential yes during the thirty-day retreat of 1927 in Whylen near Basle. Thirty years later he still recognised the tree in the Black Forest where God's call had reached him and where he, once a fan of the metaphysical poet Stephen George, was overpowered by the irresistible power of God's crucified love. It stripped him of all worldly aspirations, and as Stalder put it: 'Dès lors il se soumit sans hésitations aux exigences radicales de la vocation.'[48] The experience of Whylen was not a call to theology, not even one to the priesthood. It was a call into the existential yes, constitutive of the way in which he would conceive his life in the future. From then on it was no longer up to him to choose and plan: 'You are not to choose; you are called. You will not serve; you will be used. You are not to make any plans; you are but a tiny element in a large mosaic projected long ago.'[49] Spiritually, Balthasar relived in Whylen the experience of the grain of wheat; henceforth, death and rebirth constitute but one and the same life bringing forth God's own harvest.[50]

Later, the memento of his ordination would bear the words of the *Roman Canon: Benedixit, fregit, deditque*; it was his way to express the solidarity and common destiny between master and servant. Gradually, according to Balthasar's own understanding of things, this fundamental and existential yes undergoes a profound transformation. The Ignatian attitude of the beginnings, an attitude of almost promethean proportions, evolves and matures into a profoundly Johannine vocation, one ultimately related to his common mission with Adrienne von Speyr.

It dawned on him that at all times vocation remains God's creation, to be remodelled, even broken and reshaped, according to his inspiration and will. Yet, the same law that breaks holds the power to heal. Balthasar's withdrawal from the Company of Jesus has to be read against this backdrop. The long and painful story of

[48]   R. Stalder, 'Amour et Vision. Hommage à Hans Urs von Balthasar', in *Civitas* 20 (1964/65), p. 605.

[49]   *Pourquoi je me suis fait prêtre*, ed. Centre Diocésain de Documentation, Tournai 1961, pp. 20/21.

[50]   *Das Herz der Welt*, Arche Verlag, Zürich 1953², p. 55.

his departure resulted in the deepening and expansion of his existential yes. This yes was pronounced in the name of Ignatius and for the sake of ever greater fidelity to the original Ignatian inspiration.[51]

Balthasar is led and helped along in his decision by Adrienne von Speyr. Henceforth, there is a change in priorities: the community of St John and – after Adrienne's death – the publication of her writings take precedence over Balthasar's own literary production. But, most important, Balthasar's Ignatian attitude has been reset in a radically Johannine perspective, where *disposición* and *indifferéncia* are permeated with the qualities of *menein*, the permanent and transparent presence of God's love. Balthasar's Marian profile has its roots and takes form in the charism of Ignatius, deepened and enlivened by the spirit of John.[52]

THE MARIAN WATERMARK

Indeed, the existentially constitutive act of anthropology – affirmation, the 'yes' – bears an unmistakably Marian watermark. It is neither usurped by nor the fruit of a simplistic mariological projection. The reading of finite reality leads to the discovery of receptiveness and openness to infinity; the meditation of being opens the understanding for the ontological difference and its ultimate rootedness in love (*ens et amor convertuntur*), yet, it is in the contemplation of the history of God's self-revelation that the deep Marian configuration of human reality is most concretely and most comprehensively articulated.

And so Mary, the person who lends flesh and blood to the Marian principle, stands for anthropological concretisation and comprehensiveness. She, the 'most pure among all imaginable creatures, does not mediate anything whatsoever of the heavenly truth without the cooperation of the senses'.[53] The figure of concreteness is the unmovable cornerstone of Balthasar's christology; the figure of

---

[51]   *Zeugen des Jahrhunderts*, loc. cit., p. 19.

[52]   See *Unser Auftrag. Bericht und Entwurf. Einführung in die von A. v. Speyr gegründete Johannesgemeinschaft*, Johannes Verlag, Einsiedeln 1984, pp. 105/106 (=UA).

[53]   A. von Speyr, *Die Magd des Herrn. Ein Marienbuch*, Johannes Verlag, Einsiedeln 1969², p. 182.

totality (comprehensiveness) ultimately refers to his trinitarian theology, and the attitude of affirmation represents the foundational human act of ecclesiology.

No wonder, then, that Mary reflects the three basic ciphers, or better, figures, of Balthasar's philosophical and theological discourse: concreteness, totality and affirmation. This reminds us that she is the meeting point for a great many fundamental Christian doctrines, 'almost like a railway junction where many lines converge and where connections are established' (John Macquarrie). She is herself neither *ens concretissimum*[54] nor the totality of being. Her role in Christian life is one of concretising, as she did at the outset of the history of incarnation. She is simultaneously the 'maîtresse de la voie et du raccordement':[55] Mary connects, brings together and – most important – points beyond herself.

THE ANTHROPOLOGICAL CONFIGURATIONS (ANTHROPOLOGY *IN SITU*)

Thus, at the heart of Balthasar's anthropology we are able to locate the existentially constitutive act of affirmation and acceptance. At this point, the question may be asked: Did this act or attitude take on a special configuration in his work? Or to put it differently: Would it be possible to ascertain that the Yes-attitude has a structural and structuring character, that important configurations of Balthasar's work have been shaped by this existentially constitutive act of his anthropology? The answer to this question would seem to be yes.

ECSTASIS AND KENOSIS

The Balthasarian human existence is essentially ecstatic and kenotic: to stand and be active in God's service (kenotic dimension) one has to be enveloped and raptured by God's glory and love (ecstatic dimension). One cannot be separated from the other. *Kalon* and *agathon* belong to each other and signify – as Plato would have

---

[54]   OP, p. 196ff.
[55]   Ch. Péguy, *Tapisserie de Notre Dame. Oeuvres poétiques complètes*, Pléiade, Paris 1941, p. 698.

remarked – both the vision of the sacred and the sacred character of being.[56] Theological phenomenology – such as Balthasar's – is grounded in the act of *aisthanesthai*, meaning receptive perception. In Balthasar's understanding, this verb is connected with the Latin *audio, avisdio*, meaning to comprehend, to hear, and also with *oboedio* from *ob-avisdio*, meaning to obey in the sense of acting appropriately.[57] In 1939 already, Balthasar wrote an article bearing as title the lapidary interrogation: 'Verstehen *oder* Gehorchen?' (Understanding *or* Obeying?)[58] The answer to this question was – of course – not an either-or solution, but the typical Balthasarian *et-et*: it matters to understand *and* to obey. The article mentioned has seminal qualities and anticipates the hallmarks of both Theoaesthetics and Theo-dramatics, as well as the unavoidable and indissolubly paradoxical character of human existence.

There is then an intimate and unbreakable connection between seeing and hearing, understanding (knowing) and obeying, between Theoaesthetics and Theo-dramatics, between *ecstasis* and *kenosis*. Theology based on a like understanding of reality presents two major features: it is adoration and obedience. In and through adoration we confidently expect and receive the infinite in the finite, whereas in and through obedience we ratify and interiorise what we comprehend in adoration, so as to make it the foundation of our personal existence.

A VOCATION OF ECCENTRICITY

Each in its own way, *ecstasis* and *kenosis* testify to the eccentric disposition and vocation of the human person. In *ecstasis* we are decentred by God's loving glory, only to be re-centred in the mission of the kenotic Christ. The eccentricity of the theological understanding of the human person is our acceptance and admission into the trinitarian love-cycle. Eccentricity typifies the existential movement patterned by the laws of appropriation through disappropriation, and it is made palpable in its unity and diversity through Theoaesthetics and Theo-dramatics.

---

[56] 'Offenbarung und Schönheit', in *Hochland* 51 (1959), p. 405.

[57] 'Current trends in Catholic Theology and the Responsibility of the Christian', in *Communio: International Catholic Review* (Spring 1978), p. 81.

[58] 'Verstehen oder Gehorchen', in *Stimmen der Zeit* 69 (1938), pp. 78–85.

The double movement of emergence and immersion, of rapture and disappropriation – as the ever same and new variations of *ecstasis* and *kenosis* – has a very definite comparative character. It follows and is punctuated by the rhythms of love, where *more* means the greater glory of God and *less* the greater realisation of our own humble truth. Yet, because it is embedded in love, *ecstasis* leads to ever deeper faith and *kenosis* to ever stronger hope, meaning that faith will never pretend to be able to anticipate the final seeing of the form,[59] and hope never entertain the illusion of being already in possession of things to come.[60][61]

'SUSPENSION' (*SCHWEBE*) AND 'TENSION'

According to Balthasarian semantics, *ecstasis* results in and through *Schwebe*, a state of suspension or existential hovering. The ecstatic experience is not only the theoaesthetic experience of perception and rapture, in what Balthasar calls the 'subjective evidence' (experience of faith), but, granted that the human intellect (spirit) is essentially ecstatic,[62] human existence as a whole also lives in a state of *ecstasis*. Human beings live in suspension; literally that is, they are suspended, they are hanging from or hanging in God's mystery of love. According to the theoaesthetic code, perception and rapture are intimately linked. In a sense, to see means to be seized. It further means that theoaesthetic 'possession' is the experience of gratuity, and gratuity the experience of non-possession.

However, theoaesthetic experience (*ecstasis*) has no self-alienating effect. It eliminates, on the contrary, our experience or impression of estrangement and alienation from the source of absolute love. This existential hovering may seem uncomfortable: invited into infinity, but without having made our home there, enraptured but not alienated. Balthasar nonetheless considers this seemingly uncomfortable existential situation as whole and wholesome. Incomprehensible and mysterious as our existence in suspension may

---

[59] *2 Corinthians* 5: 7.

[60] *Romans* 8: 24–25.

[61] *Das Ganze im Fragment. Aspekte der Geschichtstheologie*, Benziger Verlag, Einsiedeln 1963, p. 354 (=GiF).

[62] *Das christliche Jahr. Text zu Bildern von Richard Seewald*, Josef Stocker, Luzern 1944 (see: Pfingsten).

be, it has a wonderfully moving and driving quality, the healing power to make us whole.[63]

Kenosis, on the other hand, is synonymous with existential tension. Where there is freedom, there is tension, especially where infinite freedom meets finite freedom. Tension is engrained in the very texture of Theo-dramatic existence, because it is simultaneously *Gegebensein* and *Aufgegebensein*, date and mandate, a given but also a challenge. In a specifically theological context there is existential tension between the first and the second Adam and, an even more typically Theo-dramatic tension (*kenosis*), between ever greater disappropriation and ever greater personalisation. The theodramatic person lives in constant tension between his identity as creature and the God-offered challenge to mature into a new personality grounded in mission.[64]

'Suspension' and 'tension' are like two faces of the same coin, and so likewise are *ecstasis* and *kenosis*. At the very foundation of both 'suspension' and 'tension' we discover the watermark of the *analogia entis*, whereas *ecstasis* and *kenosis* are figures which designate their common foundation in the comparative character of being. Being, as we read it in Balthasarian theology, is both love and freedom, which means that *ecstasis* ultimately represents the human answer to the comparative character of love, and *kenosis* the proper reaction to the comparative dynamics of freedom. And again, 'suspension' can be associated with the Johannine *menein* (existence in love) and 'tension' with the Pauline *hypomonē*.[65]

Analysing, in the 1930s, Goethe's theory of knowledge for *Apocalypse*, Balthasar distinguished two complementary facets: one is called 'gnoseological humility' and leads to an attitude of self-giving; the other corresponds to 'gnoseological asceticism' and materialises in action-orientation. The two combined result in a comprehensive attitude of growing openness.[66] It would seem that we are confronted here with still another early draft of Theoaesthetics and Theo-dramatics!

---

[63] GiF, p. 122.
[64] TD II/2, p. 212 (German version).
[65] *2 Corinthians* 6:4.
[66] *Apokalypse der deutschen Seele*, Bd. 1, loc. cit., pp. 419–26.

FIGURE (FORM) AND ROLE

The anthropological vehicles of *ecstasis* and *kenosis* are respectively *figure* for Theoaesthetics and *role* for Theo-dramatics. *Ecstasis* happens on behalf of the visible form which not only points to an invisible and mysterious depth, but which itself is also phenom-enon, meaning manifestation as well as hidden presence. Thus, the movement of *ecstasia* originates in the encounter with the visible form and from there is inexorably drawn into the depth of the reality which is also the source of what is manifest in the visible form. Ultimately, it is this double polarity of and within the figure which triggers the ecstatic movement.[67] This is well documented in the three expressions of what Balthasar calls the form of faith or Christian figure, namely, the trinitarian form, the form of the *concretissimum ens* and the most anthropological of Christian forms: the figure of Mother and Child.[68]

The artist is the one anthropological profile in Balthasar's work where the intimate relationship between form and *ecstasis* are most accurately illustrated. The true artist is literally absorbed into his own creation; his whole person is entirely directed toward his work. In the end he disappears behind or into his work. His artistic genius is one of gratuity; his highest achievement lies in the ability to point beyond himself. In this sense, the artist is a theoaesthetic facilitator; his *ecstasis* is the ecstasis of service.[69]

Similarly, the typical anthropological profile of Theo-dramatics is the actor.[70] He, too, suggests transparency and availability. His position is one of mediation. The *kenosis* of his vocation materialises in the role he plays, and his uncomfortable position between author and director, between director and spectator, creates dramatic tension. Above all, the actor is torn between his personal identity and the exigencies of his role.

The role is to Theo-dramatics what the figure or form is to Theoaesthetics. And as in Theoaesthetics the beautiful form be-

---

[67]   *Herrlichkeit, Eine theologische Aesthetik*, Bd. I: *Schau der Gestalt*. Johannes Verlag, Einsiedeln 1967², p. 144 (=H).

[68]   *Pneuma und Institution*, Johannes Verlag, Einsiedeln 1974, p. 59 (=PI).

[69]   See 'Christliche Kunst und Verkündigung', in *Mysterium Salutis I*. Benziger Verlag, Einsiedeln 1965, p. 179.

[70]   See TD I, pp. 260–74.

comes the Christian form, so in the Theo-dramatics the notion of role is replaced with that of mission.

THE MARIAN CONNOTATION

We have attempted to show how the central anthropological act of affirmation – the Balthasarian yes – can be retrieved and pinpointed in Theoaesthetics and Theo-dramatics as *ecstasis* and *kenosis*. They have not lost thereby any of their Marian connotation. The Theoaesthetics, the archetypal human experience of the Christian figure (faith) is Marian. This archetypal experience reveals a highly ecstatic profile; it is rooted in Mary's experience of motherhood:

> Seen in the light of Mary's simple experience of motherhood, which in her has become a function of the archetypal act of faith, all closed consciousness of self and all closed experience of self become problematic: the experience of self must open out, through faith, to an experience that encompasses both oneself and the other – oneself and the burgeoning Word of God, which at first seems to be growing in the self until in this growth it becomes evident that it is rather the other way around and that it is the self that is contained in the Word of God.[71]

This beautiful and archetypal example of Christian *ecstasis* leads directly into the heart of anthropology as presented in Theo-dramatics. And here again, Mary is pictured as the model of theo-dramatic existence, the archetype of creaturely *kenosis*.[72] In Mary, there is no rupture or opposition between *ecstasis* and *kenosis*; she represents, in a certain sense, the linchpin or personal unity between Theoaesthetics and Theo-dramatics. Her Self, which contained the word of God (*ecstasis*), gradually and irresistibly grew to be contained, remodelled and activated in the service of God's own Word (*kenosis*).

---

[71] HI, p. 339 (English version).
[72] TD II/2, p. 293ff. (German version).

THE CONSTITUTIVE ANTHROPOLOGICAL ARTICULATIONS (ANTHROPOLOGY *IN FIERI*)

After considering the *homo Balthasarianus in actu*, as anthropology of affirmation, after trying to locate him *in situ*, within the context of the typical expressions of Balthasar's thought and work, rendered in the ciphers of *ecstasis* and *kenosis*, we now would like to pinpoint the major constitutive articulations of Balthasar's anthropology. These articulations evolve and revolve around the notion of the human person. Simultaneously, they seem to suggest a developmental trajectory at whose starting point we find the anthropological profile of the fool whose ultimate realisation will be the saint.[73]

THE PARADOXICAL CHARACTER

Balthasar presented us with a whole gallery of fools; they come in all shapes and shades, from saintly fools like Symeon and Andrew to Dostovesky's Idiot and Rouault's Christ-clown.[74] As a rule, the fool stands for tragic human existence (sometimes in God, sometimes estranged from God), for brokenness and rupture. He reflects alienation and lives in a state of suspension where flight, cowardice and irony dominate. The fool typifies the paradoxical and unredeemed character of human existence and its manifold expressions of contradiction.

Thus the paradoxical character of human existence is no accident nor simply the consequence of human error; it is constitutive of human nature. This is particularly true for the unresolved and unsurpassable paradoxes that exist between man and woman, individual and community, between body and spirit. Human existence in action reveals a tragic fissure and resembles a human *Ou-topos*. This practical and concrete paradoxical human constitution cannot be reneged or eliminated. Yet, we are being offered an alternative, the alternative that our paradoxical status as unre-

---

[73] See J. Roten, 'Die marianischen Menschentypen in Hans Urs von Balthasar', in *Mater Fidei et Fidelium. Collected Essays to Honor Théodore Koehler on His 80th Birthday. Marian Library Studies* (University of Dayton) 17–23 (1991), pp. 424–44.
[74] See *Herrlichkeit. Eine theologische Aesthetik*, Bd. III/1: *Im Raum der Metphysik*, Teil II: Neuzeit. Johannes Verlag, Einsiedeln 1975, pp. 492–552.

deemed beings be transformed into one of redemption. The saint, thus, is a redeemed paradoxical human being, foremost because holiness is a gift from God and transcends all human categorisations.

THE LAW OF REVERSAL

The relocation of human existence within the Christian context is, according to Balthasar, the only means to free the human being from the self-imposed but impossible task to make him, or herself, whole. It is the object of Theo-dramatics to free the human person from self by engaging it in a dramatic dialogue with God. He, God, will lead the person to a more intimate understanding of self and show his/her ultimate destination.[75] Thus, the Christian perspective of anthropology is based on the Balthasarian law of reversal and descent. What it means is the Christian realisation of the unabridged version of *Gnothi sauton*. *Gnothi sauton* (know thyself), yes, but as the gods themselves want you to be.[76] Human authenticity and identity, then, means to be an active partner of the dramatic dialogue initiated by God himself, yet in full respect of the human condition.

THE EXPERIENCE OF FREEDOM

This is the appropriate place to analyse the Balthasarian dialectic between human and divine freedom, in particular the human person's discovery of his/her 'infinite finiteness', or his/her constitutive *autexousion*,[77] and further, the inevitably 'extrovert' tendency of human existence, the exit from self and the reaching out in an effort of co-existence with others. May it suffice to remark that according to Balthasar the experience of finite freedom is primarily feminine, one of existential and passive determination and experiential 'affection', and becomes masculine only in a second phase of outreaching and active determination.[78] The experience of freedom leads to *Selbstverdankung*, to existential gratitude – for a creature is

---

[75] TD II/1, p. 314 (German version).
[76] PI, p. 25.
[77] TD II/1, p. 219.
[78] PI, p. 207.

truly him- or herself only if in God. One is free if one dwells in God's freedom.[79] In other words, realisation of self and finite freedom will occur and come about only with participation in God's freedom. In conclusion then, the word 'person', in the sense of human being, 'receives its special dignity in history when it is illuminated by the unique theological meaning'.[80]

PERSON AND MISSION

'Person' is constituted during the second phase of the dramatic dialogue between God and human being, only after the discovery of election in the experience of finite freedom. Here again, a more thorough analysis would lead us to consider the difference between the 'I' (self) and one's personal role, the difference between role and mission, the passage from mission (and its vicarious functions) to person. Balthasar agrees with Denis de Rougemont when the latter says:

> Only in such a community (meaning neighbour and church) does the person exist truly. Person, act, vocation become for me virtually synonymous. The act is concrete obedience to a transcendent vocation: the vocation brings forth the person in the *individuum*. Hence this new definition: the *individuum* is the natural man; the person is the new creature, as Paul understands it.[81]

What de Rougemont calls 'vocation' Balthasar has named 'mission', stressing thus the christological foundations of his understanding of person. only in the God-Man is there identity between the 'sublime actor and the role he has to play' (Haecker). St Thomas describes this identity as the identity of *processio* (within the Godhead) and *missio* (the sending of the Son into the world). The identity of person and mission is no unverifiable abstraction. It is actualised in the humanity of Christ who came as the 'suffering

---

[79] *Der dreifache Kranz. Das heil der Welt im Mariengebet,* Johannes Verlag, Einsiedeln 1977, p. 77.

[80] 'On the Concept of Person', in *Communio: International Catholic Review* 1 (1986), p. 19.

[81] Ibid., p. 25.

servant' to do the will of the Father.[82] In the human person there is no identity between election from eternity and the actual call and mission in time and space. Called in time, the mission of the human person is limited in time, dependent on the ever more faithful entering into mission, the stripping of self and the constant exposure to grace: all these aspects constitute the human being as a truly theological and dramatic person.

THEO-DRAMATIC EXISTENCE

Participating in Christ's universal mission, the theological or dramatic person is de-privatised and re-socialised in mission. 'What we call universal (socially speaking) can only exist as the elongation (*Elongatur*) of the person, and the person in turn exists only thanks to its elongation in mission.'[83] Elaborating on the notion of mission, Balthasar remarks that the authentic human personality is not congruent with I or Self; quite to the contrary, it is constituted in and through its *work*.[84] Human existence therefore has a kenotic configuration: God in his own kenosis points out to the human person that he or she too must be subjected to the laws of kenotic existence.[85] Thus, in a new and different sense, the human person becomes an *Ou-topos*. He or she is homeless and disappropriated again, because entirely given into Jesus Christ's mission through ecclesial mediation and to the greater glory of the most Holy Trinity.

MARY – MODEL OF THEO-DRAMATIC EXISTENCE

Last but not least, we are referred to the human archetype of theo-dramatic and kenotic existence, to Mary. According to Balthasar, in Mary are concretised, in an eminently personal fashion, not only the comparative of humility, but also the comparative of love. In Mary,

---

[82] TD I, p. 525 (German version).
[83] TD II/2, p. 251 (German version).
[84] 'Existenz als Sendung: Christus und seine Nachfolge', in *Schweizerische Kirchenzeitung* 145/48 (1977), p. 709.
[85] *Katholisch*, Johannes Verlag, Einsiedeln 1975, p. 80.

highest anonymity generates – suggested Balthasar[86] – the highest expression of personality. In turn, the highest expression of personality leads to universality; it is rooted in the personal and simultaneously universal yes of the Lord's servant and is in a special way expressed in the life of the Church (office and holiness). As already pointed out for Christ, 'Mary's theological personality is no abstraction; it is embodied in Mary of Nazareth, whom the "Marian Memoria" of the Church calls "Daughter of Zion" *because* she is in the first place a Jewish girl, whom we call "New Eve" *because* she is a real woman and mother, and whom we call "Servant of the Lord" *because* she is first and foremost a concrete believer.'[87]

FRUITFULNESS

The last word on Balthasar's anthropology belongs to fruitfulness.[88] It represents the logical conclusion to an existence in mission, and likewise stands at beginning and end of the Theologics. There is no more radical way of saving oneself than in becoming fruitful. Fruitfulness is the keystone not alone of God's logic but also of his hermeneutics. Fruitfulness is first and foremost in God himself (the Triune, Jesus Christ); all subsequent fruitfulness takes its origin in him – in his trinitarian and crucified love. The God of love unites himself in a *sacrum connubium*[89] to Mary, the Church, the saints and to all who have been drawn into his fruitful kenosis. This mystery has virginal and spousal character, testifying to the primacy and the ultimate fruitfulness in the Spirit. It finds its highest, the most concrete and altogether most comprehensive expression in the eucharist, the *Verbum Caro*, and is the fruit of Christ's union with Mary-Church.

Finally, since fruitfulness is a mystery shared between man and woman, it comes as no surprise that this summit of human existence finds concrete realisation in Balthasar's own life. In the double mission of Hans Urs von Balthasar and Adrienne von Speyr, the

---

[86] TD II/2, p. 293f.; p, 322f.

[87] J. Roten, 'Memory and Mission: A Theological Reflection on Mary in the Paschal Mysteries', in *Marian Studies* 42 (1991), 111, 128–30.

[88] *Theologik II. Wahrheit Gottes,* Johannes Verlag, Einsiedeln 1985, p. 54–61.

[89] TD III, pp. 237–45 (English version).

respective roles of man and woman are directed towards the reaping of a common fruit. For them, this common fruit materialised most specifically in their secular institute, the Community of St John.[90]

HISTORICAL CONCRETISATIONS

The Marian watermark and configuration of Balthasar's anthropology is clearly legible and easy to decipher. One might even venture the following comparison: if for Karl Rahner christology is considered to be the ultimate consequence of anthropology, so, conversely, Mariology for Balthasar represents the ultimate realisation and model of anthropology. Can and should it be said: *Omne ens marianum?*[91] Whatever the final answer to this question, the following can be taken for granted: our mental structure, our ontological constitution and theological destiny – they all have, in Balthasar's grammar of anthropology, a Marian configuration.

HISTORICAL CONCRETISATION I

The Marian principle – as formulated by Balthasar – has a quasi-ideological function. It is called upon to exorcise the always looming shadows of idealism and dialectical philosophy, both of them alive and well as *neo-Buddhism* and *neo-Judaism* in Balthasar's assessment of the present.[92] For both of these last grand non-Christian worldviews the present is *un*-truth. In neo-Buddhism, transcendence operates unequivocally backward in time. The movement of *religio* binds back to the lost origin. The only palliative for the *baneful* dissipation of existence is recollection in oneself, the mysterious path inward, into the depths … into flight, ultimately, from self and reality. For neo-Judaism – steward of dialectical philosophy – transcendence is

---

[90] See UA, pp. 73–75.
[91] Klaus Hemmerle, 'Das Neue ist älter. Hans Urs v. Balthasar und die Orientierung der Theologie', in *Erbe und Auftrag. Festvortrag anlässlich des 75. Geburtstages in der Kath. Akademie Freiburg*, Beuron 1981, pp. 91–93.
[92] *Truth is Symphonic: Aspects of Christian Pluralism*, Ignatius Press, San Francisco 1987, pp. 180–89. The English version circumscribes 'Neo-Buddhism' and 'Neo-Judaism' with 'the Asiatic way out' and 'the Jewish utopian breakthrough'.

unequivocally oriented to the future. Its catchwords are 'absolute action', 'primal instinctual energy' or 'open humane being' – as the absolute dialogical reality.[93]

For both neo-Buddhism and neo-Judaism, existence – as it is lived in fact – cannot be right. And so the beginning of wisdom – in both instances – is the denial of what now is. Not so Christianity: it affirms the present, because God himself has affirmed it. In his life, death and resurrection he imparted the 'fullness of grace and truth'[94] to our here and now. He fills our present with his presence. But God's presence embraces the past and the future as well. It is in this unlimited presence that Abraham's yes became Mary's yes, that Mary's yes bore fruit in the Church's yes. That is why Mary's yes is the archetypal anthropological act. It inspires and gives ultimate legitimation to the Christian way of philosophising and theologising. Because of Mary's yes, two things are clear for Christians: (1) faith which is based on incarnation cannot have recourse to flight from this world: and (2) faith that comes wholly from God's initiative is prohibited from 'hastening' salvation only by its own efforts.

HISTORICAL CONCRETISATION II

Balthasar's map of contemporary ideologies or *Weltanschauungen* may no longer be accurate and what he calls neo-Judaism[95] may be seriously shaken by the collapse of world communism. Still, the present of western civilisation is subliminally impregnated by the seriously ailing from the Cartesian-Kantian syndrome. The ultimate irony, or perhaps tragedy, according to a commentator of contemporary history of ideas, is 'that secularism [the consequences of the Cartesian-Kantian syndrome, J.R.] has not led to humanism. We have gradually dissolved the human being into a bundle of

---

[93] Ibid., pp. 183/84.

[94] *John* 1: 17.

[95] There is no anti-Jewish penchant in Balthasar. Balthasar's dialogue with Buber resulted in an honest assessment of differences and common ground between Judaism and Christianity (see *Martin Buber and Christianity*, London 1961). In his investigations on human identity (see TD I), the dialogical principle as developed by Rosenzweig and Buber has a mediating function in the approach of biblical revelation.

reflexes, impulses, neuroses, nerve endings'.[96] Deconstructivism and reconstructivism have disassembled and reassembled the human person in an attempt to discover the mystery of the human genetic code. They have left it a shambles, unable to give us an authentic humanism. It is pathetic to see how Popper, the mastermind of critical rationalism, in the end is left with a desperate pledge to optimism, optimism understood as a quasi-categorical imperative: 'Optimism is our duty, he recently remarked, we must concentrate on the things to make and on the things to be made. We are responsible for them.'[97] Similarly but differently, Francis Fukuyama concentrates his anthropology on *thymos*, the desire and struggle for recognition. *Thymos* is 'that part of man which feels the need to place value on things – himself in the first instance, but on people, actions, or things around him as well'.[98] The social expression of *thymos* is *isothymia*, the 'human desire for equal recognition'.[99] Fukujama identifies liberal democracy as *the* typical and ultimate human situation where the needs for *thymos* and *isothymia* are and/or will be satisfied. Consequently, the *end of history* as well as the *last man* are at hand.

All three, deconstructivist secularism, critical rationalism and postmodernist political theory fail to recognise the *epochal* importance of the existential affirmation of the totality of being in its concrete expression. This, Balthasar's anthropological legacy, would seem to be the most effective antidote against the Cartesian-Kantian syndrome. It is summed up in the Marian principle: it comes alive in the freedom to listen to God's word (faith sustained by reason) and in the translation of God's self-revelation into one's personal and communal life, where meaning becomes value and fidelity reflects the continued answer to God's ongoing self-revelation. All of these attitudes are personally and archetypically represented in Mary, the 'immaculate concept' of Balthasar's anthropology.

---

[96] Henry Grunwald, 'The Year 2000' (Time-Essay), in *Time* (30 March 1992), p. 75.

[97] Interview with Karl Popper in *Spiegel* (23 March 1992), p. 211.

[98] Francis Fukuyama, *The End of History and the Last Man*, The Free Press, New York 1992, p. 163.

[99] Ibid., p. 182.

7

YOUTHFUL UNTO DEATH: THE SPIRIT OF CHILDHOOD

John Saward

Balthasar said of his friend Gustav Siewerth that he had 'the mind of a lion and the heart of a child'.[1] The tribute applies equally to himself. His leonine mind – majestic in its knowledge – roars through the vast forest of his work. But the lamblike heart is its still centre. I do not just mean that 'despite' or 'in addition to' the adult grandeur of his achievement he retained a childlike simplicity. That is true, but it is not the whole truth. In Balthasar the child's heart shapes and orders the mind. In the *Theological Aesthetic* it is young, uncluttered eyes which see the splendid form of revelation. In the *Theo-dramatic* a child is caught up into the drama of Christ's self-giving love. In the *Theologic* a little one lets himself be led by the Holy Spirit into all the truth of the Father's Word made flesh.

As a virtue, spiritual childhood graced the life of Hans Urs von Balthasar; as a theme of theology, it runs through all his writings. This essay has the simple aim of tracing its course. The subject has contemporary relevance. To a self-consciously 'adult' academic theology, jaded by its adjustments to worldly wisdom, Balthasar points the way to conversion – a renewed sense of childlike wonder at 'that than which nothing greater can be conceived'.

BALTHASAR ON CHILDHOOD: THE SOURCES

Balthasar's last book – the completed manuscript was lying on his desk on the day of his death – was on the spirit of childhood, *Wenn ihr nicht werdet wie dieses Kind.*[2] It was that year's Christmas gift to

---

[1]   *Mein Werk*, Durchblicke, Einsiedeln 1990, p. 72. All the works of Balthasar cited are published by Johannes Verlag in Einsiedeln unless otherwise stated.
[2]   *Wenn ihr nicht werdet wie dieses Kind*, Ostfidern 1988.

his friends. It was also, as his cousin Peter Henrici has said, 'his true legacy'.[3] The title places its own clear emphasis: 'Unless you become like *this* Child'. It is the Child-God, argues Balthasar, who invites us to be like himself. In him all childhood is exalted to a new and incomparable dignity. Small is not only beautiful; it is the way to heaven. This is also argued in a chapter in *Das Ganze im Fragment* and in important articles in *Communio* reprinted in *Homo Creatus Est*.[4] The concept of 'simplicity' (synonymous in the New Testament with childhood) was reviewed in a number of books and articles written in the last twenty years of Balthasar's life: *Christen sind enfältig, Einfaltungen*, 'Der Glaube der Einfältigen' (reprinted in *Spiritus Creator*).[5] Detailed studies were made of the three French prophets of spiritual childhood – St Thérèse of Lisieux, Charles Péguy, and Georges Bernanos.[6] As for the Church Fathers, it is their youthful enthusiasm for the Word of God which Balthasar most admires. Of St Gregory of Nyssa he says that his 'naïve and ardent attachment to all the beauties of earth, to all human and cosmic values ... gives his thought a note of youthfulness and a kind of morning freshness'.[7] There are no old saints. Those who are the Church's venerable Fathers are first of all her docile children. The Spirit of the risen Jesus renews their youth like the eagle's. 'How juvenile are Augustine's *Confessions* compared with Plotinus... .'[9]

<hr />

[3] 'Hans Urs von Balthasar: A Sketch of His Life' in David L. Schindler (ed.), *Hans Urs von Batlhasar: His Life and Work*, ed. David L. Schindler, San Francisco 1991, p. 42.

[4] *Das Ganze im Fragment*, Aspekte der Geschichtstheologie, new edition (1990); ET, *Man in History: A Theological Study*, London & Sydney 1968. Some of the translations from this work are my own. I shall therefore give references to both the German original and the English translation. The two *Communio* articles are 'Das Kind Jesu und die Kinder' and 'Jung bis in den Tod', *Homo Creatus Est*, Skizzen zur Theologie V (1986), pp. 165–74, 175–80.

[5] *Christen sind einfältig* (1983), *Einfaltungen*, Auf Wegen christlicher Einigung, new edition (1988); *Spiritus Creator*, Skizzen zur Theologie III (1967).

[6] See *Schwestern im Geist*, Thérèse von Lisieux und Elisabeth von Dijon, new edition (1990); 'Péguy' in *The Glory of the Lord*, A Theological Aesthetics III: Studies in Theological Style: Lay Styles, ET, Edinburgh 1986; *Gelebte Kirche; Bernanos*, new edition (1988).

[7] *Présence et Pensée*, Essai sur la philosophie religieuse de Grégorie de Nysse, new edition, Paris 1988, p. xvi.

[8] *Homo Creatus Est*, p. 179.

[9] See below, p.146f.

The theme of childhood is not confined to an obscure corner of Balthasar's works. It is omnipresent. For example, in the third volume of *Herrlichkeit*, Balthasar introduces us to the poets and philosophers, from Homer to Hegel, who have glimpsed the glory of Being. Finally, in the last fifty pages, we enter the inner sanctum of Balthasar's own metaphysics. There, waiting to show us the wonder of existence, is not a humourless Hegelian or a sober-sided Sartrean, but a smiling baby and his mother.

Balthasar's theological mission, as he never ceased to remind his readers, is inseparable from that of Adrienne von Speyr. It should not surprise us, therefore, to discover that the spirit of childhood is one of her chief preoccupations, as Balthasar explains in his introduction to the *Nachlabwerke*:

> A fourth theme is *childhood*, which is a fundamental concept in New Testament proclamation, but today, through Christians demanding 'maturity', has been quite wrongly put in the shade. Her whole life long, Adrienne retained a truly vital relationship with her own childhood – despite her almost masculine incisiveness and resolution.[10]

In *Das Wort und die Mystik* Adrienne gives an unforgettable definition of the 'little way'.

> The Son will invite believers to stay childlike before the Father. They must not be constantly stressing and thinking of their unworthiness, but in a simple, childlike way should receive and rest in the awareness of being children of God. They should move about in God's world in a relaxed way ...[11]

THE MYSTERY OF THE CHILD

'Everywhere outside Christianity', says Balthasar, 'the child is automatically sacrificed'.[12] Pagan antiquity saw the child as an

---

[10]   Introduction to *Nachlabwerke* I (1966), p. 15.
[11]   *Das Wort und die Mystik* II; Objektive Mystik (1970), p. 165.
[12]   *Das Ganze im Fragment*, p. 282; *Man in History*, p. 257.

'imperfect, half-finished human being',[13] 'a preliminary stage before full humanness'.[14] The Promethean ideologies of the modern age repeat the same terrible error. The helplessness of the infant is an embarrassment to those who glorify 'man come of age'. For example, according to Karl Marx, dependence (and therefore childhood) is synonymous with slavery. Only when a man is independent and in debt to no one is he truly himself.[15] Balthasar agrees with Bernanos that the child – and the spirit of the child – is the chief victim of dechristianised modern culture. 'Human society is built upon the tacit, thousandfold murder of the unborn'.[16]

Christianity alone truly cherishes the child. 'Only in the mystery of the Word made flesh', say the Fathers of the Second Vatican Council, 'is the mystery of man made clear'. 'Only in the light of God made child', we may add, 'can human beings fully understand and finally recover their childhood.'

> It took the incarnation of Christ to show the eternal signifi-
> cance, theological and not just anthropological, of being
> born, the utter blessedness of coming forth from a life-giving,
> bearing womb.[17]

Why is revelation necessary to bring home to man the meaning and value of his own early days? Because his intellect has been weakened and wounded by the sin of his first father. There are truths concerning man's nature, in principle knowable by reason, which in his fallen condition he finds it hard to grasp.

> Everything said here about the human child is part of human
> existence, and so it is not really an object of God's self-revelation
> in Jesus Christ. Nevertheless, much of what is deepest in man,
> because of his alienation from God, is submerged and forgotten.
> Only through the incarnation is it brought back to the light of
> remembrance and human self-understanding. In our case this

---

[13] *Das Ganze im Fragment*, p. 269; *Man in History*, p. 269.

[14] *Wenn ihr nicht werdet wie dieses Kind*, p. 9.

[15] See Ferdinand Ulrich, *Der Mensch als Anfang*, Zur philosophischen Anthropologie der Kindheit, Einsiedeln 1970, p. 11f.

[16] *Das Ganze im Fragment*, p. 276; *Man in History*, p. 251.

[17] *Homo Creatus Est*, p. 173.

takes place through Jesus' teaching about the indispensability of the truly childlike attitude if we are to share in the Kingdom of God, which he has brought near.[18]

Fallen man's estranged face has often missed his childhood's many splendours, but if the eternal Word becomes a child, then the child becomes in the framework of providential revelation the full expression of eternal truth and eternal life. In the divine person of the Word human childhood is revealed with immeasurable dignity and incomparable destiny.

> For Jesus, the state of early childhood is clearly not in any sense morally indifferent or inconsequential. On the contrary, the child's way of being human, which for the adult is submerged, represents a kind of pristine zone in which everything was right and true and good, a state of hidden security, which cannot be written off as 'pre-ethical' or 'unconscious' (as if the child's mind were not yet awake, in fact, still at the animal level, which it never is, not even in its mother's womb). Childhood represents a sphere of pristine wholeness; in fact, since the child cannot at first distinguish between his parents' love and god's, it is not only a sphere of wholeness, but a time of holiness.[19]

According to the Second Vatican Council, Our Lord Jesus Christ, the divine Word made flesh, is revelation, *mediator simul et plenitudo totius revelationis.*[20] The eternal Word is consubstantial Image of the Father and uncreated archetype of creatures, and so, says Balthasar, when he becomes true man, his every human action, experience, and stage of life is revelatory, speaks volumes of God and man.

> The Word of God walked through time. As He walked, everything was word and revelation of the Father, but also revelation of the truth of human existence … his humanity is an instrument upon which every melody can be played;

---

[18] *Wenn ihr nicht werdet wie dieses Kind,* p. 18.
[19] Ibid., p. 9.
[20] *Dei Verbum* 2.

even silence, the pause, can become a striking means of communication.[21]

When we affirm that God the Son became man, we mean not only that in the Blessed Virgin's womb he assumed a complete human nature, but also that he entered upon the whole human adventure – from conception to the last breath. 'Human life is development in time: man is seed and sapling, child and boy, man and old man'.[22]

Through its assumption without absorption by the Son of God, human nature is raised up to a dignity beyond compare. When he lives out a complete human life from womb to tomb, all the ages and stages of earthly existence receive new meaning: the entire biography of man is shown to be 'fitted in all things, apart from sin (cf. *Hebrews* 4: 15), to serve as speech for God'.[23] When God the Son becomes a child, all childhood is exalted in him. As St Leo the Great says, 'by his own beginnings he consecrated the early days of little ones'. The child is precious first of all because he is God's creature, made in his image. But the child is also, and above all, precious because of the incarnation of One of the Trinity. There is a direct link between the child, any and every child, and *the* Child.

> The child is not just a remote symbol of the Son of God. If you show love and kindness to 'one such child' (*Matthew* 18: 5, any child of all the millions that there are), and if you do it, consciously or unconsciously, in the name of Jesus, in the Spirit of Jesus, you are receiving the archetypal Child, who has His place in the bosom of the Father. Now since that Child cannot be separated from his special place, your quiet act of kindness takes you to the Ultimate Person, to the Father himself: 'Whoever receives one such child in my name receives me; and whoever receives me, receives not me but him who sent me (*Mark* 9: 37)'.[24]

---

[21] *Das Ganze im Fragment*, p. 268; *Man in History*, p. 243f.
[22] Ibid., p. 244.
[23] Ibid., p. 271; p. 246.
[24] *Wenn ihr nicht werdet wie dieses Kind*, p. 8.

The divine Child has united himself to every child, so that anyone who welcomes a little one welcomes the eternal Son, and with him, in the Spirit, the Father. We can see the Son of God in every child and every child in the Son of God. Péguy could even say: *Vous êtes tous des enfants Jésus.*

> At this age loving trust (in the people who provide for the child's needs) and unquestioning obedience intertwine as at no later stage in life. Here is the affinity with the eternal Child of the Father – in other words, a closeness to heaven, which Jesus expresses in mysterious words: 'See that you do not despise one of these little ones; for I tell you that in heaven their angels always behold the face of my Father in heaven' (*Matthew* 18: 10). Hence, too, the recommendation, which is theological and not just moral, that the community look after the helpless child: Whoever receives a child receives Jesus and in him the Father himself who sent him (cf. *Mark* 9: 37). And the lowliness of the child is a constant image of the descent from all the grown-up self-glory of the mature to humble service: 'He who is greatest among you shall be your servant' (*Matthew* 23: 11). 'Whoever humbles himself like this child, he is the greatest in the kingdom of Heaven' (*Matthew* 18: 3). When Jesus blesses the child, when he takes him in his arms, he confirms the affinity between the natural age of childhood and his eternal childhood before the Father.[25]

THE METAPHYSICS OF THE CHILD

Balthasar places childhood at the centre of his metaphysics. Both Plato and Aristotle held that the road to wisdom begins with wonder, which is the child's native disposition. One of the characters in Plato's *Timaeus* reports the opinion that the Greeks are 'eternal children', for ever 'young in [their] souls'. In the immediate context, the point is simply that the historical records of Greece, unlike those of Egypt, do not reach into the remote past, but with the hindsight of Christian culture, we can read the text at a deeper level. The patrimony of the pagan Greeks is not the 'adult' one of

---

[25] *Homo Creatus Est*, p. 172f.

making and doing, but the childlike one of absorption in the marvel of Being. In the same spirit, drawing on the insights of Gustav Siewerth and Ferdinand Ulrich, Balthasar finds the beginning of metaphysics in the child's experience in his mother's womb and arms 'of being admitted into a sheltering and encompassing world'.[26] The first metaphysician is the newborn babe.

> A baby is called to self-consciousness by the love and smile of his mother. It is, in fact, the horizon of infinite Being in its totality which opens up to him in this meeting. It reveals four things to him: (1) that he is *one* in love with his mother, and yet he is not his mother, and so Being is *one*; (2) this love is *good*, and so the whole of Being is good; (3) that this love is *true*, and so Being is *true*; (4) this love is a cause of *joy*, and so Being is beautiful.[27]

The love of mother for child, between Thou and I, opens up Being in 'its absolute unlimitedness and fullness'.[28] From his mother the child draws the whole content of metaphysics: Being is beautiful, true, and good.

Balthasar is aware that, through the weakness and sinfulness of Adam's sons and daughters, the mother/child relationship does not always fulfil its vocation.

> For a child, the real love of his parents, to begin with, cannot be separated from God. The difference – assuming every-thing takes place without trauma – has to be shown to him in the humility of his parents and their dependency on God. If the child begins to feel any disturbance – whether between the parents or between one parent and the child, the horizon of absolute Being will be confused and clouded, and so will its gift, all-inclusive created being as God's gift, because this gift becomes comprehensible for the child only in the con-creteness of his relationship of love to his parents within the

---

[26] *The Glory of the Lord.* A Theological Aesthetics V; The Realm of Metaphysics in the Modern Age, ET, Edinburgh 1991, p. 616.

[27] 'Uno sguardo d'insieme sul mio pensiero', *Strumento internazionale per un lavoro teologico: Communio* (1989), p. 41f.

[28] *Wenn ihr nicht werdet wie dieses Kind*, p. 14.

sphere of peace of the entrusted living space. Any kind of tension in this sacred realm opens up wounds that usually cannot be healed in the child's heart. The victims of divorce, and very often of mixed marriages, are always the children.[29]

To read Balthasar on the metaphysics of childhood is to be reminded constantly of Virgil: *Incipe, parve puer, risu cognoscere matrem*, 'Begin, small boy, to know by smile thy mother'. What is special about the Fourth Eclogue is not only its apparent prophecy of the birth of Christ, but also its undoubted high appreciation of the child, the unborn child. This is without precedent in the ancient world.

THE CHILD-GOD AND HIS MOTHER

The Magi found the Child with his Mother (cf. *Matthew* 2: 11), and so do we. It is not human childhood in isolation that is exalted by the Incarnation of the Son of God, but childhood and motherhood together.

> The Madonna and Child are, for the Christian, the unique, incomparable pair which places every mother and child relationship within the radiance of eternal grace.[30]

Balthasar contemplates the relationship of the divine Child and his Mother in the whole 'threefold garland' of its mysteries from Nazareth and Bethlehem to Calvary and heaven. He speaks beautifully of Our Lady's part in the shaping of her Child's human mind, the *scientia acquisita*, in which he grows in wisdom. He always knew as man that he was the Father's eternal Son.[31] From the beginning his self-consciousness was a mission-consciousness, the awareness of being the sent Son of the Father. He did not need to be 'informed' that St Joseph was not his physical father. Mary may be said to have

[29] Ibid., p. 15.
[30] *Das Genze im Fragment*, p. 270; *Man in History*, p. 245.
[31] 'It is impossible that this Child only became aware of being Son of God, of being God, at some point of time in his development. So in his earliest consciousness he must have known, however implicitly, that he was contained within the bosom of the infinite personal Father' (*Wenn ihr nicht werdet wie dieses Kind*, p. 23).

'strengthened' his awareness of his relationship with God the Father, but we should not seek to know how, by what words: 'We can leave that to the mystery of Mary's discretion.'[32] Discarding the Scholastic opinion that Christ as man did not learn from other people, Balthasar shows how Mary introduced him to the religion of Israel, above all to its prayers and Scriptures.

> If we take the incarnation of God's Word seriously, then we have to say that Jesus, like every other human child, learnt slowly and gradually: not only human language and human behaviour, but also the religion of his people.[33]

Balthasar presents a new reason for the fittingness of Christ's Virginal Conception and Birth. It is the necessary condition, he says, of his childlike devotion to the Father. To be conceived without male seed has an inner necessity for Him whose whole being, as man and as God, is towards the Father.

> Jesus is the One who is perfectly poor and perfectly childlike. He lets himself be filled and fed only by what the Father gives him. Indeed, if we think more deeply about him being the Son, we can say that he perpetually lets himself come out of the Father, for he is born 'not of blood nor of the will of the flesh nor of the will of man, but of God' (*John* 1:13). This is the most extreme form of simplicity, poverty and childlikeness conceivable. It is unique to the Son of God, and yet he does not want to keep it so himself, he wants others to share in it. To those who accept him he gives the 'power to become the children of God' (1: 12), and from being slaves they become free sons, because they 'acknowledge the truth' that the poor and childlike Son, precisely through his poverty and childlikeness, reveals the ultimate reality, the heart of the Father. For John, this and nothing else is 'the Truth'.[34]

The eternal Word is sent by the Father to make all things new, to make a sin-aged race young again in the grace and glory of sonship.

[32] *Homo Creatus Est*, p. 168f.
[33] Ibid., p. 168.
[34] *Christen sind einfältig*, p. 38.

And so he becomes man, he is conceived as man, in a new way, of a Virgin by the power of the Holy Spirit: *nova ordine, nova nativitate*, says St Leo the Great, 'in a new order, by a new birth'.

A CHILD FOR EVER

Jesus, says Balthasar, is a child for ever, 'youthful unto death' and beyond. He is a child for ever in his divine person, because he is the only-begotten of God, the eternal Son of the Father. He was always a child, 'young unto death', in his humanity on earth, because, full of grace and truth, he kept into adulthood what the sinful sons of Adam lose – his innocence and all the other spiritual goods of childhood. And he is and will be for ever a child in his humanity in heaven, because, with the scars in his body, the risen Jesus retains all the states and mysteries of his earthly life.

Jesus is a child for ever in his divine person as eternal Son. 'The youthfulness of Jesus and of those who try seriously to follow him is a mystery far surpassing psychology, because it derives from the most hidden depths of theology, from the mystery of the Divine Trinity.'[35]

> Jesus, ... grown man that he is, has never left the 'womb of the Father'. Even now, as incarnate, he 'rests' in it; in fact, it is only because he is the One who rests in the Father's womb that he can make a valid revelation of the Father.[36]

The generation of the Son is eternal, transcending all succession, abiding in the perpetual now of the Godhead. He is eternally being generated, and so he is 'a child who cannot grow out of being a child'.[37] Even when he comes forth from the human womb of Mary, he never leaves the divine bosom of the Father. The eternal Wisdom of God is 'daily' the Father's delight, 'rejoicing before him always' (cf. *Proverbs* 8: 27–31). When he enters our 'lowly world', as St Leo the Great says, he does not leave 'the glory of the Father'.

---

[35] *Homo Creatus Est*, p. 179.
[36] *Wenn ihr nicht werdet wie dieses Kind*, p. 7.
[37] *Homo Creatus Est*, p. 177.

The human child separates himself from his parents in order to grow, to be fruitful, to age. But the divine Child is the fruit, eternally springing forth, of the Father's generation, even in being sent into the world. Here there is no habituation, only perpetual wonderment, eternal gratitude, and eternal ready obedience. For the Father's act of generation is an unfathomable love which cannot be plumbed or analysed: the Son's readiness is the way he participates in the divine wisdom and omniscience. And the darkness of the cross is nothing other than the entry into the bottom of this obedience, whereby the Son takes the alienation of the world into his pure obedience.[38]

Jesus was always a child in his humanity on earth. As a stage of life, it came to an end, but as a state of mind and heart, it remained and remains for ever.

There is something of childhood about the whole gospel event, right up to the final cry of the abandoned Child of the Father on the Cross: 'Why?' – a child's question. The Wisdom of God is here a questioning child, and for a moment He can receive no reply.[39]

From conception to the cross, the entire being of Jesus, his every human word and thought and action, is centred on the Father, on the One whom he calls, in childlike fashion, 'Abba, dear Father'.

Jesus ... suffers as the Son. The child's word 'Abba', 'Daddy', becomes audible for the first time in his prayer in Gethsemane (*Mark* 14: 36). Even when the Father can no longer answer, the whole Passion, right up to the cry of dereliction on the Cross, is borne in the Spirit of childhood. And after he has been led through all the terrors of Holy Saturday – like a child lost in a frightening wood, he can proclaim in triumph on Easter Sunday: 'I am ascending to my Father and to your Father' (*John* 20: 17), for he has now succeeded in making his

---

[38] Ibid., p. 177.
[39] Ibid., p. 173f.

own sons with him, 'raised up with him and made us sit with him in the heavenly places' (*Ephesians* 2: 6).[40]

Jesus' adult teaching has a childlike, certainly a youthful quality; 'Does not the Sermon on the Mount, with its Utopian, uncompromising idealism, appear odd among all the other ethical systems of mankind?'[41] It is pervaded with wonder (*Jesus miratus est*), a human and truly childlike emotion, but with its analogue, says Balthasar to his own readers' amazement, in the Trinity.

> This astonishment stems from the much deeper astonishment of the Eternal Child, who is astonished, in the absolute Spirit of Love, at the love which rules and surpasses all things.[42]

Much that is puzzling in Our Lord's words is illuminated when we perceive that they come from a childlike heart. For example, the declaration that 'the Father is greater than I', which so exercised the Church during the Arian controversy, is the Child's pride in his Father.[43] The comparative – 'greater than I' – is significant. It means so much more than the positive or superlative. 'The comparative is the linguistic form of wonder', of the child's wonder.[44]

No man has been more mature than Jesus, none more manly. He is serenely self-controlled. He teaches with authority. He is shrewd.

> Jesus always answers the trick questions of the Jews with a disconcerting shrewdness which far exceeds the sly cunning of his questioners. And he, who when his Father's hour comes, will give himself up defenceless to his captors, before that hour eludes them.[45]

Jesus is perfectly adult in his mind not despite but because of the undying childlikeness of his heart. He is Lion in being Lamb.

---

[40] *Wenn ihr nicht werdet wie dieses Kind*, p. 47.
[41] *Das Ganze im Fragment*, p. 287; *Man in History*, p. 262.
[42] *Wenn ihr nicht werdet wie dieses Kind*, p. 36.
[43] *Homo Creatus Est*, p. 173f.
[44] *Wenn ihr nicht werdet wie dieses Kind*, p. 36.
[45] *Christen sind einfältig*, p. 41.

Spiritual childhood and psychological maturity coincide, because in Christ, Balthasar says, following St Thomas, eternal procession and temporal mission are one: 'His eternal *processio* from the Father, his being a child towards the Father, and the whole resolute seriousness of the *missio* that follows from it.'[46] The Christian, too, only becomes mature when, with childlike obedience and trust, he takes up the mission given him by the Father.

> The more we identify with the mission entrusted to us, the more deeply we become sons and daughters of the heavenly Father: the whole Sermon on the Mount testifies to that. In the great saints it can be seen immediately that Christian childlikeness and maturity are not in any kind of tension with each other. The saints retain into great old age a wonderful youthfulness.[47]

Jesus is also a child for ever in heaven, because in his glorified humanity all the historical mysteries of His earthly life are gathered up and have a permanent sanctifying power.

> Since eternal life already exists and reveals itself in his earthly life and all its changes, one can readily accept that in rising and ascending to heaven, he is able to embrace all the forms of human existence within the eternal ... True, the Son at the right hand of Father is now no longer in a physical, transitory sense the Child that once lay in his Mother's arms. But he is the eternal Child who has assumed into his eternity all the forms and stages of his earthly childhood existence, because his earthly childhood was already the word of revelation concerning his heavenly one.[48]

BECOMING LIKE A LITTLE CHILD

Balthasar wants us never to forget that he who tells us to become like children himself for us became a child. In this he follows an

---

[46] *Homo Creatus Est*, p. 170.
[47] *Wenn ihr nicht werdet wie dieses Kind*, p. 32.
[48] *Das Ganze im Fragment*, p. 272; *Man in History*, p. 247f.

important line of Patristic and medieval exegesis. Who is the child that Jesus places in the disciples' midst (cf. *Matthew* 18: 2)? It is Jesus himself, says St Bernard, the great God who became the Virgin mary's little child.

> Behold, a little child is placed in our midst. O little child desired by little children! O little one indeed, but little only in malice not wisdom. Let us endeavour to become like this little child. Let us learn from him, for he is meek and lowly in heart, so that the great God should not without cause have been made a tiny human being, have died for nothing, been crucified in vain.[49]

Balthasar suggests that our Lord's teaching on spiritual childhood flows from his own ever-present childhood. It is truly the Christ-Child who is the disciples' model.

> The grown-up Son will look back at His own childhood, which is still with him, and taking a child in his arms will embrace the eternal state of childlikeness and emphasise above all its helpless openness to the will of the Father, to the kingdom of heaven that is coming.[50]

Our Lord does not just exhort us to become like little children. As St Augustine never failed to assert against Pelagianism, God commands what he wills, but he gives what he commands. He bestows the grace of a new childhood, the Spirit of sonship, on a humanity old and grey in sin and death. In water and the Holy Spirit the Father gives us rebirth in the Son.

> The Child has received power from the Father to take others into his own birth from the Father (cf. *John* 1: 13; 3: 5–8), others who with him leave false adulthood behind and become children again. It is not an empty figure of speech, but the deepest reality in Christianity: we have received the

---

[49] *In Laudem Virginis Matris* 3, 14.
[50] *Das Ganze im Fragment*, p. 277f.; *Man in History*, p. 253.

Spirit of Childhood, who enables us to cry 'Abba, Father' (cf. *Romans* 8: 15f.).[51]

Only in Christianity, only in Christ, is the poets' yearning for a new childhood fulfilled. 'O das ich lieber wäre wie Kinder sind', cried Hölderlin in the night of his madness. Henry Vaughan made the same confession: 'O how I long to travel back, And tread again that ancient track.' In the sacrament of baptism we are given second birth, the new and unconquerable childhood of sonship in the Son. In the sacrament of penance the grace of the risen Jesus rejuvenates us out of the ageing ravages of sin. While we still breathe, we have the chance of travelling back.

> Now the backward glance to lost childhood – as cultivated by Christian poets – is no longer just a romantic dream, but a longing for a lost innocence and intimacy with God that Jesus and Mary never lost, and which through the depths of the grace of Baptism and the ever-renewed forgiveness of sins also always lies before us. Only the Christian view of the mystery of childhood can offer a counterweight to the heedlessness of the delusion of progress, whether it appears in anti-Christian, or neutral, or even Christian guise.[52]

For the members of the Body, as for the Head, spiritual childhood is not childishness, but the very condition of maturity. To be mature is to preserve 'the "super-moral" holy goods of our beginnings into adulthood'.[53] 'For a Christian, being grown up means abiding in God, the source of one's growth'.[54] St Paul has the balance right: 'Brethren, do not be children in your thinking; be babes in evil, but in thinking be mature' (1 *Corinthians* 14: 20).

Once spiritual childhood is perceived as the shaping principle of Christian life, mystical theology can wrest itself from the self-consciousness and psychologising to which, in the present as in the past, it has so often been prone. This was the great achievement of St Thérèse of Lisieux. The Dark Night is transformed tenderly into

---

[51] *Homo Creatus Est*, p. 174.
[52] *Das Ganze im Fragment*, p. 282f.; *Man in History*, p. 257f.
[53] *Wenn ihr nicht werdet wie dieses Kind*, p. 10.
[54] *Homo Creatus Est*, p. 178.

the sleep of the Child Jesus: 'What did he do while he slept so sweetly, and what became of his abandoned little ball?'

THE LITTLE WAY

But what *is* spiritual childhood? How do sons-in-the-Son walk the 'little way'? Balthasar answers this question by explaining the affinity between the Father's eternal Child and every human child.

> The life of both is the unaffectedness of letting themselves be given and owing themselves. Jesus has to lead the adult and mature back into this unaffectedness without relieving them of the burden of their responsibilities. But it must be the right burden they carry. Not anxiety 'about your life, what you shall eat or what you shall drink, nor about your body, what you shall put on'. In this they can be children: 'The Gentiles seek these things; and your heavenly Father knows that you need them all.' Real responsibility lies elsewhere: 'Seek first the kingdom of God' (*Matthew* 6: 28), as the order of the Our Father, the children's prayer, teaches.

In the Spirit of the obedient Son, the childlike soul lives in the present of the Father's holy will. He gently lays aside remorse for the past and fear of the future. He tries to honour the 'sacrament of the present moment'.

> The present world, teeming with adulthood and maturity, does not understand this any more. Futurology is the first and most necessary of the sciences. In political theology the kingdom of God is identified with concern for eating and drinking and clothing the poor. In the final analysis, such a theology has lost its sense of childlikeness, however many plausible reasons it may produce for its scale of values.[55]

To be a child is to be indebted. To be childlike is to acknowledge one's debts by the unfailing prayer of petition and thanksgiving.

---

[55] Ibid., p. 172f.

Jesus stresses the 'Say Please', 'Say Thank You' of childhood, not because otherwise the gifts would be refused, but so that they will be acknowledged as gifts. 'Ask, and you will be given …' (*Matthew* 7: 7) with such assurance that, in the very asking, you can give thanks for what you have received (*Mark* 11: 24).[56]

To be a childlike Christian is to live gladly and gratefully in the real, visible, hierarchical Church, Christ's beloved Bride and our Mother and Teacher. Spiritual childhood is the very soul of Catholic life.

Here is a new dimension of Christian childlikeness: the reception, in the Church, of the sacraments authorised by Christ, of the proclamation of his Word, and of the leadership decreed by him. It is clearest in the case of the sacraments. In the Church God alone holds the great Eucharistic banquet, to which we are invited as children; he alone in the sacrament of penance bestows the forgiveness of sins and the Holy Spirit; he alone takes the promises of fidelity pledged in marriage into the indissolubility of the marriage bond between Christ and his Church; he alone consecrates a man to sacramental powers or to a life-long dedication in definitive vows. Every person who approaches a sacrament is, like a child, a pure receiver; even if he has to make a contribution of his own, that is nothing other than the perfect readiness of the child.[57]

THE CHILDLIKE MOTHER

There is a strange paradox in the gospel. We are called to be the children of the Father, sons-in-the-Son, brothers and sisters of Christ. And yet Jesus says that anyone who does the will of his heavenly Father is his *Mother* (cf. *Matthew* 12: 50). This is a paradox, but not a contradiction.

---

[56] *Wenn ihr nicht werdet wie dieses Kind,* p. 39.
[57] Ibid., p. 41.

The intertwined images of motherhood and childhood have been applied to the believing soul, most impressively in German mysticism since Eckhart, but already quite clearly in Origen. Whoever takes the Word of God into his soul becomes his Mother and, through grace, can help to give him birth. But he can only do this because at the same time he is drawn into the eternal birth of the Son from the Father, in which, through grace, he becomes brother and sister of the Word. 'Of his own will [the Father] brought us forth by the Word of truth' (*James* 1: 18). The Father does this by the free choice of his grace, not by nature, as he begets the Son, the Word. yet he does it through the Word that he addresses to us and lays in us, and in such a way that there is not creation but 'bringing forth', a participation in the generation of the eternal Son, for James continues: '… that we should be a kind of first fruits of his creatures'.[58]

The dogma of the Immaculate Conception sheds light on this mystery. By the anticipated saving power of her Son's Cross, Our Lady is given the grace of adoption, the Spirit of sonship, at the first moment of her existence. She is made the Father's beloved daughter precisely to prepare her to be Mother of the Son: *filia in Filio* in order to be *Mater Filii Dei*. In spiritual childhood, as in all else that is Christian, Mary is our motherly model. Like Our Lady and with her help, we are first to be children-in-the-Child, so that we may then be mothers of the Child – mothers-in-the-Mother of the Child.

God the Father gave his Word in the Holy Spirit as the fleshly seed which grew and became perceptible in her, which claimed her totally and towards which she could and did regard herself as mother, precisely because her Son drew her into the same child-relationship with the Father. If all this is so, why should not the Word be given to us also as a child? In his quiet powerlessness the Child-Word can be so easily and by a thousand means rejected and aborted, almost without the pious noticing (just as human society is built upon the tacit, thousandfold murder of the unborn, as if

---

[58] *Das Ganze im Fragment*, p. 275f.; *Man in History*, p. 250f.

there were no need to waste words on that foundation). The Child-Word clings to us and seeks refuge and protection from weak human flesh. 'Not as a conqueror did He come, but as one imploring refuge. He lives as a fugitive in me, in my safe-keeping, and I have to answer for him to the Father' (Bernanos).[59]

For Balthasar, Mary is more than just the Church's model and mother. She truly *is* the Church, the embodiment and personification of the Church's deepest identity and final destiny. The coincidence in Mary of childhood and motherhood will, therefore, be reproduced in the Church, not least in her celebration of the Eucharist. It was with childlike trust that the incarnate Son offered himself to the Father on the Cross. In the same spirit of childhood the Bride, through the ministry of the priests, sacramentally renews that sacrifice on her altars.

> Childhood has a primacy in the event of redemption. It takes the Son of God from his human childhood, through his public works and rejections, to his high priestly office on the Cross. It also takes up the Church, born as a child from his wounded side, into the consenting priestly cooperation with the Cross (ever new in the Eucharist and daily life). This primacy shows clearly that the whole work of redemption, in all its supreme seriousness, can ultimately only be accompanied in the childlike attitude of the God-Man and in the childlike faith of his Bride, the Church ... The Church, as our Mother, must never forget that no girl is born as a mother. Motherhood does not fall ready-made from Heaven. So the Church's motherhood of grace rests on her primary, unforgotten, and abiding childhood.[60]

THE SPIRIT OF CHILDHOOD IN BALTHASAR

In all that he wrote, in all that he was and did, Balthasar strove to heal what he called the most tragic divorce in the history of the Church –

[59] *Das Ganze im Fragment*, p. 276; *Man in History*, p. 251.
[60] *Wenn ihr nicht werdet wie dieses Kind*, p. 49f.

the separation of theology and holiness. Those who knew him well would without hesitation agree that the spirit of childhood of which he wrote so beautifully was the most striking quality of his life.

> For all his greatness and towering knowledge, he was able to remain 'uncomplicated', humble, indeed childlike ... But he did realise and acknowledge his gifts. He saw them as just that – pure gift, something bestowed on him, for which he had to be thankful, which he had simply to put into service.[61]

Nur das Ganze: the definition of catholicity and the fundamental principle of Balthasar's theology. What is that if not the child's plea that something beautifully complete and whole be not shattered? In the Child born of the Virgin, God the Father has given us his all, says St Bonaventure, all his truth and grace, all his mercy and love. Like a child welcome the Child, echoes Balthasar. Let the Father's gift be not diminished. Let the Catholic whole abide.

---

[61]   Peter Henrici, S.J., see note 3, p. 141.

8

THE LOGIC OF DIVINE GLORY

John O'Donnell, S.J.

INTRODUCTION

The aim of this Chapter is to introduce the reader to the last part of Balthasar's trilogy, his *Theologik*. Here at the outset, we could mention that this last part of three volumes. The first, with the subtitle 'Truth of the World' was originally published in 1947 and was reissued as part of the *Theologik* in 1985. This first volume essentially offers a philosophical account of truth. The second and third volumes mark the shift from philosophy to theology. Volume II, entitled 'The truth of God' addresses the question of how Jesus Christ can express God's truth in the categories of human language. The final volume, 'The Spirit of Truth' presents an overview of Balthasar's pneumatology, explaining how the Holy Spirit interprets the truth of Jesus Christ for all ages. The continuity between the two parts is seen in Balthasar's fundamental insistence that truth, whether in the philosophical or in the theological sphere, is the revelation of love.

In the space of this short essay, it will obviously be impossible to give anything like a comprehensive account of Balthasar's theological logic. What I propose to do therefore is to highlight some of the more important themes in each of the three books in order to give the reader a taste for the richness of Balthasar's understanding of logic.

TRUTH OF THE WORLD

The first point of note in the philosophical account of truth is Balthasar's presentation of his method. On the one hand, he excludes in this volume a specific appeal to the data of revelation. On the other hand, he does not wish to exclude *a priori* all dimensions of the supernatural from his account, for as a Christian he recognises that the world is impregnated with God's grace. He proceeds therefore phenomenologically, limiting himself to the truth of the world while acknowledging that as a Christian he may see some things that a non-believer may miss.

One of the goals of his reflection is to show the coinherence of the three transcendentals: truth, beauty and goodness. Although here his account is centred on the true, he recognises that there is no recognition of the truth without a corresponding commitment to the truth. The ultimate logic is the logic of life where one is called to choose the good and exclude evil from one's existence. The choice of evil would ultimately be the most radical form of contradiction.

At the same time every perception of the true opens us to the dimension of beauty. To understand this point, we must grasp that for Balthasar, truth happens when Being unveils itself. In this unveiling, an essence appears. The mystery of Being makes itself felt in a concrete appearance. In this appearance there is a correspondence between essence and appearance, but what is more important for the aesthetic dimension is the transparency of Being in the appearance. The man or woman who knows never ceases to be astonished by the inexhaustible depth of Being revealing itself. Beauty derives from the radiance of Being in its manifestation.

As I already indicated in the introduction, one of the more fascinating aspects of Balthasar's approach to logic is the link he finds between truth and love. If truth is an unveiling then this fact presupposes freedom. This unveiling can happen only if the essence freely wishes to manifest itself. Balthasar is no naïve realist. For him there is a priority of the objective over the subjective. But at the same time he insists that every being possesses a minimum of freedom. Every being whatsoever, in some sense, is a for-itself and hence free. For Balthasar, the beings of the world can only realise themselves insofar as they present themselves to a human knower. However, this they can do in freedom. At the same time we should also note that truth can only happen when the human subject opens himself or herself to the appearance of Being. Without a surrender of myself to the world which is there, truth can never happen. The event of truth thus involves the double surrender of freedom, that of the object and that of the subject. This mutual surrender can rightly be called an event of love.

Another point which Balthasar stresses in his account of truth is the mystery character of this event. The ultimate explanation for this mystery must be sought in God, in the fact that finite beings share in the infinite depth of God the creator. But what this means for the truth of the world is that the subject can never exhaust the essence of anything whatsoever. Moreover, even if he could do so, he would be confronted with the ultimately unfathomable mystery that a being is. Before this mystery he can only stammer in wonder.

A further conclusion that can be drawn from the fact that knowledge can only happen in freedom is the direct proportion that exists between knowledge and faith. Already in the *Theological Aesthetics* Balthasar had stressed that *gnosis* and *pistis* always go together. I can only know Christ as the form of divine beauty insofar as I surrender myself to the evidence but in the surrender I really do know. Even in the realm of human truth it is clear that knowledge presupposes faith and faith culminates in knowledge insofar as knowledge can only happen in the surrender of freedom. This account means that we must not take an empirically scientific account of truth as normative. Our technological world can give the impression that knowledge is basically mastery of reality. For Balthasar, on the other hand, the deepest account of knowledge is not to be found in domination but in surrender.

A further thesis which Balthasar develops in this first volume is that love is creative of truth. The lover sees the reality of the other which does not yet exist but which can exist by the affirmation which love gives. One thinks here, for example of the wife of the composer Edward Elgar who so believed in the genius of her husband that her love enabled him to compose works of genius. After her death his creativity almost completely disappeared. Even more to the point is how God's love creates the truth of the creature enabling him or her to be conformed to Christ's likeness. Moreover, such creative love lets the false image sink into nothingness. This is exactly what happens when Christ obliterates the distorted picture of our humanity which sin has established and restores his image in us.

THE TRUTH OF GOD

An important key for interpreting the second and third volumes of the *Theologik* is the Johannine perspective. Balthasar consistently interprets theological truth in the light of the Fourth Gospel. What strikes us straightaway at the beginning of the second volume is the leap from a philosophical account of truth to the astounding claim of Christ: 'I am the truth' (*John* 15: 6). Such a staggering affirmation can only be accepted on the basis of God's revelation from above. Nevertheless, the first part of the second volume looks at various approaches from below which prepare the way for the revelation of the Christian understanding of truth.

A key dialogue partner in this first section is Hegel. I would suggest that Balthasar is both fascinated and repulsed by the Hegelian system. Its pretension to be all-embracing fascinates Balthasar's spirit but fundamentally he judges it to be a perversion of the truth. Balthasar argues that Hegel misses the mark because his system does not do justice to love. For Hegel the other is basically a necessary means to the self's own realisation. The other is a logical necessity. Hegel is never completely comfortable with love, for in his view love always demands the sacrifice of the I, a sacrifice which the self must make which it makes always a bit unwillingly. Balthasar consistently argues that the I does not have to go out of itself to reach the other, for in fact the I always finds itself from the beginning in the presence of the Thou.

In this perspective, therefore, it is clear that the dialogical philosophers (Büber, Rosenzweig and Ebner) come far closer to the Christian understanding of truth which is ultimately rooted in the Trinity. In Balthasar's judgment, Büber comes closest to the Christian vision with his insistence on the Zwischen (the between) which makes dialogue between the I and the Thou possible.

Balthasar marvels that so little attention has been given in philosophy to the generation of the new human being in the act of love. In his opinion the sexual union of husband and wife is the best human analogy for the Trinity. The Trinity, which is the ground of all truth, is basically the mystery of the ever-greater fecundity of the love of the Father and Son which overflows in the procession of the Holy Spirit.

Turning now to the revelation from above, we see that Christ is the truth because he perfectly expresses in human language the reality of God. Balthasar never explains how this is possible. Indeed no explanation is possible since here we are face to face with a mystery. What he does is continually circle around the mystery of God in human flesh.

First, he stresses with Nicholas of Cusa that God is not *aliud* since God is the source of everything which is and outside of God there is literally nothing. On the other hand, since God is totally transcendent, God is *alius*. Here we confront the mystery of Jesus. As God, he is totally other than us. But as human, he is totally similar.

Hence the mission of Jesus is to express in human language the otherness of God. Here we come to the problem of myth and the question of anthropomorphism. Balthasar follows the suggestion of C. S. Lewis that Jesus is myth as fact. The classical myths divinise the cosmic powers. The force of the myths lies in their concreteness. But the myths are not historical. Christ, on the other hand, is thoroughly worldly and thoroughly historical. His every word, gesture and deed is expressive of the divine. Jesus is the divine in the human. Balthasar cites Schelling with approval: either no anthropomorphism or a radical anthropomorphism.

What is astounding about Jesus' language is that it is totally familiar and simple, lucidly clear for even the most uneducated audience. Jesus talks about things of everyday life to bring to speech the reality of the kingdom of God. His language is anything but unintelligible. Why then was he not understood? Balthasar suggests two approaches. First, because his full word was not completely uttered until the moment of his death when the word was fulfilled in the deed. Secondly, because of the lack of faith of his hearers. Hence the need for another Paraclete who would interpret Jesus to the world after his departure.

If Jesus is God's word in a human word, or as Barth would say, the analogy of faith, what place does the analogy of being have within Balthasar's theological logics? Balthasar has always insisted upon the necessity of maintaining the doctrine of *analogia entis*. God can only enter into a covenant with humankind if the human partner is autonomous. The creation retains its place within the analogy of faith.

Moreover, Balthasar argues that created being even reflects the trinitarian Being. The mystery of the Trinity is the mystery of one indivisible divine substance in three divine persons. Within the absolute unity of God there are the infinite persons. Within the absolute unity of God there are the infinite 'spaces' between the divine persons. Balthasar finds the mystery of triune unity and differentiation reflected in the created order in the real distinction between existence and essence. Finite being (non-subsistent being) is only found in the endless variety of the diverse created essences. Moreover, for Balthasar, God's life is a paradox of fullness and poverty. The Father and the Son are so rich in their divine being that they give away their being to each other. In not retaining divinity for themselves they are poor but their poverty is an expression of infinite overflowing love whose fruit is the Spirit. Likewise, non-subsistent being is poor in that it gives itself away, expressing itself in the beings and yet each limited expression reflects the abundant richness of being.

In the mystery of the Incarnation and of grace the infinite distance between God and the creature remains. For example, the Council of Chalcedon teaches that the natures are unmixed. And yet they exist within the unity of the divine person. The same is true for grace. The creature remains a creature but his or her creaturehood is inserted into the life of the Trinity, into the infinite space which separates the three divine persons. Hence the analogy of being is not denied but is rather integrated into the analogy of faith.

Let us now turn to the polar opposite of analogy, the doctrine of dialectic. For Balthasar the root of the term dialectic is disunion, being torn asunder and in this sense contradiction. The whole point of this second volume of the *Theologik* is that Christian faith admits of no dialectic in this primordial sense of term. Combining the Johannine and the Pauline perspective, Balthasar argues that Jesus not only took on our physical flesh but also the flesh of sin. Citing one of his favourite texts, he argues that God made Christ sin (cf. 2 *Corinthians* 5: 20--21). This means that Christ fully entered into the condition of God-forsakenness which sin implies. God can only cast the lovelessness of sin from his life. But in identifying with our sinfulness on the cross, Christ does not enter into contradiction with the Father. Rather he remains a pure obedience and hence utters his word of love even under the conditions of lovelessness. Thus, his death represents the triumph of dialogue even when the Word is brought to silence upon the cross.

Developing the same perspective for the Christian life, Balthasar trenchantly rejects the dialectical position of Luther. The Christian is not a *simul iustus et peccator*. The Christian life is not contradiction. Genuine Christian existence is letting Christ live in one so that the believer passes from death to life in the new capacity received in grace to love the neighbour.

As a final point in this section we can mention Balthasar's fascinating treatment of the whole question of the *via negativa* in

Christian theology and asceticism. Here he not only enters into dialogue with Christian mysticism but with the negative way of the Oriental religions such as Buddhism and with the Christian appropriation of neo-Platonism as well. For Balthasar the way of negative theology is the supreme temptation for any serious philosophy of religion. If God is to be God, then God must be wholly beyond the world. The One is beyond the creation and the only way to reach it is to leave the world behind in a soaring flight to the Absolute.

The difficulty here is that such a flight does not do justice to the reality of love. For in such an approach there is no place for the supreme value of the Thou. The smile of the mother, which brings the I into consciousness of itself for the first time, is definitively left behind. Balthasar finds that the *via negativa* is fundamentally based on resignation. The Christian approach to God is always founded on the fundamental conviction that we creatures have been found by God. The first experience in faith is affirmation. From this affirmation there grows the never-ending search for the ever-greater God. Here once again we see the radical importance which the Trinity has in Balthasar's system. For a Christian the ultimate reality is not the lonely One without the Other, the One who must find in the world a partner of dialogue. Rather God is the triune community of love. For a Christian God is not the formless One of Plotinus but the Super-Form of a community of divine persons.

THE SPIRIT OF TRUTH

This third volume like its predecessor is guided by a Johannine perspective. Balthasar builds his pneumatology around two key texts of John's Gospel and two key motifs. The first is *John* 16: 13, 'The Spirit will lead you into all truth'. In this text Balthasar sees the fundamental mission of the Holy Spirit, namely to lead the Christian community into the truth who is Christ. The second text is taken from the same sixteenth chapter of John, 'The Spirit will take what is mine and will declare it to you' (v. 14). The importance which Balthasar attaches to this text is found in the link which John emphasises between the Spirit and the Son. The Holy Spirit is and will always be none other than the Spirit of the Son.

With this background, let us once again highlight a few of the more interesting perspectives which Balthasar opens up for us in this volume. And we can begin with his understanding of the inner-trinitarian life.

The first point which we can consider is how Balthasar understands the inner-trinitarian life, especially the rôle of the Holy Spirit in the immanent Trinity. Looking at the great Western tradition of theology, Balthasar notes how the persons of the Trinity have been understood in their subsistence. The persons of the Trinity are really distinct, each being a hypostasis for and in itself. The theology of the Middle Ages stressed the fact that the persons are distinct because of their relations of origin, the Son being from the Father, the Spirit being from the Father and from the Son. Balthasar argues that today we must give equal weight to the goal of the relations. Person is always oriented to the Thou. Hence the Father is ordered to the Son and the Son is ordered as response to the Father while the whole being of the Father and the Son is towards the Spirit. As we have already seen, the Spirit is the surplus or super-abundance of their love. In this sense the Spirit opens the love of the Trinity outwards to the world and toward the economy of salvation.

While dealing with the life of the Trinity, Balthasar devotes some fifteen pages to the problem of the *filioque*. Suffice it to say here that he argues for the necessity of this theological development in order to make clear the character of the Trinity as community of love. While respecting the Greek tradition that the Spirit proceeds through the Son and while willing to agree with Augustine that the Spirit proceeds *principialiter* from the Father, Balthasar nevertheless argues that the Son cannot be alien to the procession of the Spirit. Minimally this would mean that the Father is never without the Son and that the Spirit receives from the Son (Epiphanius would say he receives his form from the Son); maximally the *filioque* would mean that the Son is active in the procession of the Son.

In this last volume, Balthasar returns to a point which he had already developed in the *Theodramatik*, namely what he calls a soteriological inversion with regard to the Spirit's work in the economy of salvation. If in the inner-trinitarian life the Spirit proceeds from the Father and the Son and hence is passive-receptive, in the economy the Spirit is active. The act of the incarnation, for example, happens while the Son is passive. The passivity of the Son here corresponds to the Son's personhood as obedience. Then during his life-time Jesus obeys the Father by surrendering to the inspirations of the Spirit. His ultimate surrender is his death on the cross in the power of the Spirit (see *Hebrews* 9: 14). From the moment of the resurrection there is a new inversion when the Son again becomes active pouring out the Spirit upon the Church.

A large part of this last volume is devoted to what Balthasar calls objective and subjective Spirit. Already in an early collection of essays *Pneuma and Institution* (Einsiedeln, 1974), Balthasar had dealt with this theme. In his view the Holy Spirit always has an objective and subjective dimension. And these two dimensions are rooted in the life of the Trinity. In the Trinity the Spirit is the subjective love of the Father and Son. In this sense the Spirit represents love-act and event. But the Spirit is wholly referred to the Father and to Son. The Spirit is the fruit of their love, the result of their love act. The Spirit has no face of his own but always bears a christological face. In Balthasar's opinion, the fact that the Spirit is normed by the Father and the Son is the ground of everything 'institutional' in the economy of salvation.

The double aspect of the life of the Spirit is then reflected in God's history with his people. Wherever there is the Spirit, there is love. This is the essence of the Church, represented especially by the figures of Mary and John. The Church of love is most visible in the free bestowal of the charisms by the Spirit, in the special missions received by the saints and in the life of prayer. But the Spirit manifests his presence also in an objective or institutional way. This presence of the Spirit is seen in the hierarchy, in the sacraments, in the written word of sacred Scripture and in the magisterium. To be sure these dimensions of the Church are thoroughly christological. For example, Christ established the priesthood and works through the sacraments. But Balthasar argues that these dimensions are not just christological, they represent the objective presence of the Holy Spirit, the Spirit whose face is so hidden that Christ's from is made visible. The strength of Balthasar's position is that it makes clear the complementary character of objective and subjective Spirit. These two dimensions are inseparable, for both are ultimately rooted in the unity-in-difference of the inner-trinitarian life.

Having spoken of the objective presence of the Spirit in the Church, Balthasar also considers the relation between God's Spirit and the creation. Here once again he seems to be pursued by the figure of Hegel with his doctrine that the world is objective Spirit. In a section entitled 'Spirit as World-Soul', Balthasar recalls the ancient question debated in theology whether there is such a thing as a world soul. He notes how some contemporary thinkers such as Pannenberg see the Spirit of God as a field of force making itself felt in the cosmos. In this sense, for Pannenberg the Spirit becomes a cosmic principle. Something similar can be found in Teilhard de Chardin who sees the Spirit as the driving force in the universe responsible for the upward thrust of evolution. Balthasar is extremely critical of these approaches, for he believes that they neglect the christological and soteriological foundation of all thinking about the Spirit in the New Testament. In the Scriptures the Spirit is always the Spirit of Jesus, hence the Spirit of self-emptying and of service. If there are waste products in the upward spiral of evolution, such wreckage cannot be attributed to the Holy Spirit. In Balthasar's view, if there is something like a world-soul, it is better to see it as an immanent principle within the creation rather than the Holy Spirit of the Trinity.

At the end of the *Theologik* Balthasar asks where all of God's salvific work is leading. His answer is clear. Everything is destined to return to the glory of the Father. As Ignatius of Antioch put it, 'A living water murmurs within me; in the depths of my being it summons me: Go to the Father' (Ad. Rom. 7, 2). The work of the mediator is therefore none other than to lead us to the Father. But when we return to the house of the Father, what shall we see? The New Testament consistently affirms that God is invisible (see 1 *Timothy* 3: 16). Nonetheless, the First Letter of John says that in the end 'we shall see him as he is'. (1 *John* 3: 2). But who is the he of whom John is here speaking? Balthasar argues that it is the Son.

In the final analysis the goal of the Christian life is the vision of the glory of God revealed in the face of Christ. In the beatific vision we shall see the Son but the Father will always remain shrouded in mystery. Still this state of affairs does not weigh down the Christian, for he or she grasps that the meaning of truth is love. Hence the Christian only wants to know what the beloved wants to reveal. Whether in this life or the next the last word belongs to love and not to knowledge. And thus the comprehension of the truth cannot take place through the mastery of reason but only through the surrender of the self in freedom to the Father revealed in Jesus Christ and continually made present to us in his Spirit. Thus, our understanding the truth begins here on earth, but its completion is reserved for heaven when we will be definitively taken up in the contemplation of the Son and so into the everlasting adoration of the Father.

9

BARTH AND BALTHASAR: AN
ECUMENICAL DIALOGUE

John Thompson

Karl Barth has been described by Pope Pius XII as 'the greatest theologian since Thomas Aquinas'.[1] Whether that is true or not, as a Swiss theologian in the Reformation tradition who lived between the years 1886 and 1968, he became world famous for his rediscovery and reinterpretation of the Bible and his own tradition and writing the massive tomes of the *Church Dogmatics*. At the same time, he applied his new insights to Church and State – the latter notably against Nazi aggression and tyranny. It is also a fact that Barth saw the twin errors which he had to counter if a proper theology was to emerge as Neo-Protestantism and Roman Catholicism in its pre-Vatican II traditional garb. He carried out an intensive and mostly critical study of Catholic teaching for the greater part of his working life. He even called the *analogia entis*, which many Catholic theologians accept, and which posits some similarity between God and man, as 'the invention of Antichrist'.[2] With this background and approach, it requires, therefore, some explanation, indeed imagination, to see how one can even begin to speak of ecumenical dialogue. Wherein lies the answer? Certainly not primarily in Barth's negative attitude towards what he regarded as these twin dangers, nor even in Vatican II and its ecumenism, for Barth died three years after the end of the Council. Rather, it is to be found in three aspects of his life and experience of the European church scene.

---

[1]   Karl Barth, *Evangelical Theology: An Introduction*, Trs. Grover Foley, London and Glasgow: Collins 1963, p. 1.
[2]   *CD*, 1/1, p. xiii.

First, despite clear disagreements between Barth and Catholicism, he and its representatives entered into dialogue as far back as 1928.[3] He gave a lecture entitled 'Roman Catholicism: A Question to the Protestant Church', delivered in Bremen on 9 March of that year. This dialogue was continued with Eric Przywara[4] on the whole disputed area of the nature of analogy. Secondly, in the 1940s and 1950s there was considerable change in the theological stance of many Protestant and Catholic theologians, including Hans Urs von Balthasar, who sought to shed the Scholastic trappings of much western theology, its dualistic framework and static conceptuality, and express the faith more in line with Holy Scripture.[5] Thirdly, there was the towering figure and achievement of Barth himself and the whole nature of his theological task. He was regarded by Balthasar as the most authentic voice of the Reformation in the twentieth century and therefore, if one wishes to have dialogue, he was the obvious partner. At the same time he saw in Barth's theology a universalism and holistic vision as most authentically Catholic. It was factors such as these that made it possible for Barth and Balthasar to come together and find considerable common ground. A not unimportant aspect of this was the personal friendship which developed between the two men which, despite many disagreements on theology, continued from 1940 when Balthasar came to Basle as Catholic Chaplain to the students in the University – a friendship which lasted until Barth's death in 1968. Eberhard Busch in his fine biography of Barth[6] writes of this close relationship which included Adrienne von Speyr the mystic visionary. It shows that a friendly ecumenical relationship and dialogue may be about theology but is carried out between people and these personal friendships are invaluable, indeed absolutely indispensable, to proper theological encounter.[7] Those of us in our own difficult situation and divisions in Ireland who engage in similar dialogue have had precisely the same experience.

---

[3] Karl Barth, *Theology and Church: Shorter Writings*, Trs. Louise Pettibone Smith, London: SCM Press 1962, pp. 307–33.

[4] Eberhard Busch, *Karl Barth: His Life from Letters and Autobiographical Texts*, Trs. John Bowden, London: SCM Press 1976, pp. 182ff.

[5] G. C. Berkouwer, *The Second Vatican Council and the New Catholicism*, Trs. Lewis B. Smedes, Grand Rapids, Michigan: Wm. B. Eerdmans 1965, pp. 34–56.

[6] Busch, op. cit., p. 362.

[7] Ibid.

Balthasar was twenty-one years younger than Barth and was clearly largely influenced by him rather than vice versa, though the latter may also have been true. Balthasar attended a seminar of Barth's in 1942 on the Council of Trent, read the *Dogmatics* avidly and in 1948/49 gave ten lectures on Barth, one of which I was privileged to hear and several of which Barth himself attended.[8] Barth found in Balthasar one who wanted to look in a new way to the centre in God's revelation in Jesus Christ and, as Barth wrote, 'use him like a Trojan horse to bring about change in Catholicism'.[9] The result of Balthasar's lectures was his book *The Theology of Karl Barth*[10] and his article 'Christian Universalism'[11] which appeared in 1956 in *Antwort*, the Festschrift for Barth's seventieth birthday. Barth had considerable respect for Balthasar who more than most realised the importance of Barth's early commentary on Anselm[12] and the influence it had on the *Church Dogmatics*, especially in the sphere of methodology. Barth writes of Balthasar as 'my expositor and critic'[13] and regarded him as possibly the most astute Catholic interpreter of his wrings. These are only some ways the two related to and influenced each other.

Before coming to the main themes for the discussion, I want to indicate in brief and general terms, areas of common approach seen in the lives and work of these two theologians. There was, first, the profound spirituality of both. Balthasar had also a mystic strain, learnt partially from Adrienne von Speyr and developed through his repeated use and exposition of Ignatius Loyola's 'Spiritual Exercises'.[14] Barth's was based on prayer and worship and obedience to the Word. He quoted often the words of Calvin, 'All knowledge is

---

[8]   Ibid.

[9]   Ibid.

[10]   Hans Urs von Balthasar, *Karl Barth: Darstellung und Deutung Seiner Theologie*, Cologne: Jakob Hegner 1951, ET *The Theology of Karl Barth*.

[11]   Balthasar, 'Christlicher Universalismus', *Antwort: Festschrift zum 70 Geburstag von Karl Barth*, Zurich: Evangelischer Verlag 1956, pp. 237–48.

[12]   Karl Barth, *Anselm: Fides Quaerens Intellectum, Anselm's Proof of the Existence of God in the Context of His Theological Scheme*, Trs. Ian W. Robertson, SCM Press 1960, Preface to the Second Edition, p. 11.

[13]   *CD*, IV/1, p. 768.

[14]   Balthasar, 'In Retrospect', *The Analogy of Beauty: The Theology of Hans Urs von Balthasar*, John Riches (ed.), Edinburgh: T&T Clark, pp. 196–97. Balthasar speaks of coming in this way 'closest to the sense and inspiration of the Reformation, from Luther to Karl Barth'.

born in obedience'.[15] Further, both wrote for and within the context
of the Church, sought its renewal through a new understanding of
God's acts in revelation and redemption,[16] and both acted throughout in pastoral and preaching roles as well as in academic theology.[17]
At the same time, both remained close to the essence of their
respective traditions. Their position may be summed up in a phrase
I have coined from Barth – 'respectful freedom in relation to
tradition'.[18] Theologically, Barth began *a posteriori* and not *a priori*
from some given scheme or ideas. That means he began within the
faith, seeking understanding of it, *Credo ut intelligam* and Balthasar
went a very long way with this view of theology and its doctrines.
Listen to what Balthasar wrote, 'You do good apologetics if you do
good central theology, if you expound theology effectively, you have
done the best kind of apologetics. The word of God is self-
authenticating, proof of its own truth and fecundity and it is
precisely in this way that the Church and the believer are inserted
into one another'.[19] Here are words which are almost identical with
what Barth himself had expressed at the beginning of his theological
writings.[20] And finally, both wanted a church open to the world and
not closed in on itself.[21] But neither wanted a Church or theology
concerned with the world in such a way that its agenda was largely
determined by it, or simply took over aspects of the world and treated
them as if they belonged to the Church, i.e., baptised the Enlightenment into Christ and so effectively destroyed the essence of the faith.[22]

I turn now to four aspects where both Balthasar and Barth made
significant contributions to theological thinking. The first and the
fourth bring out considerable disagreements as well as agreements,
in the second and third they are in virtual unanimity.

I. THE NATURE OF THE KNOWLEDGE OF GOD

One of the effects of the work of Karl Barth on the whole theological

[15] Barth, *Evangelical Theology*, p. 18.
[16] *CD*, IV/4, pp. 7ff. Balthasar, 'Another Ten Years', *The Analogy of Beauty*, p. 223.
[17] Busch, op. cit., pp. 62ff., 90ff. et al.; Balthasar, op. cit., p. 227.
[18] *CD*, 1/2, pp. 597ff.
[19] Balthasar, op. cit., p. 227.
[20] *CD*, II/1, pp. 8, 93ff.
[21] Balthasar, *Retrospect*, pp. 194–95.
[22] Ibid., pp. 197–201.

scene was to force a rethink on the questions of revelation and natural theology. His own position is well known – only through God is God known.[23] Sinful human beings can never reach a knowledge of God, but in their search for a reality to worship only create an idol.[24] Hence, the old theistic arguments and the whole realm of natural theology are questioned and indeed are rejected by Barth. God alone can break down the barriers of our sin and ignorance and does so exclusively in Jesus Christ by the Holy Spirit. In this way, he opens up human beings for knowledge of himself and in the same act demonstrates his own existence. This 'christological concentration', as Barth himself called it,[25] has had profound effects in making the Church and its theology reassess its position and the place, if any, for the old argument for a *praeambula fidei* or for a *De Deo Uno* approach before one reaches the *De Deo Trino*. It is clear that Balthasar goes a very long way with Barth on these matters which raise several issues of prime importance for faith and theology – the nature of revelation, its relation to our humanity and the knowledge of God, what place does the human play in all this and what kind of creaturely correspondence or analogy reflects God's action for and his relation to us? In other words, how are nature and grace related to one another?

Walter Kreck, in an important book on Barth and his theology, speaks of Balthasar as 'one of Barth's most penetrating critics and admirers'.[26] 'It is astonishing', he writes, 'how close Balthasar comes to Barth even in relation to natural theology'.[27] It is, however, closeness but not full unanimity and it was a closeness in marked contrast to the official Church theology of Catholicism prior to Vatican II. Kreck points out this close approximation in three ways:[28]

---

[23]   *CD*, II/1, pp. 3ff.

[24]   *CD*, IV/1, pp. 177f.

[25]   *Karl Barth 1886–1968, How I Changed My Mind, Introduction and Epilogue by John D. Godsey*, Edinburgh: The Saint Andrew Press 1966, p. 43.

[26]   Walter Kreck, *Grundentscheidungen In Karl Barths Dogmatik, Zur Diskussion Seiner Verstandnisses von Offenbarung und Erwahlung*, Neukirchener Verlag 1978, p. 150.

[27]   Ibid.

[28]   Ibid., p. 153. Balthasar, *Karl Barth*, p. 296, German Edition.

1. a common christocentric theology,
2. the predisposition of the creature, of humanity, including reason, by the grace of God towards the revelation of God in Jesus Christ as their real centre and goal,
3. the possibility of an *analogia fidei*, i.e. a correspondence in human faith to the activity of God.

At the same time, Balthasar believed that Barth went too far so that his christological concentration became 'a christological construction',[29] as he called it, giving too little place to human cooperation with grace on the basis of prevenient grace. Balthasar does not believe in or accept the older form of natural theology as a basis for faith. He interprets the natural theology of Vatican I as speaking of the creaturely possibility for and not the fact of natural knowledge of God, an interpretation which can naturally be queried. In this he moves towards Barth and away from the traditional tendency towards dualism between nature and grace.

Balthasar sees our creaturely nature having both a formal and material aspect.[30] The formal is the presupposition with which grace operates and the material is the reality of sin. Because God is not only our redeemer but also our creator, Balthasar sees an intimate interrelationship between them. He writes: 'The whole order of reason is embedded theologically in the order of grace just as creation is. Our ability to know God is due to prevenient grace. To come to a personal relationship of knowledge and will with the God of creation means to be placed before the God of Jesus Christ and no other'.[31] In other words creation and we as creatures are christologically orientated. The possibility of our knowledge of God comes first from God's prevenient grace in creation and forms the starting point from which we come to a true knowledge, a deeper knowledge in Jesus Christ his Son. There is, therefore, something in nature which enables us to know God but that something is itself the action of God's grace in the creaturely realm. Barth, on the other hand, sees creation and redemption related through the covenant. Creation is the outer ground of the covenant and the covenant is the

---

[29] *CD*, IV/1, p. 768.
[30] Kreck, op. cit., p. 155. Balthasar, op. cit., p. 331.
[31] Ibid., p. 154. Balthasar, ibid., p. 335.

inner ground of creation and the covenant is fulfilled in reconciliation.[32] There is, for him, no point of contact on the basis of
prevenient grace such as Balthasar indicates. There is only one grace
of God which, by the Holy Spirit, enables faith which corresponds
to the reality of revelation. Hence Barth could not and did not
perceive or accept analogies in creation outside of faith. His was an
analogia fidei and *analogia relationis*. Balthasar believed that the
analogia fidei which he also accepted, based on revelation, did not
exclude but involved an *analogia entis*.[33] He felt that Barth should
come to the same conclusion since he accepted some form of
creaturely presupposition for our knowledge of God in the fact of
the creation itself and the humanity of Christ.

The question that arises here between Balthasar and Barth is a
complex one but I can put it only in brief outline. Is there a
correspondence, an *analogia entis*, in the very being of our
creatureliness between humanity and God however dissimilar the
creation and Creator may be? Balthasar answers yes and this is due
to the prevenient grace of God in creation which enables a certain
human aptitude or capacity for God. Barth denies this *analogia entis*
and sees all correspondences or analogies grounded only in God's
revelation in Christ and perceived through faith and this is a
position which he would seem to have accepted and retained
throughout the whole of his life though some deny this. Hans Küng
speaks of Barth no longer mentioning the *analogia entis* from the
mid-1950s onwards.[34] This is in fact correct but does not necessarily
mean that he endorsed it. That he maintained his own view to the
end is set out in a very able, lengthy article by Eberhard Jüngel in
1962.[35]

Balthasar claimed in the preface to the second edition of his book
The Theology of Karl Barth that the dispute between them had been
resolved but the judgment of John Riches in this regard is, I believe,
essentially correct when he writes, 'He (Barth) remained deeply
suspicious of the dangers of a natural theology which would

[32]   *CD*, IV/1, pp. 22ff. *CD*, III/1, pp. 42ff.
[33]   Balthasar, *Karl Barth*, p. 313. Kreck, op. cit., p. 153.
[34]   Hans Kung, *Theology for the Third Millenium: An Ecumenical View*, Trs.
Peter Heinegg, Harper Collins 1991, p. 266.
[35]   Eberhard Jüngel, 'Die Moglichkeit Theologischer Anthropologie auf dem
Grunde der Analogie, *Ev. Th.* 22/10 (1962), pp. 535–57.

ultimately control a theology of revelation, a suspicion greatly
fuelled by his battles with theologians like Brunner and Althaus who
advocated a doctrine of orders of creation. And Balthasar himself
was fully alive to such dangers. He was to live to see the way in which
the opening up of the Church to the world which he and others had
fought for could easily lead to the erosion of that which was
distinctively Christian. Hence, his fierce reaction, notably in *Cordula*
to Rahner's development of the notion of 'anonymous Christians'.[36] Thus a presupposition for grace which itself comes from a
form of grace in nature must not be seen as a natural capacity
however it may be regarded as a form of search for God and however
that search may be seen as taken up into and fulfilled in revelation
in Jesus Christ.

The nub of the difference which comes up also in the doctrine of
the Church is an area for further dialogue. It is a question of the place
of the human and human action in relation to grace. Both Eberhard
Jüngel and Walter Kreck point out how in his last Volume IV on
Baptism Barth maintained a strong emphasis on the human faith
requesting baptism for the person.[37] Jüngel believes that because of
Barth's emphasis on the human being as the subject of his faith there
is a place where Barth and Catholicism have the possibility of further
genuine ecumenical dialogue. Furthermore, Barth did not dispute
that in the sphere of creation there could be 'parables of the
kingdom' by which God could and did speak to humans.[38] But he
insisted that this was not a natural theology but a possibility that was
left open to God to speak when, where and as he pleases. However,
when he does so, and if he does so, this will conform to the truth
given to us in Jesus Christ without which these others would have
no revelatory significance whatsoever. This was in fact Barth's
ultimate reply to Balthasar's and other's criticism of his continued
rejection of natural theology.

---

[36] John Riches, 'Hans Urs von Balthasar' *The Modern Theologians, An Introduction to Christian Theology in the Twentieth Century*, Volume 1, ed. David Ford,
Oxford: Basil Blackwell 1989, p. 248.

[37] *CD*, IV/4, p. 73f. Eberhard Jüngel, 'Karl Barths Lehre von der Taufe', *Barth-
Studien*, Zurich: Benzinger, pp. 269–70.

[38] *CD*, IV/3, 1, pp. 128–29.

II. CROSS AND RECONCILIATION

Both theologians see the divine revelation in Jesus Christ centred and fulfilled on the cross. Incarnation moves inexorably towards the Passion.

There are three aspects where Barth and Balthasar are in substantial agreement, namely the divine *kenosis*, the teaching on the descent into hell and the universality of reconciliation.

KENOSIS

Both theologians see the Son of God in obedience to the Father's will becoming incarnate for us and our salvation.[39] But this has two facets; it corresponds to an obedience of Son to Father in the life of the triune God – an eternal filial response of love. This manifests itself in time in the incarnation which moves inexorably to the cross, to the depth of our sinful disobedience. If the centre of God is in Jesus Christ, the centre of Christ is the cross. The possibility of all this is in the divine nature, will and act of God.

Both reject nineteenth century kenoticism and link their views rather with Patristic theology which sees the whole divine drama of our salvation as *kenosis*. Balthasar is so much in agreement with Barth here that he expressly states 'We may leave to Karl Barth the closing words on the doctrine of *kenosis* and its theological consequences'.[40] What then are these for Barth? Since the divine *kenosis* reaches to the cross and embraces all our sin and suffering it at one and the same time reveals the true nature of God, the height of his deity in this lowliness, the divine in this humiliation. Jesus Christ surrenders himself to abandonment by the Father on the cross but not to ultimate separation, a theme widely debated in modern theology. Barth writes of what happens here, in Christ 'God gives himself but he does not give himself away.... He does not cease to be God. He does not come into conflict with himself'.[41] In fact, it is here precisely and supremely that he is known as God always in the light of the resurrection.

---

[39]   *CD*, IV/1, p. 184; Balthasar, *Mysterium Paschale, (MP) The Mystery of Easter*, Trs. with an Introduction by Aidan Nichols O.P., Edinburgh: T&T Clark, pp. 49–89.

[40]   *MP*, p. 79.

[41]   *CD*, IV/1, p. 185.

To some extent, Balthasar takes this line of thinking further though in substantial agreement with Barth.[42] With Barth he fully accepts Chalcedon but sees what happens on the cross not merely as the man Jesus suffering and dying in our place. This is something which happens to God, to one of the Trinity who suffers and dies. This has been described as the New Chalcedonianism by Rahner, who was against it, but Balthasar does point in this direction and Barth is close to it.[43] Here both are more careful and reserved than Moltmann who is largely dismissive of Chalcedon and sees the divine self-giving as so great that it almost looks like a cleft in God.[44]

THE JUDGMENT AND HOLY SATURDAY – THE DESCENT INTO HELL

The depth of self-giving on the cross leads to Balthasar's original treatment of Holy Saturday.[45] On the cross the whole power of our sin and evil battle against Christ who is active in love, suffers and prevails. In the descent to dead, the Son is in passive solidarity 'with those damning themselves',[46] who wish to live apart from God in an impossible loneliness but now find that he is with them and for them in their godlessness. In this way and in no other Jesus preaches to the spirits in prison.[47]

He enters into solidarity from within with those who reject all solidarity; He descends into hell. Barth comes close to this view in his exposition of the Apostles' Creed[48] where he interprets the descent into hell as Christ bearing the just judgment of God on our sin to the uttermost.

It is clear that both Barth and Baltahasar see a soteriological aspect to the cross. In fact, the whole conception of hell is raised by both

[42]   Balthasar, *MP*, pp. 49ff.
[43]   Karl Rahner, 'Jesus Christus – Sinn der Lebens', in *Schriften* 15 (1983), pp. 206–16.
[44]   Jürgen Moltmann, *The Crucified God*, trs. R. A. Wilson and John Bowden, SCM Press, 1976², pp. 235ff.
[45]   Balthasar, *MP*, pp. 148–88.
[46]   Balthasar, *Pneuma und Institution*, pp. 401–4, 407–9. See *The Von Balthasar Reader*, p. 153, Medard Kehl and Werner Löser (eds.), trs. Robert J. Daley and Fred Lawrence, Edinburgh: T&T Clark 1982.
[47]   Ibid.
[48]   Karl Barth, *Credo*, tr. J. Strathearn McNab, London: Hodder & Stoughton 1936, p. 91f.

as a kind of negative aspect of what is the most positive thrust of God's great Yes and Amen to our humanity in reconciliation.

RECONCILIATION

Barth views God's action as one which in Christ reconciles the whole of humanity and the universe to himself. He accomplishes this in the exclusive action of incarnation and the cross but includes the whole of creation in this embrace.[49] These perspectives are important for Balthasar as well. Kehl comments, 'Because of his doctrine of universalistic predestination Barth has become for Balthasar the great catalyst of his own sketch of a "theology of history"'.[50] Balthasar thus sees Christ as 'the central and integrating source of meaning for all of history'.[51] Barth here goes back against and beyond post-Reformation views of Calvinism's limited atonement to the reformers and from them to patristics and the New Testament.[52] This in fact is one of the 'Catholic' aspects of Barth which is most congenial to Balthasar and where he feels they are most at one.

One can sum up these three aspects of Barth's theology in the terms of Berthold Klappert in four ways.[53] In his actions in Christ God affirms Himself and manifests His glory – He is *pro se*. Is this not the theme of *Herrlichkeit* in Balthasar? Secondly, He is *pro nobis*, for us and our salvation (again at the centre of Balthasar's thought). Thirdly, He is *contra nos* – in judgment – a further interest in Balthasar and finally, He is *pro me*, for each of us personally, perhaps not so much emphasised with Balthasar as Barth but true nonetheless. Here at last, as Barth says, Bultmann comes to his own. But this subjective, existential element by the Holy Spirit is only true in the light of the above total perspectives, much of which Bultmann omits or interprets otherwise than our two theologians. It is also only true

---

[49]   *CD*, IV/1, p. 317f. cf. *CD*, II/2, on Election.
[50]   Medard Kehl, 'Hans Urs von Balthasar: A Portrait', *Von Balthasar Reader*, p. 28.
[51]   Ibid., p. 30.
[52]   *CD*, IV/2, p. 277.
[53]   Bertold Klappert, *Die Auferweckung des Gekreuzigten, Der Ansatz der Christologie Karl Barths im Zusammenhang der Christologie der Gegenwart*, Neu Kirchen 1971, pp. 234–35.

of the centre in the cross as it is seen retrospectively in the light of the resurrection.

III. THE TRINITY

It will not be surprising if Barth and Balthasar, who have so much in common in Christology and the atonement, have similar views on the Trinity and this is in fact the case. Both work largely within the western tradition and are deeply indebted to Augustine and Aquinas. Yet both move away from the more static conceptuality of that tradition to find and express the character of the triune God in a more dynamic way. Barth sees God as a being who acts,[54] the one God in the activities of the three persons – more akin to eastern thought – and affording, as T. F. Torrance points out, another ecumenical bridge in a different direction.[55] Balthasar by his conception of a liveliness in God expresses a similar concern which does not endanger in any way the ontological reality of God's being.[56]

A second aspect common to both is the definitive role the Trinity plays in their theological thinking as a whole. For Barth it is an implicate of revelation and stands at the forefront of the *Church Dogmatics*[57] informing the whole so that whether dealing with creation or anthropology or the Church the trinitarian form emerges. Werner Löser points out how Balthasar's theology has similar traits and a basic trinitarian character. He writes: 'His whole theology has trinitarian contours'.[58]

Thirdly, while Barth lived before Rahner's dictum that the economic Trinity is the immanent Trinity and vice versa[59] he would

[54] *CD*, II/1, pp. 257ff.

[55] T. F. Torrance, 'Karl Barth and Patristic Theology', *Theology Beyond Christendom, Essays on the Centenary of the Birth of Karl Barth*, ed. John Thompson, Allison Park: Pickwick Publications 1986, pp. 225–26.

[56] Gerard O'Hanlon, *The Immutability of God in the Theology of Hans Urs von Balthasar*, Cambridge University Press 1990, pp. 112ff.

[57] *CD*, I/1, pp. 295ff. Claude Welch, *The Trinity in Contemporary Theology*, London: SCM Press 1953, pp. 161ff. describes Barth's view with the heading, 'The Trinity as the Immediate Implication of Revelation'.

[58] Werner Löser, 'Trinitatstheologie Heute, Ansatze und Entwurfe', *Trinitat, Aktuelle Perspektiven der Theologie*, Wilhelm Breuning (ed.), Freiburg, Basel, Vienna 1984, p. 39. See Balthasar, *Theo-dramatik IV – Das Endspiel (TD)*.

[59] Karl Rahner, *The Trinity*, Trs. Joseph Donceel, London: Burns & Oates 1975[2], pp. 21ff.

not have agreed with it simpliciter though there are places when he comes close to this view and emphasises the economic aspect strongly. Nor did Balthasar agree with Rahner here as elsewhere.[60] The position they took up can be described as a unity and distinction between the immanent and economic Trinity. It is in the event of reconciliation on the cross that the true character of God is seen. The Trinity is, therefore, to use the modern way of putting it, 'the mystery of salvation'.[61] There is, of course, only one triune God, one Trinity but what God does in salvation shows us who he is in himself in the fullness of the divine being before creation existed. In my view, unity and distinction is a better way of stating the relationship between economic and immanent Trinity than Rahner's where the gracious condescension of God can be unintentionally given too little stress.[62] Fourthly, since it is in the economy of salvation that we see God as He is, the event of identification with our sin shows us the relation of the Son to the Father by the Holy Spirit.[63] In the event of God-forsakenness of the Son on the cross Barth and Balthasar see the nature of God's love taking sin and suffering so fully into the being of God as almost to lead to a division – a danger obviated by the prior reality of their union by the Holy Spirit.[64] Both see the suffering of the Son as indicative of the fact that God is no apathetic Being but one who enters fully into our lot and suffers for and with us.[65] Barth can speak of there being a true aspect of the Father being involved with the Son and His suffering on the cross, the *particula veri* of the old patripassianism.[66] Balthasar sees the triune love of God on the cross embracing and taking to itself the whole sorrow, alienation and God-forsakenness of humanity, almost to the point where he is in danger of a form of panentheism.[67] At the same time,

---

[60] O'Hanlon, op. cit., pp. 36ff.; *TD*, III, pp. 253–62, 298–99.

[61] Eberhard Jüngel states that 'The mystery of the Trinity is the mystery of salvation'. 'Das Verhaltnis von "okonomischer" und "immanenter" Trinitat', *Entsprechungen: Gott-Wahrheit-Mensch*, Munich: Ch. Kaiser 1980, p. 270.

[62] Thomas F. Torrance, 'Towards An Ecumenical Consensus on the Trinity', *Theologische Zeitschrift*, 31/6 (1975), p. 337.

[63] *CD*, IV/1, pp. 199ff.; O'Hanlon, op. cit., pp. 118f.; *TD*, IV, p. 48ff.

[64] *CD*, IV/1, p. 185f.; O'Hanlon, ibid., p. 33.

[65] *CD*, IV/2, pp. 225, 357; O'Hanlon, ibid., p. 69f.; *TD*, IV, pp. 196–99.

[66] *CD*, IV/2, p. 357.

[67] O'Hanlon, op. cit., p. 471; *TD*, III, pp. 420–21.

while there is suffering in God, one cannot attribute our human suffering univocally to the Trinity as is the tendency in Moltmann, a view which Balthasar sees as in danger of mythologising.[68]

Eberhard Jüngel, interpreting Barth, has described God's being as a being in becoming.[69] Balthasar is chary of this view but by this Jüngel does not mean that God has become something that He is not and so changes. Rather it indicates the movement and living fullness of life in the relationships between Father, Son and Holy Spirit, which the terms 'generation' and 'procession' indicate. Balthasar intends the same when he speaks of God as a trinitarian process, a process of trinitarian drama with an event character.[70] Being and happening must be thought together, a fully Barthian conception corresponding to the event and dramatic character of the cross and discussed particularly in *Theo-drama* II.

Fifthly, Father, Son and Holy Spirit are one God in personal relationships. Both theologians come from their western perspective close to the eastern conception of Zizioulas and others based on the Cappadocian view of the Trinity as 'Being as Community'.[71] The relational basis of Christian faith in the persons of the Trinity is the paradigm for Church, anthropology and society since we live as God does in no lonely isolation but with and for one another. Balthasar developed this possibly more than Barth as a dialogue in drama between the divine persons and to be manifested in our human life in a similar way.[72] Again, in line with more recent trends Balthasar goes beyond Barth in showing the relationship of the persons in God as capable of being described as receptivity, interaction, mutuality, a giving and receiving in God.[73] And beyond this

[68] O'Hanlon, ibid., p. 39.

[69] Eberhard Jüngel, *The Doctrine of the Trinity: God's Being is in Becoming*, trs. Horton Harris, Edinburgh and London: Scottish Academic Press 1976; O'Hanlon, op. cit., p. 91; *TD*, I/2, p. 143–45.

[70] J. J. O'Donnell, *The Mystery of the Triune God*, Heythrop Monographs 6, London: Sheed & Ward 1988, pp. 167f. Where he discusses and compares Jüngel and Balthasar, cf. *Theo-dramatik* IV, pp. 66–67.

[71] *CD*, III/2, pp. 222–85. cf. Stuart D. McLean, Creation and Anthropology, *Theology Beyond Christendom*, ed. John Thompson, pp. 111ff. McClean writes of Barth's views, 'relationship is the key to understanding God and persons', (ibid., p. 112). Balthasar writes, 'this unity (of the triune God) is nothing other than pure being-for-one-another', *Von Balthasar Reader*, p. 226.

[72] O'Hanlon, op. cit., pp. 33–37, 66–64, *Pneuma*, p. 402, *TD*, II/1, p. 171.

[73] Ibid., pp. 121ff.

again, as G. O'Hanlon has clearly demonstrated, Balthasar seeks with great care and nuanced thought to develop a view of the Trinity where God in some measure can be seen to change yet always remains the same, to be 'ever more' yet the one constant triune God.[74] The tradition is here stretched to the limits and possibly beyond them.

Here one can discern a similar analysis and interpretation by Balthasar and Jüngel. Jüngel suggests the example of human love where people enrich one another and grow in community as they meet and live with one another.[75] Analogously this is applicable to the triune God. There is joy involved, self-giving and even surprises, mystery and 'ever more' of the same. Sixthly, an interesting further line of agreement between Barth and Balthasar is what Colin Gunton calls 'space' in God – otherness and freedom.[76] Barth uses this conception in his doctrine of the Church where the Holy Spirit, distinct from the Church, yet mediates Jesus Christ the Son of God to its members.[77] Since the Spirit is divine, this reflects His place and work in the Trinity. The Spirit is distinct from the Father and the Son, over against them in one sense, and yet with them in their unity and fellowship with each other. There is, says Barth, mediation and distance, communication in confrontation, unity in partnership in God and this forms the basis of His actions which leave space for a cosmos, creaturely being other than God yet related to Him. Balthasar uses this idea, and most likely takes it from Barth, when he speaks of each person in the Trinity as having an otherness, a space in which it allows the others to be and, as G. O'Hanlon puts it, 'within this space we find our home'.[78] If by this is meant that we share through fellowship with the triune God in eternal life this is an acceptable way of putting it, but if it means the existence of creation in God this is more doubtful. What, however, is quite clear from the foregoing is that the whole nature and conception of the

---

[74] Ibid., pp. 110ff.

[75] Eberhard Jüngel, *God as the Mystery of the World: On the Foundation of the Theology of the Crucified One in the Dispute Between Theism and Atheism.* trs. Darrell L. Guder, Edinburgh: T&T Clark 1983, pp. 318ff.

[76] Colin Gunton, *The Promise of Trinitarian Theology,* Edinburgh: T&T Clark 1991, p. 132f.; O'Hanlon, op. cit., pp. 116ff.

[77] *CD*, IV/2, pp. 341ff.

[78] O'Hanlon, op. cit., p. 55.

action of the triune God in creation and redemption are seen by Balthasar and Barth in very similar ways. Balthasar has been able, post-Barth, to carry the debate further in line with more recent Catholic and Protestant thinking on the relationship of the Trinity and the cross, the Trinity and the death of God and what this means for us.

IV. THE CHURCH

In speaking of the Church, we come to an area where many continuing agreements are to be found yet where the interpretations also seriously divide. I look first in a more general way at some basic agreements. Both see the Church as christologically grounded – Jesus Christ by the Holy Spirit bringing it into being. Barth calls it, 'the earthly-historical form of his (Christ's) existence'.[79] Both see the person and work of Christ as incomprehensible without the Church – for Barth it is always Christ and His own,[80] for Balthasar Christ always appears surrounded by a group of disciples, apostles, a constellation of followers, of believers.[81] For both he is the Head, the Church is the Body of Christ. Again, for both, the Church does not simply exist for itself but for the world in mission and service since Christ died not simply for the Church but has effected a universal reconciliation.[82] For both, the Church is, as Barth calls it, 'the provisional representation of what is God's will for all'.[83] These form a considerable common basis from which to have ecumenical dialogue.

I look now a little more closely at four areas – the unity, catholicity and ministry of the Church and ecumenical dialogue.

UNITY

Both Barth and Balthasar see the Church as a given concrete unity

---

[79] *CD*, IV/1, p. 643.
[80] Ibid., pp. 663ff.
[81] M. Kehl, *Von Balthasar Reader*, p. 38; Balthasar, *Der Antirömische Affekt*, Freiburg: Herder 1974, pp. 115–23.
[82] *CD*, IV/1, 2, 3; Balthasar, *Retrospect*, pp. 194–95; *MP*, p. 263.
[83] *CD*, IV/3, 2, pp. 681; Balthasar, *MP*, ibid.

corresponding to its basis in the one unique person of Jesus Christ.[84] The New Testament metaphors and images of body, bride, temple, etc., bear clear witness to this. It is a visible unity in space and time, but also a communion of all the saints in heaven and on earth. Division is quite simply a sin against Christ and a plurality of different churches contrary to its nature. Balthasar applauds Barth's view here and gives a lengthy quotation in *Theo-drama II* on this issue. 'If we listen to Christ we do not exist above the differences separating the churches but in them... . One should not want to explain the multiplicity of the Church at all. One should deal with it as one deals with one's own and other's sins. One should understand it as guilt.'[85] For Balthasar as against Barth, the human origin of the Church is in the willing obedience of the blessed Virgin Mary.[86] Balthasar is strongly Marian in his churchmanship, Barth clearly is not.

CATHOLICITY

This slippery word which has presented so many problems shows also a considerable measure of agreement between the two. It is related first to the wholeness and fullness of the life given and available for us in Christ.[87] At the same time, it is a call and demand to be what we are; to seek to attain that stature which is ours as gift in Christ.[88] For Balthasar this is fully exemplified in Mary, for all others it must be striven for.[89] Catholicity also means that it is supranational and seeks to embrace all people in its fold. For Balthasar, as for Vatican II, this means bringing the riches of the peoples into its embrace.[90] For Barth it means simply universality embracing all nations[91] and therefore also transcending nation, class, creed and other differences. Further, catholicity means visibility, a given structure, clear guidelines. For Barth it is a matter of

---

[84]   *CD*, IV/1, pp. 667ff.; Balthasar, ibid., p. 230; *TD*, II/2, pp. 406–10.
[85]   Balthasar, *TD*, ibid.
[86]   M. Kehl, op. cit., p. 40.
[87]   *Von Balthasar Reader*, pp. 247ff.; *CD*, IV/1, p. 713.
[88]   Ibid.
[89]   Balthasar, *Retrospect*, p. 205; *Das Katholische in der Kirche*, pp. 10–15.
[90]   'Lumen Gentium', *The Documents of Vatican II*, Walter M. Abbott, S.J. (ed), London: Geoffrey Chapman 1966, S.13.
[91]   *CD*, IV/1, p. 707.

faith.[92] We believe the Holy Catholic Church, we cannot prove it, but trust in God to make it visible in time. Catholicity also means *semper eadem*, a oneness of being in this and every age, a succession in continuity. For Balthasar this form of oneness and succession is seen in the whole structure of Roman Catholicism, papacy, hierarchy, apostolic succession, offices, gifts.[93] For Barth, the succession is the succession of apostolic witness in obedience to the word,[94] something also included by Balthasar. Here, clearly in outline many areas of agreement also bring before us profound and subtle, far-reaching differences.

MINISTRY

One of the fascinating things about comparing Barth and Balthasar is that each seeks to base his theological position on Scripture; Balthasar certainly there but more tied to tradition than Barth; Barth seeking to base his wholly there if this is a fair judgment. Balthasar is quite clear that from the very beginning of the Church, post-resurrection, it was hierarchically structured with a Marian, Petrine and apostolic character already built into it which was to be handed down to succeeding generations, a highly debatable area between Roman Catholicism and the Reformation. Balthasar writes, 'Thus from the very outset this Church was *hierarchically constituted*.'[95] Peter was given the primacy of office, Mary the embodiment of faith, exemplar mother of the Church and John the disciple and representative of love. In this the Church is really both masculine and feminine in Peter and Mary with the women at the tomb.[96] The community of love of the Spirit is not without its institution and various biblical passages are so interpreted, e.g. the race to the tomb and Jesus' commission to Peter.[97] The Apostles sit on twelve thrones, already a college of bishops who hand on their authority to their successors.[98] Clearly in outline and in character the Catholic

92 Ibid., p. 708.
93 *MP*, pp. 255ff.
94 *CD*, IV/1, pp. 714ff.
95 *MP*, p. 255.
96 Ibid., p. 257.
97 Ibid.
98 *Von Balthasar Reader*, pp. 209–10.

Church in the form of Roman Catholicism is there from the beginning though to be developed more fully later. Barth's views are in sharp contrast and opposition.[99] He certainly does not exclude institution altogether but the whole thrust is in a quite different direction. The Church, he defines, as the living community of the living Lord Jesus Christ in the fulfilment of its existence, where Christ is the true witness and servant and where ministry is certainly a succession of preaching, teaching and serving but where this is much more the work of the whole people of God. There are commissioned and appointed leaders, and in the New Testament it is clear that a succession of ministry and witness is also evident but that it takes the particular form Balthasar suggests is an area of very great difference and dispute in biblical interpretation. As far as the actual form of the polity or ministry of the Church is concerned Barth follows closely the idea which comes from the New Testament and has been stated by P. T Forsyth, T. M. Lindsey and others within Protestantism that each local community represents the outcrop of the universal Catholic Church and therefore has a certain amount of autonomy. In other words, Barth's is almost a congregational polity, the apostolate that of the laity, the whole Church in the service of Christ in the world.

ECUMENICAL DIALOGUE

Balthasar writes about such a dialogue in words which are close to the intention of Barth, 'Ecumenical dialogue can bear fruit only if it seizes on what is most deeply Christian and, faithful to its utter seriousness, develops a sense for what is secondary and relative, for what therefore can be conceded on both sides'.[100] Now these are fine statements but leave open the question as to what is distinctively Christian, what is primary and what is secondary. Honest facing up to our divisions in the light of what is in Balthasar's phrase 'most deeply Christian' is certainly the way forward. Presumably both Barth and Balthasar mean that what is most deeply Christian is God's coming and action, His revelation of Himself in Jesus Christ by the Holy Spirit, the revelation of the triune saving God in the

---

[99] *CD*, IV/1, p. 666f.
[100] Balthasar, *Retrospect*, p. 203.

midst of our rebellion and disobedience. But does the Roman Catholic structure which Balthasar so obviously supports belong intrinsically to that? If so, then here Barth again would disagree.

Thus, while there is much common ground the differences in application are also clear. Barth readily welcomed the changes in the Roman Catholic Church at Vatican II[101] which were in line with Balthasar's continuing concerns, namely, a greater emphasis on revelation than on reason and the desire for the renewal of the Church. However, Balthasar set out a view of institution, authority and churchmanship Barth could not accept. Balthasar sees the Church as a kind of person, a corporate personality with a mission and goal both *ad extra* and *ad intra*.[102] *Ad intra* it is to rescue the sinners within the Church; *ad extra* to exemplify and to convey to others in doctrine and in life the fullness of the Catholic faith. Others who are 'separated brethren' have breached the unity of the Church. In practical terms this means that, since the papacy is the visible symbol of unity and division leads to plurality of views, this moves one away from that centre of unity, from that corporate personality embodied in Catholicism.[103] For Balthasar, there is ultimately only one path for meaningful ecumenical activity: the representation of the Catholic Church's own principle in exemplary lived holiness. For Balthasar it meant an organic wholeness where the unity and catholicity of the Church formed by the Spirit as its soul is many faceted.[104] Each aspect of its total being is necessary to the fullness of Christ and the faith. This given form, as understood by Balthasar, was clearly unacceptable to Barth. Even post-Vatican II Barth set out his contrary views on several major issues of dispute. In *Ad Limina Apostolorum*,[105] a small book written after his visit to Rome in 1966 at the age of eighty, he asked a set of highly critical, searching questions of his hosts. The answers unfortunately are not recorded. In answer to a letter he received on Mariology, which is not published in the book, he writes, 'I am still obliged as before to reject your presupposition as such, the possibility, justification and

---

[101] Karl Barth, *Ad Limina Apostolorum: An Appraisal of Vatican II*, tr. Keith R. Crim, Edinburgh: The Saint Andrew Press 1969, pp. 65ff.

[102] Balthasar, 'Another Ten Years', *Retrospect*, p. 229.

[103] Balthasar, *TD*, II/2, pp. 406–10.

[104] Ibid.

[105] Barth, *Ad Limina Apostolorum*, pp. 19–37.

necessity of Mariology'.[106] Barth summed up his critique of Marian dogma in his *Dogmatics*. It was in his view the cental question at issue, the human creature cooperating with grace on the basis of prevenient grace. He writes that 'the Mother of God of Roman Catholic Marian dogma is quite simply the principle, type and essence of the human creature cooperating servant-like (*ministerialiter*) in its own redemption on the basis of prevenient grace and to that extent the principle, type and essence of the Church'.[107] Or, to put it otherwise, the Church in its being and structure, *in persona Christi*, in a measure duplicates on earth the functions of Christ. Barth's reply to Marian dogma is his quiet debate with Catholicism in the *Church Dogmatics* IV/2 where he puts the humanity of Jesus as the exalted human at the centre, the one wholly sinless person in total fellowship with God.

Another serious objection which Barth had to the continuing doctrines of Roman Catholicism was the papacy and despite many complimentary words spoken about new trends in Vatican II, especially the trends towards the Bible, he writes, 'At the beginning of everything, beclouding everything stands the dogma of papal infallibility',[108] though he notes in passing a new flexibility in the interpretation of this and other dogmas. A further area where Barth's views are poles apart from the Catholic views is in his sacramental teaching.[109] It is generally agreed by his commentators that his christological concentration lead him to speak of Christ as the one sacrament and baptism and the Lord's Supper as signs pointing to that. In fact he desacramentalised the sacraments as seen in his rejection not only of infant baptism but of baptism as a sacrament.[110] It is, rather, a human request for water baptism as a sign of the grace of God given already by the Holy Spirit but not a means of grace. He did not live long enough to write fully on the Lord's Supper (or the Eucharist) but his views would have been very different from the sacrifice of the mass. These are deep and far-reaching divisions with little sign of rapprochement. Another area

---

[106] Ibid., p. 60.
[107] *CD*, I/2, p. 143.
[108] Barth, *Ad Limina Apostolorum*, p. 71.
[109] *CD*, IV/4.
[110] Ibid.

where Barth was critical of Balthasar was on his views of the saints. While commending Balthasar's emphasis on Christ he is concerned lest his conception of the Saints as possible and actual repetitions and reenactments of Christ will in fact lead 'not in theory but in practice' away from the centre and become 'the object and origin of Christian faith'.[111]

However, these differences were not the last word that either Barth or Balthasar believed had to be spoken about ecumenical dialogue or inter-church relations. Another more spiritual view of ecumenical dialogue must be brought to the fore and understood as even more important than attempts to reconcile diverse views on dogmas and doctrines. Barth saw Vatican II as a genuine attempt at renewal and in that light made a plea for a similar renewal, which he did not see, within his own Church and other Christian communions.[112] This would by no means obviate the necessity for continuing serious doctrinal dialogue and debate but that discussion would then be undertaken in the light of God's revelation in Christ which includes us all and in the power of the enabling grace of the Holy Spirit. It was for that kind of genuine ecumenical dialogue that Barth and Balthasar both worked and lived and prayed. Here at this most deeply Christian centre where, as Barth said,[113] we put the truth of Christ as the arbiter and judge of all the churches is the place we must begin, continue and end.

---

[111] Barth, *Ad Limina Apostolorum*, p. 72f.
[112] Ibid.
[113] *CD*, IV 1, p. 681f.

10

THE WIDER ECUMENISM: CHRISTIAN PRAYER AND OTHER RELIGIONS

Bede McGregor, O.P.

'And if, finally, one is seeking (always in line with the Council) the doctrinal framework needed before beginning the dialogue with the non-Christian religions and the various forms of modern atheism, one can safely go to Balthasar.'[1]

One of the major themes of mission theology since the Second Vatican Council is inter-religious dialogue. There are many types of dialogue with our non-Christian brothers and sisters. There is the dialogue of life in which people of different religious persuasions live together and enrich each other through the faithful practice of the values of their various religions. There is the dialogue of collaboration in social concerns inspired by religious motives, such as in the study and execution of development projects and in initiatives to foster justice and peace. There is intermonastic dialogue in which, for example, Catholic monks and Buddhist monks live together for some time and share with each other their respective religious and monastic experiences. There is the dialogue of scholars from the various traditions. There are the endless kinds of formal and informal meetings between the followers of the different religious traditions that are becoming a normal part of the life of a growing number of missionaries.[2]

---

[1] Henri de Lubac, S.J. *The Church: Paradox and Mystery*, Ecclesia Press 1961, p. 104.

[2] See Bulletin: Secretariatus pro non-christianis, xx/2, pp. 124f. This Bulletin is now issued under its new name by the Pontificium Consilium pro Dialogo Inter Religiones and is an indispensable guide to what is going on in this area of the Mission of the Church.

But the deepest meeting takes place at the level in which a person opens out to God, the place of prayer or meditation and where there is a sharing of this ultimate religious experience. We are invited to listen to the human person in all the diversity and richness of his cultures and religions, at its deepest level, 'where its conscience is formed and upon which is founded the moral action of all people'.[3]

This meeting of followers of the different religions to pray, each in his own way, has been called for by John Paul II and indeed his example at the famous meeting held in Assissi on 27 October 1986 gives us a relatively new model of inter-religious dialogue. It is precisely in this area of Christian prayer in the context of other religious traditions that Balthasar showed a life-long interest. Throughout his life he passionately defended the primacy of the contemplative dimension of human life and specifically of the Christian life, which costs nothing less than everything. He writes: 'Therefore the contemplative life is essential and central to the life of the Church as a whole. For the Christian there can be no external action without inner contemplation (which is the existential dimension of faith), since it is quite possible to fulfil his life by inner contemplation without external activity. The contemplative act is the permanently basic act of all external action: it is active and effective, fruitful and missionary beyond all external undertakings of the Church.' He continues with a certain sharpness:

It is devoutly to be wished that the Church won't sell its deepest mysteries and highest privileges for the mess of potage of external apostolic satisfactions; that it won't abandon for the sake of psychological, sociological and statistical considerations the ultimate risks that can be justified only on theological grounds. The voice of the Holy Spirit is not heard when the message of Thérèse of Lisieux, Edith Stein and Charles de Foucauld is thrown to the wind. The witness that would be abandoned then is not primarily a witnessing to the exclusively contemplative form of life, which will always remain the affair of a few people with a special vocation; it is the witness for the contemplative foundation of every Christian life, as I have tried to show.

---

[3]   John Paul II, *L'Osservatore Romano*, 27–28, Ottobre 1986, p. 2.

Anyone who is not prepared to listen to God in the first place has nothing to say to the world.[4]

There is surely no more radical impoverishment of the dignity and quality of life of the human person than when the contemplative heart of it has been diminished or has died completely. This is true in every religious tradition.

CHRISTIAN THEOLOGIES OF NON-CHRISTIAN RELIGIONS

But before going into the question of the relationship between Christian prayer and the religious experience of other traditions as it is found in their ways of prayer and meditation, although some religions, like some forms of Buddhism for instance, would scarcely use the term prayer or its equivalent, it may be helpful to briefly refer to the various Christian theologies of these religions. The particular theology of other religions will usually determine the emphasis that one gives in the various theories and practice of dialogue. Balthasar's critique of Rahner's theory of Anonymous Christianity is well known and crucial. These two theologians represent what is best in two opposed, or at least different, theologies of non-Christian religions and nearly all other catholic theologians can be grouped around them. I cannot take the pluralist position as a serious catholic position, indeed, even as a Christian one although the questions it raises are important and may contribute eventually to a greater consensus in the formulation of a Christian theology of non-Christian religions.

Basically the question revolves around the way in which one relates grace and nature, redemption and creation, reason and faith,

---

[4]   Hans Urs von Balthasar, *Who is a Christian?* Burns and Oates 1968, pp. 75–81, cf. also, Hans Urs von Balthasar, *Prayer*, Ignatius Press 1986, chapter 1: 'The Necessity of Contemplation', pp. 13–31; Hans Urs von Balthasar, *Elucidations*, SPCK, 'An Apology for Contemplatives', pp. 126f. Perhaps the strongest expression of his theology and conviction about the primacy of contemplation is evidenced in the communities he co-founded with Adrienne von Speyr. That the secularised nature of modern life requires more, not less, emphasis on the contemplative dimensions is a theme that crops up frequently in the work of Balthasar.

salvation and history, time and eternity, God, the world and the human person. The starting point, as in so many theological problems, is pivotal. Both Rahner and Balthasar are obviously in complete agreement on the defined presupposition that God wills to save everyone without exception and that the cross is the concrete and effective sign of this universal salvific will. The problem is how the non-Christian attains to faith in the specific content of Christian revelation in the absence of the adequate hearing of the gospel. In response to this precise question Rahner starts with the subjectivity of the human person and his infinite spiritual horizon. Balthasar starts with God and his revelation of Himself. Rahner seems to accentuate the continuity between the human spirit and the gift of God's revelation but of course he makes all the necessary distinctions so that revelation is not seen as a demand implicit in the human spirit but as a totally transcendent gift having its origin in the sovereign freedom of God and in no way originating in the human person. He explains the relationship between nature and grace in terms of the obediential potency so dear to scholastic theology but in the context and language of his transcendental methodology. Balthasar is not convinced and thinks that Rahner subordinates or subsumes the truths of faith under a philosophical system and does not do justice to the event of the cross and redemption, at least in the context of his Christian anthropology, whatever about other places. Here only and not necessarily in other parts of his work he seems to think Rahner is guilty of a relativisation of the cross of Christ and of the Church.

Balthasar, on the other hand, begins with God and puts forward a magnificent theology of the mystery of the Trinity, incarnation, cross and resurrection of Christ. He emphasises the discontinuity between the creature and creator, between creation and redemption and while he insists that creation loses nothing of its intrinsic value in the work of redemption, and strongly affirms the spiritual openness of the human person to God, his critics think he does not do justice to the positive values of the non-Christian religions and the graced outreach of the human person to God. The debate between these two great scholars seems to have similarities with the notorious problem of harmonising the sovereignty of God's grace and human freedom. If one begins with God's grace it can be difficult to establish the autonomy of human freedom and if one begins with the affirmation of human freedom one tends to find it hard to argue logically to the primacy and sovereignty of God's grace.

Both Rahner and Balthasar use the principle of the analogy of being and of faith to relate nature and grace, the openness of the human spirit towards the infinite and the utter transcendence of God's revelation and the event of redemption but they differ in the way they use it. Rahner's explanation is already well known and repeated by his many followers[5] but I think Balthasar's position is less frequently stated or appreciated so it is worth putting it as clearly and as fairly as possible and few people do it more faithfully and sympathetically than Medard Kehl, S.J. He writes:

> In every analogous correspondence between nature and grace, between the orders of creation and redemption, Balthasar highlights both the uniqueness and the incomparability of the definitive self-revelation of God in Jesus Christ. Even if the creature represents a presupposed reflection of the creator and his love, the historical event of God redeeming us in Christ does not result from this presupposition. The positive content of the analogous correspondence between the created order of nature and the historical order of salvation lies precisely in the (gratuitously given) openness for the, once again, 'totally other', underivable completion of the self-revelation of God in Christ which could never be calculated from creation itself and which is thus to be received only as pure gift. This takes place by no means as a self-perfection of creation, but as a totally free act of the loving God for his creature. The revelational form of his love, Jesus Christ, is absolutely unique. All that creation can produce in love, in meaning, in truth and beauty, does not converge on this figure of Christ in such a way that it would

---

[5]   Whatever is said or written about the interpretations of Rahner by some of his followers I think the core of his theology can be defended against some of the objections of Balthasar and while I prefer the starting point and emphases of Balthasar, I think it is important to do justice to Rahner especially on his understanding of the relationship between grace and nature and what he means by the supernatural existential and the dictum that all is grace which is sometimes attributed to him. A fine exposition of his position can be found in several places but especially in his *Theological Investigations* vol. 4, pp. 212f.

logically, so to speak, grow out of it. No, everything created remains fragmentary in itself; it comes up against a not to be transcended limit that is native to all imperfect and ephemeral things. Only the historical 'new beginning' of the loving God himself brings, with Christ, the possibilities of creatures to their definitive fulfilment. It is exclusively in God's reaching to us that our stretching to God reaches its goal.[6]

In the words of Balthasar himself: 'Precisely in the movement that the creature sees and feels itself drawn to the heart of God, does it experience unto the depths its own not-being-God, does that all dominant relationship of absolute and relative, of divine and worldly being get brought home to it relentlessly and without any possibility of appeal.'[7] The revelation of God in Christ remains – despite every possible demand for it and in every real fulfilment – still the absolutely unimaginable new and other which is already given in no 'transcendental experience'. In summary fashion one could say that the major difference between Rahner and Balthasar is that Rahner builds his whole theological system or synthesis in almost exclusively philosophical language and concepts, without neglecting basic revealed principles such as the universal salvific will of God, on the concept and reality of his famous *Vorgriff.*[8] This is a pre-comprehension or apprehension of supernatural revelation by the human person under the movement of grace in a non-thematic and implicit way if he consents to the openness of his nature to transcendence in the context of the supernatural existential. This access to revelation is available to non-Christian and even atheist. On the other hand Balthasar starts with the God of revelation and builds everything around the total mystery of Christ, as absolutely unique and universal in its salvific outreach, incomparably and utterly new, and always unexpectedly and astonishingly Good News.[9] It is interesting that neither of them had any first-hand or

---

[6]   *The von Balthasar Reader*, T&T Clark 1982, p. 22.
[7]   Balthasar, *Glaubhaft ist nur Liebe*, Einsiedeln 1966, p. 30.
[8]   Winfred George Phillips, 'Rahner's Transcendental Deduction of the Vorgriff', *The Thomist*, vol. 56, no. 2, April 1992.
[9]   A typical passage of Balthasar aimed at Rahner and his followers is as follows: 'In every human religion, of course, there lie approaches to an intimate relationship to God, since the non-divine creature can understand and reflect on himself essentially only as a deficient "image" of the Absolute, longingly calling out to its

continual contact with the great religious traditions of humankind although Balthasar studied sanskrit at university level under the great Indologist von Glasenapp and has a greater theoretical understanding of the eastern traditions than many of his critics.

It is not difficult to see how one can construct a mission theology centred on the necessity and urgency of proclaiming Christ and him crucified from this premise of the absolutely incomparable and unique mystery of Christ and his redemptive work. It seems less problematical than the position that sees the content of revelation as already present implicitly in some way, although non-conceptually and non-thematically, in the human person who consents in freedom and under grace to the openness to transcendence that constitutes his very being as created by God. Here, mission is the task of facilitating the transition from implicit to explicit knowledge and awareness of the saving truths of faith. It simply involves going from unthematic to thematic faith. It comes as no surprise to read a follower of Rahner write: 'Despite the various orders of mediation of the mystery of Christ – perfect and complete in the ecclesial community, imperfect and incomplete outside the same – we must observe that the differences do not place Christians in an advantageous situation with respect to salvation.'[10] In this type of climate of theological thought it is not easy to formulate a motive for mission that would move one to evangelise at all costs even if it involves the risk of martyrdom. If there is no advantage in being an explicit Christian with regard to salvation does it really matter ultimately whether one is explicitly and knowingly a Christian or not. It could seem that one religion is as good as another in this view in the sense that it is Christ who saves in any religion and the form of mediation

original. God's saving acts in history are not "transcendentally" (hence "known" but not "in consciousness") etched into this longing, however – even if it had always been under the guidance of grace (supernatural existential) – in such a way that man, on witnessing God's mighty deeds, for example Jesus' resurrection, would not be impelled to wonder and adore, but could say to himself; after all on the basis of my own constitution, I have actually been expecting this all along. In trying to satisfy his yearning precipitously and on his own initiative, what he represents as religious objectifications is, according to the testimony of the Bible, not an approach to the image that God has set up of himself, but rather its miscarriage and perversion: an "idol", a "false god".' Balthasar, *New Elucidations*, Ignatius Press 1986, p. 85.

[10] Jacques Dupuis, S.J., *Jesus Christ at the Encounter of World Religions*, Orbis Books 1991, p. 146.

is not of absolute importance. Hans Kung has in fact argued that the non-Christian religions are the normal ways of salvation and Christianity the extraordinary way for relatively few people.[11]

I have tried to indicate, however briefly, the principles of Balthasar's theology of non-Christian religions. I did this in the conviction that Balthasar sees the relationship between Christian prayer and non-Christian meditation simply as a practical application of these general principles. Strictly speaking Balthasar does not give us a comparative study of Christianity and the non-Christian religions, nor a general history of religions; his main purpose is to put into relief the specificity of the Christian gospel, to underline the absolute uniqueness of Christ and the universality of Christian redemption, and the ultimate incomparability of God's self-revelation and communication in Christ, with any other approach or religious tradition. Whatever the possible analogical similarities, the dissimilarities are even more striking. In the context of dialogue with the secular world and other religious traditions the most urgent and profound need is to appreciate the distinctiveness of our own Christian faith. This is particularly true when he comes to discuss Christian prayer in the context of non-Christian forms of meditation and prayer.

CHRISTIAN AND NON-CHRISTIAN FORMS OF MEDITATION AND PRAYER

Balthasar begins his book *Christian Meditation* with the words: 'The decisive question is whether God has spoken to the human race – about Himself, of course, and likewise about His reason for creating man, the world – or whether the Absolute remains the Silence beyond all the words of the world.'[12] The Christian stakes everything on the fact that God spoke and continues to speak to us. Above all that He speaks most perfectly and fully in Christ. Christian prayer is in function of revelation and grace. It is not simply poetic or philosophical religious experience; it is not something engen-

---

[11]   Hans Küng, *Christian Revelation and World Religions*, ed. J. Neuner, S.J., Burns & Oates 1967, p. 25f.
[12]   Balthasar, *Christian Meditation*, Ignatius Press 1989, p. 7.

dered by various techniques, eastern or western, nor is it simply a psychological state of harmony or rest achieved through an increasing number of relaxation exercises or programmes or psychotherapy; more obviously it is not the experience that is consequent on the use of certain drugs whatever the apparent and occasional similarities in effects at the psychological level. Christian prayer begins with God and his Word. It is first divine initiative and gift before being a graced response. It is interpersonal of its very nature, involving two freedoms and therefore two loves, divine and human. There is a Christian apophatic prayer but it must be theologically understood in the context of the revealed word of God and cannot bypass the humanity of Christ or sideline the Christian community. Indeed all forms of Christian prayer whether kataphatic or apophatic can ultimately only be taught by God himself. The request, 'Lord, teach us to pray' is always and everywhere put to the Church too. The reply of Jesus is the core of the gospel, and when you pray, say Our Father. There is no other comparable experience offered to humankind and it forms the central privilege of being a Christian and what one is called to share with those to whom he or she is sent.

Rahner writes: 'If the doctrine of the Trinity were to be suppressed as false, the greater part of religious writing, (and what is even more sad, the very life of Christians) would remain almost unaltered.'[13] The very opposite would be true of Balthasar. Remove the doctrine of the Trinity and there is nothing left of any significance; his writings would make no sense at all. This is particularly true of his theology of Christian prayer. Because it is trinitarian, it is christocentric or vice versa and here lies the specificity of Christian prayer which is put in high relief in the context of other forms of prayer or meditation. When the Christian prays he or she shares in the prayer of Christ to his Father; not only in the prayer of Christ in his humanity but as the eternal Son of the Father in the Spirit. He enters into the communion between the Father, Son and Holy Spirit dwelling within him or her.

---

[13] K. Rahner, *Mysterium Salutis*, vol. 3, Brescia 1969, p. 404.

CHRISTIAN AND ISLAMIC PRAYER[14]

Perhaps the specificity of Christian prayer can be highlighted now by reviewing it in the context of other religious traditions. Let us start with Islam. In some real sense the Christian is instinctively thankful to God for the gift of Islam. In the absence of the preaching of the gospel hundreds of millions of people have come to a belief in the one transcendent God through the traditions of Islam. The practising Muslim prays five times a day, he fasts and gives alms, he enters the way of poverty through pilgrimage, he is attached to the prophets especially the prophet Muhammed, he is thankful for the world wide Islamic solidarity, but above all these things stands the incomparable God and his revealed word as uniquely understood in Islam. The Quran shapes the consciences of Muslims and guides them in the deepest *jihad* of conquering themselves in order to submit more fully to the will of God always and everywhere. In the absence of the Gospel Islam surely keeps the faithful Muslim very close to God

The prayer life of this monotheistic faith is indeed impressive and the Christian rejoices at it. Still, a meaningful dialogue and sharing with Islam on the topic of prayer and therefore on nearly every other religious subject is often experienced as very difficult. The reason is simple and apparently insurmountable. For Muslims, to claim that Jesus Christ is the Son of God is *shirk* or blasphemy, the greatest of all sins. All the other difficulties stem from this one at the very core of Christian faith. To explain our faith that God is Love we find it necessary to say that God cannot be Love and at the same time absolute solitude and if He is not Love then human existence is ultimately intolerable even if we are offered the beautiful Quranic teaching that God is closer to us than our jugular vein. If God needs creation to show his love then he cannot truly be God. So our task is to try and explain the monotheistic faith of Christians in terms of God as infinite love and therefore as interpersonal communion and we do this through the mystery of the Trinity as it is revealed to us

---

[14] Balthasar has no extended exposition of Islamic prayer although he has many references to Islam. This is in accordance with his general position that his role is to explain to the Muslim the specific nature of Christian prayer and not the nature of Islamic prayer which the Muslim will know from his own tradition. He then focuses on what he sees as the main differences and difficulties.

in and through the total mystery of Christ. The sovereignly free and infinite love of God for us is made visible to us precisely in the death and resurrection of Christ. Here lies the deepest core of our Christian existence both in prayer and action. This is quintessential Balthasar. For him 'Only Love is Believable'. He does not really have any other message. That is the challenge of our mission to our Muslim brothers and sisters, indeed to everybody and anybody. Christian prayer is simply allowing ourselves to be loved infinitely, personally, intimately, tenderly, eternally by the Father in the Son and through the Holy Spirit and to live the whole of our lives out of and on that faith experience. The gospel of Christian prayer is the offer of a created sharing in the triune life of God as Love. It is important to note that Balthasar never uses the language of superiority for Christians over non-Christians but only the language of love and humble service.

The words of God are thought of as mediated to us by the Archangel Gabriel, through Muhammed in Islam, and through the law and the prophets in Judaism. But for Christians God speaks through the Person of his Word, the eternal Son of the Father in the Holy Spirit. This is decisive for Christian prayer. The Epistle to the Hebrews sums it up:

> At various times in the past and in various different ways, God spoke to our ancestors through the prophets; in our own time, the last days, he has spoken to us through his Son, the Son that he has appointed to inherit everything and through whom he made everything there is. He is the radiant light of God's glory and the perfect copy of his nature, sustaining the universe by his powerful command; and now that he has destroyed the defilement of sin, he has gone to take his place in heaven at the right hand of divine majesty. So he is now as far above the angels as the title which he has inherited is higher than their own name (*Hebrews* 1: 1–4).

CHRISTIAN PRAYER AND THE NON-BIBLICAL RELIGIOUS TRADITIONS

Balthasar sees Islam as in some way part of the Judaeo-Christian tradition and he treats it accordingly. With regard to the non-biblical religions, he generally characterises them in comparison with Christianity as follows:

1. In non-biblical religions the human person seeks out the sacred, the mystery, God or transcendent reality, whereas in biblical religion God takes the initiative and searches out the human person. The contrast is between the human person going to God and God coming to the human person. The non-Christian religions are anthropogenetic and the Christian faith is theogenetic.

2. Because the human person initiates the search in non-biblical religions, the movement tends to be towards the transcendence of the empirical world, of a flight to the other worldly, whereas in Christianity the initiative comes from God and the movement is the free choice of incarnational descent. In the Old Testament one has the divinely inspired words of God about himself and in other religions and cultures the *logoi spermatikoi*, the seeds of the Word but in Christianity one has the presence of the Personal Word of God which definitively discloses the inner nature of God as triune Love.

3. The terminus of non-biblical religions is towards the Absolute conceived as abstract and impersonal, whereas Christianity gives witness to the concrete and fully personal presence of God in his Son whose acceptance of one Father is completed in the Holy Spirit.[15]

Before leaving Balthasar's general description of non-Christian religions I want to add two further points that he makes to avoid possible misunderstandings by his critics. First he emphasises two basic trends: One ascending: man's intrinsic disposition to seek by his very nature God and God's ways. The other descending: God's disposition to seek man by a condescension that man could not expect. Secondly, he writes that he never denied it, rather he said it often that God's free grace in Christ embraces all mankind. If men humbly seek their God, this grace can be well received and lived by non-Christians. The missionary Church has found many traces of Christ's grace among many peoples. This is the old teaching of the *logos spermatikos*, given, he thinks, more likely to those who trustingly and simply ask for it from above, than those who employ complicated techniques to obtain it.[16]

---

[15]   The above classification of Balthasar on non-biblical religion is substantially based on the very helpful article of Kenneth L. Schmitz in *Communio* 5/1 (1978), pp. 44-51.

[16]   Balthasar, 'Response to my Critics', *Communio* 5/1 (1978), pp. 70–75.

Finally, it is important to indicate the precise perspective from which Balthasar formulates his various theses.

> It is a Europe that is undergoing a change. Its Christian substance is being hollowed out by inroads of eastern meditation methods, to such an extent that in many monasteries meditation has become merely a technique of correct posture and breathing control. Thus the Church and the world are being deprived of much-needed repentance and intercessory prayer. In this Europe, the unique and indivisible 'form' of Catholicism – has been waived with the justification of pluralism in theology (applied already to Scripture) and the existence in other religions and cultures of certain analagous elements (Anonymous Christianity), 'all religions are roads to salvation', etc.[17]

Taking for granted the profound positive elements in the non-biblical religions especially the eastern ones such as Hinduism and Buddhism and the theological principles that facilitate this positive evaluation such as God's universal will to save everyone; the fact that we are all loved into existence by the creative love of God; and the human person is made in the image and likeness of God; every human being is always seen by the Father in the Son with the love who is the Holy Spirit; the teaching that no-one is outside the redemptive love of God; the universal presence of the Holy Spirit; the long experience of the missionary Church of such positive values; it is important for the Christian to be aware of the difficulties and differences when it comes to the mutual sharing of our religious experiences in the context of dialogue.

Let us take for example all those eastern religions which over thousands of years have developed the concepts of *samsara* or *maya* and their equivalents. It is difficult for them to see how the Absolute One or Being can enter the world of *samsara*: the empirical, changing, relative, disposable, illusory, consumer world – a world radically marked by cyclic time and inevitable, unrelenting decay and dissolution. The deepest desire of the human person is to seek *moksa*, liberation from such an oppressive, wounded existence and

---

[17] Ibid., p. 69.

entrance into an invisible sphere of absolute unchanging being and peace, where all desire is ultimately extinguished because there is nothing more to desire in the absolute stillness or emptiness of *nirvana* or its equivalent. The human person in these great religious traditions seeks to escape from this world but the Christian proclaims a God who so loved this world that he desired not only to enter it but to assume it in all its creaturely fragility and limitation. In one particular moment of history and through one particular humanity the total reality of salvation is mediated and the Absolute knocks at the door not just of the enlightened one, the *jivan mukti*, but the sinful one, the failure, the undeserving poor and desires with a great desire to sup with him and speak with him as one friend does to another in his heart. The scandal of particularity is very marked in the East especially when the Absolute One desires to be enmeshed with his sinful creature.

Our non-Christian brothers and sister have a right to hear from us the gospel of Christian prayer and not only to hear of our emphatic and reverent understanding of their religious vision and techniques. It is not easy to sustain the inter-personal nature of Christian prayer in the context of Advaitic or Buddhist thought. But it is surely worth the effort of trying and Balthasar does it so beautifully and so often. He insists that the first of God's gifts, the basis of all the others, is that which I call my own 'I'; I owe him not merely everything I have but also everything I am. He writes:

> But then it is true that the 'I', knowing that it is affirmed and loved by the eternal 'I', must in the end affirm itself to be the one to whom God says 'Thou' in an absolutely personal relationship that cannot be confused with the relationship I may cultivate with any other person. The always unique God calls me by my unique, unrepeatable name. But this means that the biblical God is creator in order to reveal himself; and, as a consequence, creation is the foundation of his self-communication.[18]

All this points to the conviction in Balthasar that the whole of creation and particularly my personal 'I' are not simply an aspect of

---

[18] Balthasar, *New Elucidations*, Ignatius Press, p. 152.

reality that is intrinsically ephemeral but the very creational basis for Christian prayer in all its interpersonal beauty and intimacy. There is a difference of kind between the oneness of *Tat tvam asi* or *Aham Brahma asmi* of some eastern traditions and the union of the I and Thou in Christian prayer. Even in its mystical or ecstatic phases our personal I is never so absorbed with the Divine Thou that there is some kind of identity rather than communion.

If we take the law of Karma that is also a fundamental part of the religious perspective of many oriental religions it will lead us to emphasise other aspects of Christian prayer. This law determines the whole of empirical existence, including our own bodily and psychological makeup in the sense that what we become is the direct result of what we have done. *Moksa* or salvation or more precisely liberation is determined by what we have done. It is not a personal God who rewards or punishes but it is a universal law that inevitably and infallibly achieves its effect. Intercessory prayer, forgiveness, and grace do not easily fit into this scheme of things. And even in Mahayana Buddhism, and some forms of Hinduism where there seems to be something analogous to grace in the concept of *prasad* or its equivalent, the dissimilarity is even more astonishing. There is nothing even remotely comparable to the image and reality of a God who holds nothing back but gives everything to us and whose infinitely passionate love for us is demonstrated by his willingness to die for us. I have not been able to find even an analogical sketch of a crucified God so in love with us while we are yet sinners in any other religious tradition. Prayer is a graced response in faith to this love. Redemption is always a gift and never something achieved by our own initiative and from our own resources. All theories of self-redemption from the more gross forms of Pelagianism and its more masked forms – and the law of Karma certainly moves in this direction – make prayer difficult to engage in.

Balthasar continuously lampoons anything that even appears to reduce prayer to some form of mechanistic process of technique whatever good effects it may seem to possess. Even when these techniques are distinguished from prayer itself and clearly non-magical in the way they are used, he seems to be ill at ease and merely allows that they may help us to relax and at most prepare the way for prayer in our hyper-active western modern culture. But he always appears to be astonished at the neglect of our own rich Christian traditions of forms and methods of prayer. And then he goes on the attack as in this not untypical and trenchant example:

> Here it suddenly becomes clear how much everything that in
> the required readiness smacks of technique is opposed to the
> gospel's grace of childlikeness. Whoever uses or exercises
> techniques to achieve 'concentration', 'detachment', 'to find
> himself,' for expansion of his inner space – whether by
> 'transcendental meditation', yoga, Zen, or any other exercise,
> is not poor in spirit. Rather he is full of ability and capability,
> he belongs to the 'rich' who do not pass through the eye of
> the needle, to the 'wise and clever' from whom the Father has
> concealed it. He is ultimately a Pharisee who relies on his
> works instead of entrusting himself to God in faith, for
> technique is achievement, even if its goal is 'attainment' of
> inner poverty. Precisely because one who mediates in eastern
> fashion has nothing before him that actively imparts infor-
> mation out of itself about itself, he must attain passivity by his
> own efforts. In the Christian contemplative, on the other
> hand, that which reveals itself has already in advance accom-
> plished a truth that is not alien to him, but his own most
> intimate truth, which he needs only to recognise.[19]

If these objections could be sustained by theological argument not
a few retreat centres and houses of prayer would have to close down
or completely change!

In contrast with the above passage Balthasar frequently insists
that the Christian can in open dialogue, learn much that is valid
from other religions, but invariably adds that one does not have to
relativise the objective content of his faith or suspend in 'methodological doubt' its validity. My disappointment with Balthasar in this
precise area is that he does not give examples of what we might learn
from these other religious traditions apart from the observation that
their sincerity, fidelity to their conscience and persevering practice
of prayer or meditation should stimulate us to a deeper commitment
and understanding of our own traditions. So despite all his words to
the contrary there remains a lingering doubt that he truly believes

---

[19] Balthasar, 'On Unceasing Prayer', *Communio* 4/2 (Summer 1977), p. 108f.

the Christian has really anything to learn from non-Christian forms of meditation or prayer.[20]

When one thinks of Balthasar on prayer the Pauline declaration to the Philippians comes readily to mind:

> As for the law, I was a Pharisee; as for working for religion, I was a persecutor of the Church; as far as the law can make you perfect, I was faultless. But because of Christ, I have come to consider all these advantages that I had as disadvantages. Not only that, but I believe nothing can happen that will outweigh the supreme advantage of knowing Christ Jesus my Lord. For him I have accepted the loss of everything, and I look on everything as so much rubbish if only I can have Christ and be given a place in him. I am no longer trying for perfection by my own efforts, the perfection that comes from the law, but I want only the perfection that comes through faith in Christ, and is from God and is based on faith. All I want to know is Christ and the power of his resurrection and to share his sufferings by reproducing the pattern of his death (*Philippians* 3: 6–10).

When Balthasar contemplates the crucified and risen One everything else recedes into the background. In other contexts, he clearly upholds the relative autonomy of reason and philosophy, the contribution of the behavioural and other sciences but in the sphere of the Christian mystery everything else seems to fade away and there remains only Jesus. I would not presume to judge whether

---

[20]   There are several passages which seem to me to barely conceal a sneer when it comes to commenting on eastern mediation e.g.: 'The author of this work is writing as a Christian theologian, and only as such. Like every Christian who tries to live his faith, he has certain Christian experiences; but he has none in non-Christian meditation. In some respects this is an awkward point of departure, especially since it is evident that eastern meditation (with which we are principally concerned here) has very much more technical know-how and method at its command than does Christian meditation, just as an acrobat knows how to do many more stunts than an ordinary person does.' *New Elucidations*, Ignatius Press 1986, p. 141. In other articles he makes the same point that eastern meditation and yoga are mainly characterised in comparison with Christian prayer as acrobatic stunts or gymnastics. On the other hand in more substantial work he is more respectful of non-Christian religions and their contributions, e.g. *The Glory of the Lord*, III, p. 107, etc.

Balthasar or Rahner expresses more perfectly the radical christocentrism of the Ignatian charism that is at the heart of both their theologies and lives but I would argue that they both make a contribution that resonates throughout the whole Church and indeed beyond its visible frontiers.

It would be impossible to touch on all the essential aspects of Balthasar's theology of prayer even in the specific context of the religious traditions of mankind in a single paper. There is the profound Marian dimension of prayer that is so central to Balthasar. It is Mary who saves us from a purely abstract Christ or a purely spiritualising asceticism and mysticism; her prayer is the antithesis of the process that leads to the total disintegration of the human person in a complete absorption or identity with the Absolute. Her prayer is the prayer of the Church at its most authentic and profound and Balthasar never ceases to write of it. There is the missionary character of all prayer, liturgical and personal since the intimacy of personal encounter with Christ may never occur at the expense of his universal aim and outreach.

Perhaps one of the favourite themes of Balthasar in connection with prayer, and which I have found very helpful in retreat work with non-Christians who have a strong tradition of ancestor reverence and friendship, is the communion of saints or the active role of the whole Church in Christian prayer. I will quote just one example from many possible passages to illustrate this theme:

> In the life of the Church there is very much that is personal but nothing at all that is private. Every prayer is made in the communion of saints, supported by it and, together with it, oriented to God. A Christian who attempts to sound out a gospel mystery knows that numberless people have already done so and that above all the Church in heaven is at this moment doing it with him and has an insight into depths that he seeks to fathom only with effort. Accordingly, invoking this holy Church will unfailingly help him to find the treasure for which he is digging in the field. And if he knows that the communion of saints is assisting him, this will serve as a reminder that he himself is a member of this communion and has to assist the others. He is occupied with one of the Lord's mysteries; this Lord, however, is not a detached individual but the head of his Church, with the result that anyone who

remains with the Lord likewise remains always within the space of the Church. All his gospel words and deeds, miracles and sufferings have been realised and accomplished in view of the Church and, through her, of mankind as a whole. And not only his external acts but also his internal states, and even his humanity in itself, are for the sake of all those who are to be redeemed. Together with the personal Christ we always find the social Christ.[21]

By way of conclusion I will give a brief summary of the main thrust of this chapter and end with a final quotation from Balthasar himself. While he makes numerous references to non-Christian forms of meditation and frequently shows an astute understanding of them, there can be no doubt that his main preoccupation is to underline the uniqueness of Christian prayer and its value and not to give an exposition of other forms of prayer of which he has no first hand experience. Non-Christians have a right to hear this gospel of Christian prayer and especially certain characteristics of it. These are the trinitarian and christocentric nature of prayer, the Marian paradigm of praying, the communion of saints, mission, the giftness of prayer and its interpersonal nature in knowledge and love, it is a communion between persons, never a total absorption and never mechanistic or magical.

There will often be a fear for students of Balthasar that they have not and cannot do justice to him. The fare he gives is too much and too rich. In order to make sure of being a little less unjust to him I quote him once more in a vein that marks his whole writing on the theme of inter-religious dialogue at the level of prayer and medita-tion. The rationalist can no longer pray, only rationalise, and in the end only criticise. But he who can no longer pray is incapable of even beginning a dialogue with one of the world's religions, let alone of showing in this discussion that more truth, because more absolute love, is present in the Christian religion.

Today the Christian people (or what is left of it) is searching with a lamp for persons who radiate something of the light, something of the nearness of the source. It has long since had enough of the modernities, lacking all religious instinct, which trumpet at it from the press, the radio and often enough from the pulpit. It is sad because untended, and an all too justified fear torments it that the 'one thing necessary' could be totally blocked off and made inaccessible by the 'experts', or the many dilettantes and apostates who pose as such. Often these are poor wretches, who must shout so loud in order to justify to themselves their inner predicament of no longer being able to pray. And the people has a sharp ear for spiritual sour notes.[22]

Surely Balthasar is one of those persons in the church today who radiate something of the light, something of the nearness of the source and who should be given a greater hearing in circles where there is such a profound need for more solid grounds for hope and Christian renewal.

[22] Balthasar, *Convergences*, Ignatius Press 1983, pp. 14–15.

11

THE SYMPHONIC UNITY OF HIS
THEOLOGY: AN OVERVIEW

Thomas Norris

The various contributions in this volume underline the sheer vastness of the Balthasar bibliography and the enormous range of the subjects addressed therein. As if self-conscious of this vast output, he added an epilogue in 1987, the year before his death, to the fifteen volumes of his trilogy. The purpose of the epilogue was to provide a 'peep through' the trilogy, as it were, and, in particular, 'a justification for the presentation of the traditional theological tracts on the basis of the transcendental colours of being, a presentation which results in an easy transition from a true (and therefore religious) philosophy to the biblical theology of revelation'.[1] Such a 'peep through', however, is no digest. He suggests the unity of thinking, but does not attempt a summary. Accordingly, one is well advised to aim at describing the unity of his thought and not to try to provide a resumé.

This unity, however, is not easily grasped, 'so varied is his work, so complex'.[2] As well as this difficulty there is also the danger of betraying his underlying intentions, central insights, and overall viewpoint which aspires to be dynamic rather than static, encompassing rather than partial, dialogical rather than monological, and practical as well as theoretical. There is, however, an all-pervasive and unifying concern in his work: 'everything is squandered so that the personal meeting with God may be arrived at without delay'.[3]

---

[1] *Epilog*, 7.
[2] Henri de Lubac, 'A Witness of Christ in the Church', *Communio* 3 (1975), p. 230.
[3] Ibid., p. 232.

In the title of one of his well-known little volumes he employs an adjective which is most helpful in the search for the elusive unity of his thinking. The adjective is 'symphonic'. A symphony tells a story in the medium of music. As that telling proceeds, a range of themes and melodies are both singly played out and collectively interwoven to produce the unity of the symphony. The analogy of symphony provides the clue as to the kind of unity one might expect to find in the life and thinking of Fr Balthasar. In this chapter, then, I shall attempt to detect key movements in that symphony, their interrelationship and their dynamic unfolding into the finished symphony of his work.

While attempting this brief sketch of the symphony, it is imperative to remember that 'von Balthasar's most important works, at least in his own eyes, are not his writings, but his foundations'. Behind the author there is the pastor, for he was 'a theologian only to be a pastor',[4] a pastor busy in the manifold apostolate of publication and the foundation of lay institutes whose purpose was to radiate to the maximum degree possible the reality of Christ by means of the closest possible following of Christ. As we will see, the unfolding symphony of his life and activity provides both the context and cadence of his staggering literary output. A recent reviewer gave much encouragement when he wrote, 'Balthasar's writings are founded upon intuitions about the Christian revelation which are as simple as they are primal, and, for all their diversity, they present a compelling unity. The "whole" is indeed visible in the "part" ... it seems that at any point on the surface we quickly discover that we are falling into spiritual and intellectual recesses of infinite depth'.[5] The following are the movements of the symphony which I will highlight:

1. The Discovery of divine Aesthetics: Only Love is Credible.

2. From Aesthetics through Dramatics to Logics.

3. The Unity of Philosophy and Theology.

4. The Whole is in each Part: The Form and Radiance of the Catholic.

5. The Catholic Fullness of Faith in the Marian Church.

---

[4]   Peter Henrici, *Communio* 3 (1989), p. 306.
[5]   O. Davies, *The Tablet* 23 February 1991, p. 244.

6. The Face of Christ for Today: Theology in Dialogue with Culture.

7. In Conclusion.

I. THE DISCOVERY OF DIVINE AESTHETICS: ONLY LOVE IS CREDIBLE

The young Balthasar studied literature and music. For his doctorate he investigated the eschatological issue in German literature. This massive work of almost 1,700 pages is an odyssey through the whole of German literature. What fascinated him was the phenomenon of the *capolavoro,* whether in literature, art or music. 'The question that claimed my thoughts most was this: there are many good works of literature, music and art, and of other spiritual or human activities. How can we recognise a masterwork that, though belonging to a particular category, transcends it and becomes unique?'[6] To mention a few examples, what makes the *Magic Flute* of Mozart so superior to all other Viennese musicals? What makes Goethe's poem about night so unique and incomparable among the thousands composed on the theme? And what makes Plato still stand so high in spite of the two and a half millennia that have passed since his time? In a word, what is the key to the masterpiece? Those trained in the appreciation of music or art gradually develop a sensorium, a certain ability to discern the incomparable. Of course the lay person can enjoy that piece of Mozart, that poem, or that sculpture of Michelangelo. However, he does not have the unerring ability to detect the objective excellence that makes a particular work unique.

During that time Balthasar 'found the keynote that later became central in his theology as *Gestalt,* an expression hard to translate: form, figure, shape'. There is something very like *Gestalt* in Hopkins' notion of 'inscape' by which 'the mind sees an organised whole, with all the articulation of detail necessary for the comprehension of the basic idea manifest in its fullness'. And he noticed the same in the case of human relations of authentic love, as portrayed in Rudolph Allers and, later on, in Karl Jaspers and Martin Buber. True love always presupposes and lives from the irreducible unique-

---

[6]   Balthasar, 'Theology and the Aesthetic', *Communio* 1 (1981), 62; see 'Why I am still a Christian', passim.

ness of the other. 'True love can recognise and hold fast the beloved's uniqueness within the species.'[7] In particular, the I does not master the Thou, who always remains Other. 'No I has the possibility or the right to master intellectually the Thou who encounters him in his own freedom.'[8]

Here Balthasar saw an opening for an original presentation of Christianity. That presentation involved a transition from the humanities to theology. If the created person is irreducible to any formula whatsoever, a fortiori is Christ: he is utterly unique, not explainable by any calculus.

'The fascination is with Jesus Christ – if one sees Christ as he presents himself – with his uniqueness that cannot be compared to anything else in world history'.[9] Christ is the *Gestalt* of Christianity: in his face the glory of God shines and from there radiates into the heart of Christians (2 *Corinthians* 4: 6). In Balthasar's own words, 'he is the one and only exposition of God (*John* 1: 18), infinitely rich and of a paradoxical simplicity that integrates all the elements. He is absolute sovereignty and absolute humility; he is infinitely approachable who can be reached by everyone and infinitely inaccessible, ever beyond reach'.[10]

Interestingly, Balthasar notes that this fascination does not derive from the religious sense which exists in every person, however latent or overlain. All people have this *naturale videndi Deum desiderium*. Rather it begins from the concrete phenomenon of Jesus Christ, from the *Gestalt* which he is and which 'the eyes of the heart' (*Ephesians* 1: 18) perceive as absolutely special, indeed a divine-human masterpiece, without parallel or rival in the whole of world history. The task of theology is 'to read the Figure of Christ'.[11] This means that 'theology can only perform its task by circular repetitions of that which is ever greater. Parcelling it out in isolated individual tracts is a certain death'.[12] The truth is that Christ is the *persona qua major cogitari nequit* (St Anselm).

---

[7]   Ibid., pp. 63–4; see *The Glory of the Lord*, I, p. 550.
[8]   *Love Alone: The Way of Revelation*, p. 44.
[9]   'Theology and the Aesthetic', p. 64; *The Glory of the Lord*, I, pp. 463–525.
[10]   'Theology and the Aesthetic', pp. 64–65; see 'God is his own Exegete', *Communio* 4 (1986), pp. 280–86.
[11]   *The Glory of the Lord*, I, Section III: pp. 429–684.
[12]   John Saward, *The Mysteries of March*, London 1990, p.xvii.

He is 'the perfect whole', and without him theology loses its necessary unity. He is the cornerstone of the whole theological edifice, being 'the holistic norm for theology'. He is this to a degree we are not perhaps prepared to notice or admit. Thus Balthasar loves to show that Christ is both the form and norm of the person, society and history, society being the person written large, and history being society written long, and all this not only on an ethical level but also and more importantly on an ontological level. From the *Gestalt* of Christ we arrive at Balthasar's fundamental intuition, namely, 'to render the Christian message in its unsurpassable greatness ... because it is God's human word for the world, God's most humble service eminently fulfilling every striving. God's deepest love in the splendour of his dying so that all might live beyond themselves for him'.[13] From here one gains access to the unifying core of his thought, to what Henri de Lubac sees as the very secret of Balthasar – 'a loving search for an objective grasp of the Mystery'.[14]

II. FROM AESTHETICS THROUGH DRAMATICS TO LOGICS

Balthasar contends that 'Christianity is destroyed if it lets itself be reduced to transcendental presuppositions of man's self understanding, whether in thought or in life'.[15] The trinitarian God manifested and 'exegeted' in Christ (*John* 1: 18) is not only the answer to the cosmological search for completion and the anthropological quest for answers. The truth is that he is the answer that questions all answers, since 'in his body lives the fullness of divinity' (*Colossians* 2: 9).[15] Revelation shows that 'Christian love is God's final word about himself and about the world ... The world wants to live and rise again without dying; but Christ's love wishes to die,

---

[13] Rechenschaft (1965): English translation in J. Riches (ed.), *The Analogy of Beauty*, Edinburgh, 1986, pp. 195–96; henceforth *Analogy*.

[14] Henri de Lubac, 'Hans Urs von Balthasar: A Witness to Christ in the Church', *Communio* 3 (1975), p. 243.

[15] *Love Alone*, p. 43; see 'Current Trends in Catholic Theology', *Communio* 1 (1978), p. 80.

in order that through death, it may rise again beyond death in God's form'.[16]

Called glory in both the Old and New Testaments, his love is at the heart of theology. That is why Balthasar uses as an epigram Pascal's adage, 'Tout ce qui ne va point à la charité est figure. L'unique objet de l'écriture est la charité'.[17] This divine charity engages human freedom which is humankind's greatest gift. 'God's covenant is the struggle of his love *with* sinful man' for 'it can only be God's action, continuing the drama between God and man begun in the old covenant.'[18] In the volumes on the aesthetics he has already broached the phenomenon of drama. This God of the Evermore[19] 'comes towards us, drawing nearer and nearer, ever more giving and demanding'.[20] His self-communication in Christ is no mere object to be looked at and observed. Rather, it is His action, His activity in the world and on the world which can be understood and expressed only if the world acts in response. Balthasar states succinctly the progression from the aesthetics to the dramatics and the logics

Theophany	–	Aesthetics
Theopraxis	–	Dramatics
Theology	–	Logics

Of course these elements do not admit of separation: 'the *Aesthetics* has taken up so much space' because 'it always had to show the encountered reality *at work* – as theo-praxy.' At the same time, the two volumes which deal with the Old and New Testament 'largely anticipated the development of the drama of revelation and naturally enough employed concepts and words – theo-logy.'[21] The truth is that the unfolding of revelation under the guiding cipher of glory (*kabhod* in the Old Testament and *doxa* in the New) was already a

---

[16] *Love Alone*, p. 112; see K. Hemmerle, *Thesen zu einer trinitarischen Ontologie*, Einsiedeln 1976, pp. 7–8.

[17] For *Love Alone*, see treatment of Pascal in *The Glory of the Lord*, III, pp. 172–238.

[18] *Love Alone*, p. 58.

[19] See H. Heinz, *Der Gott des Je-Mehr*, Frankfurt, 1975.

[20] 'Theology and the Aesthetic', *Communio* 1 (1981), p. 67.

[21] *Theo-drama*, I, pp. 15–16.

light which one could not pass by, an attraction both irresistible and fascinating, which drew one powerfully towards itself. In this way the aesthetic is dynamic. It dramatically engages our freedom and flows naturally into the realm of the dramatic where the God of the covenant encounters and draws humanity into communion with himself.

The God of revelation dramatically pours forth his goodness. 'This goodness is the content of theo-drama. God's action is salvation fulfilled, the reconciliation of the world with himself in Christ (2 *Corinthians* 5: 19), and this out of an initiative that is pure self-giving'.[22] Such a *bonum* consists neither in looking nor in speaking, for the looking can be beautiful and the speaking true but the good simply requires the action the giver on the receiver. Revelation confirms this since it consists in a continuum of events and words which set up a history of God with humankind and in humankind. As this history develops God joins its march, locates himself in the geography of the world until, finally, he becomes flesh in order to lead all flesh into the life of the divine Trinity. 'The proof that you are sons in that God has sent the Spirit of his Son into our hearts: the Spirit that cries, "Abba, Father"' (*Galatians* 4: 6).

Already in the Old Covenant the revelation of God's glory to Israel occurs in a highly dramatic context (*Exodus* 3; 33–34; *Isaiah* 6). The God of the Ever-more meets an increasing resistance from the side of Israel. This is the dramatic context for understanding the fact of the prophets in Israel as, under the influence of the Holy Spirit, they speak against the infidelity of Israel. Thus the whole of Hosea employs the metaphor of adultery in order to underscore the apostasy of Israel. 'God roars from Jerusalem and speaks against the whole family he brought out of the land of Egypt', is the message of Amos (1: 2; 3: 1). Isaiah for his part engages heaven and earth as jurors while he accuses Israel of being dumber than the ox and donkey (1: 3–6). The prophets carry the dynamic word of the faithful, but scorned, God of the covenant. This involves them in a crossfire between God and Israel. The symbolisation of this crossfire in terms of the obedient Suffering Servant in Second Isaiah drama-tises the battle-struggle between the incoming God of the covenant and the resisting, rejecting chosen people. Here 'the two paths cross:

<hr>

22   *Theo-drama*, I, p. 18.

the path of God to the sinful human being and the path of the sinful human being to God. These crossing paths are hostile to each other unto death; but that they should even meet requires a wholly real "battlefield" where the conflict can be decided. For as real as the institution of the covenant of God and his offer of salvation to men and women are, just as real is their refusal to dwell in this sphere of grace'.[23] The situation of the Servant is in prophecy the situation which will eventually be occupied by the beloved Son. It is a situation of doubly borne wrath – that of solidarity with the rebel sinful people for whom He substitutes himself, and that of the earlier more primary solidarity with the spurned and rejected God of the covenant whose passions are transferred to Him: anger, love, concern, disgust and even perplexity.[24] Balthasar quotes the telling words of Nicholas of Cusa: 'After this mighty voice had grown continually louder through centuries up to John, the voice of one crying in the wilderness, it finally assumed human form and after a long succession of modulations of teachings and miracles which were to show us that of all frightful things that most frightful had to be chosen by love, namely death, it gave out a great cry and died'.[25]

Already in the *Aesthetics* Balthasar brilliantly portrayed the dramatic quality of Christ's existence 'which, in the unity of claim, cross and resurrection, remains an unsplittable atom'.[26] In the volumes of the *Theo-drama* he formally expounds 'the dramatic character of existence in the light of biblical revelation'. It is the dramatic action of the 'dramatis personae' which discloses the real character of each actor in the theandric theatre that is Christianity. Here Balthasar seems to re-echo Cardinal Newman who wrote, 'Christianity is a history supernatural and almost scenic: it tells us what its Author is by telling us what he has done'.[27] The various acts in the drama of the Old Covenant, culminating in the incarnation, death and glorification of Christ, all of which constitute but one revealing Word, are like so many scenes of a drama which must be followed

[23] *Spiritus Creator*, p. 55.

[24] See ibid.; see *Epilog*, pp. 28–32.

[25] *Excitationes* 1, 3; quoted in *Man in History*, p. 282.

[26] *Theo-drama*, II, pp. 9–10.

[27] John Henry Newman, *Discussions and Arguments*, London 1872, p. 296; see *Theo-drama*, II, p. 11.

and taken in before one knows the plot, appreciates the conspiracy and perceives the characters in their true colours.

What is most striking about this theandric drama, however, is that the spectators become protagonists. Or are invited to do so. They are not to look on idly. The divine action draws them from the floor of the theatre on to the stage for the action. 'In the perception there lies the enrapturing.' Balthasar rules out any suggestion of a philosophical emanation and return of the world to God, such as one finds in Plotinus or Hegel. The truth is that 'there is a titanic opposition, which will be strongly emphasised, on the part of humankind against its involvement in the mystery of the cross. Since the very time of Christ the anti-Christian attitude exists, 'If I had not come and spoken to you, you would be without sin'.[28]

Having investigated the history of drama and literature Balthasar presses his newfound categories into the theological service of revelation. As with the cipher of glory which he first reads in the revelation and only then connects with the philosophical category of beauty, so too in the realm of drama: the data of the New Testament already show the precedence of the Son's mission to, and self-substitution for, sinners over their philosophical and literary counterparts. Jesus Christ presents himself as a man who lives and dies in order to fulfil the mission received from the Father in the Holy Spirit. This mission of the Son is identical with his hypostasis, the incarnation being the extension into time and space of his procession before all time from the Father.[29] As the protagonist of the drama in which the Father is the author and the Holy Spirit the director, Christ lives by and from his mission from the Father. 'My food is to do the will of him who sent me and to accomplish his work' (*John* 4: 34).

Christ's ministry runs in the direction of the greatest possible solidarity with human beings. The Synoptics, St Paul and St John all concur in this, each one bringing out particular dimensions of this solidarity. In Jesus the eternal Son takes on our human nature, and our human condition, as St Leo the Great loves to say. In the ultimate analysis such solidarity becomes a *Schicksalgemeinschaft*

---

[28] *Theo-drama*, III, II; see *Epilog* pp. 24–32.
[29] See E. Babini, 'Jesus Christ, Form and Norm of Man', *Communio* 3 (1988), p. 447; John O'Donnell, 'The Form of his Theology', ibid., pp. 458–74.

(solidarity in destiny) as well as a *Stellvertretung* (substitution).[30] Balthasar does not accept a soteriology which is 'content with the bland image of a God "already always" reconciled with man'.[31] His soteriology 'takes with the utmost seriousness the whole human drama in its radical need for salvation'. The self-substitution by the eternal Son is grounded in 'the eternal attitude of devotion and self-offering (*Selbsthingabe*) of one divine Person to another'.[32] It is precisely here that Balthasar locates the sense of the pre-Pauline and Nicene *pro nobis* (for us).

As the drama unfolds through the mission of the Son and his solidarity with the human condition to the point of self-substitution for each and every human being, the utter uniqueness and singularity of the Christ figure begins to stand out in relief. 'The Fathers', he insisted, 'worked on this golden background. They had the feeling for the dialectic of that which is always greater'.[33] Of course the reconciliation offered to humankind and actually wrought in humankind in virtue of the Christ event meets the human search for freedom and forgiveness 'from below'. It is another thing, however, to suggest that this search could reach its goal of itself and by itself. Neither can it be the measure of what is offered. 'The universality of the redemption derives from its singular position.'[34] It is the *concretum universale personale*.

The drama of redemption does not impair human freedom, which is actually highlighted. Balthasar loves to contrast the approaches of Origen and Augustine to this question. The former emphasised the impact of the redeemer's self-substituting love to the point where the freedom of the individual is overwhelmed by the sheer might of the Saviour's loving, while Augustine underlined the interactions of divine and human freedom to the point where human freedom could frustrate the very love that took its place in order to pay for the sinful abuse of freedom. Balthasar steers a middle course between these two positions and stresses Christ's 'solidarity from within with those who reject all solidarity'.

---

[30]   See *Theo-drama*, IV, Foreword.
[31]   E. Babini, ibid., p. 452; *Epilog* '... das Mysterium des Kreuzes ... wunderbarer Platztausch', p. 94.
[32]   *Pneuma und Institution*, p. 401.
[33]   See 'God is his own Exegete', *Communio* 1 (1986), pp. 280–86; *Science, Religion and Christianity*, p. 99.
[34]   E. Babini, ibid., p. 455; see *Epilog* pp. 95–98.

In a striking section in the first volume of the *Theo-drama*, Balthasar shows how his idea of theological dramatics is capable of unifying many contemporary tendencies in theology. He lists no less than nine: theologies of event, history, orthopraxis, dialogue, politics, future, the functional, role, and of freedom and evil. *Theo-drama* has the capacity to incorporate all of them in a higher integration.[35]

From aesthetics through dramatics to logics. The theological logics considers 'the possibility of expressing the mysterium in humanly understandable and responsible language'.[36] Just as the Apostles saw first, then followed Christ and finally spoke about what they had seen with their own eyes and watched and touched with their hands (1 *John* 1: 1), so too Balthasar completes and crowns his trilogy with the Theologics.

THE UNITY OF THESE CATEGORIES: SURPRISING IMPLICATIONS

Balthasar has developed new categories. He has also developed a new synthesis and unity between them in such a way that the aesthetic, the dramatic and the logic are capable of incorporating more traditional categories. The advantages and benefits of this unity are as surprising as they are undoubtedly fruitful.

First, the unity of the aesthetic and the dramatic has the happy consequence of uniting prayer and action, contemplation and living. In the aesthetics Balthasar shows that the first task of theology is to perceive what is revealed (*Ephesians* 1: 17) in the theandric *Gestalt* of Christ and the glory of God shining from his face (2 *Corinthians* 4: 6). The light emanating from this figure is the source both of prayer and of the enrapturing that leads to discipleship and action. The glorification of crucified and trinitarian love inspires us all to live for one another (*John* 13: 34–5; 15: 12; 1 *John* 4: 19). A new ethic, a new moral theology comes into view[37] as the Christian becomes a fellow-actor with Christ who 'let his glory be seen and his disciples believed in him' (*John* 2: 12).

---

[35] *Theo-drama*, I, pp. 23–46.
[36] E. Hill, 'Theology as Drama', *Doctrine and Life*, 1990, p. 243.
[37] *Love Alone*, p. 49.

Next, Balthasar overcomes the tragic dichotomy of theology and life, and reconnects theology and the fundamental call to holiness. The parting of the ways between theologian and saint since about the fourteenth century he deplores.[38] This separation has brought about a mutual impoverishment, the net result of which is that when he writes the third volume of *The Glory of the Lord* covering the whole period since the great scholastics and which is significantly subtitled 'Lay Styles', he has to pick theologians who are not professionally such at all. Thus Dante, Pascal, Hamann, Péguy, Hopkins, St John of the Cross and Soloviev correspond since the age of High Scholasticism with Irenaeus, Augustine, Dionysius, Anselm and Bonaventure of the previous millennium. This explains why in an activist like Madeleine Delbrêl, in contemplatives like Charles de Foucauld and Thérèse of Lisieux, Balthasar underlines the lived unity of faith-vision (theology) and discipleship (spirituality and action).[39]

In the third place, the sequence Aesthetics-Dramatics-Logics shows that theology as the adequate speaking about God is difficult, even dangerous. It is so easy to distort by exaggeration and to falsify by reduction. Theologians must be converted and live as disciples of Christ, like all sincere Christians, if they are to unpack the riches of Christ for the Church. Here Balthasar's thinking makes common cause with that of Bernard Lonergan whose monumental *Method in Theology* lays the foundations of the whole theological enterprise in the threefold of intellectual, moral and religious conversions. In investigating revelation and in mediating its riches to ever-changing cultural settings, the theologian cannot leave out of his work his own lifestyle.[40]

Fourth, Balthasar's method unites the various disciplines that compose the general area of theological study. Such a unification is most timely and welcome. It is timely since we live in an age of increasing specialisation and consequent fragmentation within the world of theology, and welcome in that many students of theology today complain that they cannot see the links between the many

---

[38] 'Theology and Holiness', in *Verbum Caro*, II, pp. 49–86.
[39] See *Analogy*, p. 205f.
[40] Bernard J. F. Lonergan, *Method in Theology*, London 1971, pp. 130–31, 144, 168, 365.

subjects they study in theology courses.[41] An English theologian writes well of this achievement of Balthasar, 'This dramatic concept ... embraces everything that, in St Thomas' expression, "belongs to the Christian religion". The celebration of the Liturgy has obvious affinities with drama ... The living of the Christian life, by individual believers and by Christian communities, is our playing our parts in the whole tremendous drama ... Church history and Patristic studies clearly fit easily into this dramatic structure ... What dogmatic theology engages in is the appreciation and proper understanding of the major themes of the drama and its chief characters: God, Jesus Christ, the Church, creation, redemption, grace, eschatology, humanity'.[42] Balthasar's method provides a theologically sophisticated and a dramatically comprehensive vision of Christian faith, life and celebration. It would enable us to achieve the ideal proposed in the Council, namely, a living grasp of the total mystery of Christ which is articulated in Scripture, lies at the heart of the Church and is principally exercised in the apostolic ministry of bishop and priest.[43]

Finally, the Balthasarian principle that theological aesthetics sublimates the philosophical transcendental of beauty and initiates the whole of the faith-elaboration called theology, has a valuable significance. The loss of the dimension of beauty,[44] theological and philosophical, in both Catholic and Protestant theology, 'resulted in the dessication of theology. What theology needs is to be steeped anew in the very heart of the love mystery of Scripture, and to be remoulded by the force it exerts'.[45] St Augustine highlighted this steeping, as also did Newman.[46] Balthasar borrowed St Thomas' analysis of beauty and its components of *integritas, proportio* and *claritas* in order to highlight the unity-fullness of each area of faith.[47]

---

[41] Komonchak, Collins, Lane (eds.), *The New Dictionary of Theology*, Dublin 1987, pp. 1011–27.

[42] E. Hill, 'Theology as Drama', *Doctrine and Life*, 1990, p. 243.

[43] Vatican II, *Optatam Totius*, p. 14.

[44] *The Glory of the Lord*, I, p. 9, '... how impoverished Christian thinking has been by the growing loss of this perspective which once so strongly informed theology'.

[45] *Word and Revelation*, I, p. 162.

[46] St Augustine, *In Joannem 26: 4–6*; John Henry Newman, *Discourses to Mixed Congregations*, London 1921, pp. 67–72.

[47] St Thomas, *Summa* I, Q. 39, A. 8.

Thus, for example, a treatise on the Eucharist would have to be bathed in this beauty-glory, with particular attention being paid to the three components of beauty.[48] Only in this way could one have a theology formed 'out of the originality of love, which God Himself is'.[49]

III. THE UNITY OF PHILOSOPHY AND THEOLOGY

In the *Epilog* which he appended to his trilogy in 1988 shortly before he died Balthasar wrote, 'Our trilogy of aesthetics, dramatics and logics is built upon the mutual enlightenment existing between the theological categories and the philosophical transcendentals. What one identifies as the qualities of Being encompassing each and every existent (the transcendentals), seem to open up the most appropriate access to the mysteries of Christian theology'.[50] With Walter Kasper he struggles for a 'truly theological theology',[51] in other words, a theology written out of the absolute originality of the crucified-trinitarian love revealed in the event of Christ. Klaus Hemmerle can say of his opus, 'I found in his work an alternative to a merely anthropological presentation of theology'.[52] This explains the fact that Balthasar works out a solidly biblical theology of revelation. He notices that God in revealing himself showed forth his glory, dramatically poured forth his goodness, and uttered the ultimate truths about himself, humankind and the history of humankind in the world. 'Christianity is at once ... adoration of God's beauty, conflict in blood, truth embodied'.[53] Balthasar does not begin, then, with a philosophy of beauty, of drama and of truth in order to apply the resulting categories to the data of revelation. His method pre-empts any suggestion that he is interested in producing an aesthetic theology or a dramatic theology. Such theologies would have to fit into, and so be measured by, philosophical categories!

---

[48] See A. Nichols, *The Holy Eucharist*, Dublin 1991, pp. 120–24.
[49] K. Hemmerle, *Thesen*, p. 6.
[50] *Epilog*, 37; see TL, I, pp. vii–xxi.
[51] W. Kasper, *Irish Theological Quarterly* 2 (1989), pp. 85–98.
[52] K. Hemmerle, *Thesen, p.* 7.
[53] John Saward, *The Mysteries of March,* London 1990, pp. 20–21; see *Theodrama* II/1, p. 31.

He is quite fascinated, however, by the correspondence of the biblically revealed categories with the transcendentals of Being. Devoting two out of the seven volumes of *The Glory of the Lord* to metaphysics, he traces 'the veins and sinews of Being' with the conviction that someone who has become blind to Being cannot be other than blind to God. With the development of science, on the one hand, and the disappearance of the sense of the metaphysical on the other, 'only the Christian vision of love can enable us to recover a sense of the beauty and the wonder of the world'.[54] Balthasar investigates the loss of this sense of Being and then proceeds to expound the whole metaphysical tradition of the West from Thales to Heidegger, ending with his own succinct (for him!) metaphysical statement.[55]

The unavoidable metaphysical question is, why is there something and not simply nothing? First formulated by Leibnitz, then given fresh and influential currency by Heidegger, it highlights the fact *that* things are. It emphasises the priority of this fact over *what* things are and *how* they are which is the concern of science. The great pioneers of science have seen this distinction[56] but the practitioners sometimes have not. Science takes its objects for granted, the metaphysician is struck by the fact that they exist in the first place, and this engenders a spirit of wonder which, as Plato and Aristotle saw, is the beginning of all knowledge. Existence or Being thus precedes essence or whatness and is distinct from it. '*Esse est aliquid simplex et completum sed non subsistens*: Being is something simple and complete but not subsisting'.[57]

From here Balthasar can outline his understanding of the analogy of Being. 'The doctrine of the analogy of beings thinks of the relationship between God, man and the world in such a way that these three poles neither glide into one another (as in pantheism) nor stand over against one another as pure polarities of contradiction (as in dialectics).'[58] Within this horizon one notices both the unity and diversity of Being: while there is an analogy between God and

[54] John Riches, 'Review of *The Glory of the Lord,* V, VI & VII', *The Tablet* 28 September 1991, pp. 1179.
[55] *The Glory of the Lord,* V, end.
[56] See S. L. Jaki, *The Savior of Science,* Washington DC 1988.
[57] St Thomas, *De Potentia,* 1, 1.
[58] W. Löser, 'Being interpreted as Love', *Communio* 3 (1989), p. 482.

creatures (for both are), there is an even greater difference within this very similarity.

In order to lead us towards the meaning of Being and existence Balthasar invites us to reflect on the key experience of childhood. 'For Balthasar the primordial human experience is that of the Thou, the moment where the child for the first time becomes aware of the smile of its mother and so becomes a *Geist*. In that moment the child becomes an I.'[59] This experience 'awakens in the child not only the consciousness of its worth (*dignitas individui*) but also precisely that of its own uniqueness'.[60] And with this uniqueness there is also given the experience of the Thou, of existence and of the world. 'The horizon of infinite Being opens itself up for him revealing four things to him: that he is at once in the love of his mother at the same time as this love is not his mother; that this love is good and therefore all Being is good; that this love is true and consequently Being is true; and that this love provokes joy and happiness and therefore all Being is beautiful.'[61] These experiences of the One, the Good, the True and the Beautiful, which are preconceptually perceived by the child in the primordial mother-child bond, are in fact the very colours of Being and are designated as the transcendentals, for they go beyond all the limits of essences and are co-extensive with Being.[62]

Everything that is, then, is one, true, good and beautiful. In God these attributes will be infinite, while in all creatures they can only be participatory. In God there will be the fullness of the One, the True, the Good and the Beautiful, while the limited creature will only share in a fragmentary way in the transcendentals.

Balthasar stresses the interlocking of the transcendentals. They imply each other and complete each other. The True needs the splendour of the Beautiful, and the Good needs the *voluptas* (attraction) of the Beautiful. The Beautiful is pleasing because it is rooted in the Good and the True.[63] Beauty has a certain primacy, since it is the radiance of Being and 'a manifestation of the real'. If

---

[59] *Love Alone*, passim.

[60] John O'Donnell,'Hans Urs von Balthasar: The Form of his Theology', *Communio* 3 (1989), p. 458.

[61] Address, Madrid 1986, in *Communio*, Italian edition, I (1989), p. 41.

[62] *Epilog*, 35–41; *The Glory of the Lord*, IV, p. 21.

[63] See St Thomas, 'Pulchra enim dicuntur quae visa placent', *Summa*, I, Q.5, A.4, ad 1.

beauty is neglected, truth loses its persuasiveness (*suasio*, Irenaeus), goodness its attraction (*voluptas trahens*),[64] and Being its very credibility. Beauty, then, is the integrating and unifying transcendental of Being, for it goes beyond the 'neutrality' of the True and the 'subjectivity' of the Good.

In the *Epilog* Balthasar writes pages fascinating for the manner in which they order and align the transcendentals. All worldly Being has an epiphanous character since its first action is to show itself. 'The life principle of a tree, invisible to itself, manifests itself in the form, growth and unfolding of the appearance of the tree.'[65] He quotes Claudel, 'the poet is able to say what everything wants to say' simply by being itself. Every visible reality has this epiphanous character, and this is its beauty. Beauty is thus the 'appearance', 'presentation' and 'self-manifestation' of the real. Since the transcendentals, which penetrate the whole of Being, imply each other, any manifestation or showing of the beauty of Being leads at once to the giving of Being. 'What shows itself (beauty), communicates itself and gives itself (goodness).' The goodness of Being is manifest in its gift-quality.[66]

Not only does Being show and give itself, it also articulates itself. In the human being endowed with self-consciousness, this speaking completes and perfects his self-manifestation and self-giving. Self-expression in human words is a final moment where the Truth articulates both the Beauty (of the self-manifestation) and the Goodness (of the self-giving).

THE CORRELATION OF THEOLOGICAL AESTHETICS, DRAMATICS AND LOGICS WITH THE BEAUTIFUL, THE GOOD AND THE TRUE

What impressed Balthasar was the striking correspondence of theological aesthetics with the transcendental of Beauty, of theological dramatics with the transcendental of Good, and of theological logics with the transcendental of Truth. Revelation witnesses to the truth of the Blessed Trinity's self-showing, self-giving and self-articulation, for in Christ, 'the Lord of glory' (1 *Corinthians* 2: 8),

---

[64] St Augustine, *In Joannem* 26:4–6.
[65] *Epilog*, p. 45.
[66] Ibid., pp. 52: 64f.

God sets forth his infinite beauty, goodness and truth. These correlations, then, are the precise form and content of the relationship of theology and philosophy. They also explain how the philosophical transcendentals do not measure or even provide the foundation for the revealed realities. In that way Balthasar avoids what one contemporary theologian diagnoses as 'the primary stumbling block in theology today, among both traditionalists and dissenters ... the fact that almost all of us treat the Catholic faith as something to be "added on" to some already-existing understanding of reality garnered from some source outside the revelation itself'. To attempt 'to trim the sails of Christ's revelation to someone else's mind' is to put cosmological and anthropological considerations in the way of letting God be God in the way God decides to be God![67] Balthasar studiously avoids such 'reductions' simply because Christ leads us to 'the knowledge of a love that is beyond all knowing' (*Ephesians* 3: 19), and he provides an answer to the search for beauty, goodness and truth that questions all other answers to this very search.[68] At the same time his theology remains truly dialogical: it not only takes culture and history seriously, it actually reads the anthology of culture in order to show, give and say more about the *mysterium fascinans, tremendens et adorabile.*[69]

Love and Being

The Christian faith confesses the monotheism of the Old Testament and in that way makes common cause with Judaism. However, their respective understandings of the Godhead differ radically. The God of Israel enters into the covenant with Israel motivated by his love (*hesed*) and faithfulness (*emeth*) (*Hosea* 2: 19; 22; *John* 1: 14), only to experience the treacherous ingratitude of his elected partner. The question insinuates itself at once, 'Is God dependent upon Israel, his creation, in order to love? If he is, is he then God? One recognises that one cannot philosophise about Yahweh without turning him into a serious problem. And this

---

[67] Joyce A. Little, in *Fellowship of Catholic Scholars Newsletter*, Vol. 15, No. 3, June 1992, p. 4.

[68] See *Love Alone*, chapters 1 and 2 on 'cosmological' and 'anthropological' reductions, respectively.

[69] See *The Glory of the Lord*, II, Epigram from Francis Thompson, p. 8.

explains the derailments of Jewish theology into unification mysticisms, theosophy and atheism'.[70]

With the revelation of the New Testament, however, space has to be made in this God of Abraham, Isaac and Jacob for a second who is this same God and for a third who is the very same God, and who are not mere manifestations or modalities of the one God. 'God does not exemplify loneliness but ecstasy, a complete going-out-from himself'.[71] This is the only condition of possibility for the apostolic conviction that 'God is Love' (1 *John* 4: 8f.). Since Christ reveals God as a Trinity of persons, a new and radical vision opens up for faith. 'The mystery of the Trinity has opened to us a totally new perspective: the ground of Being is Communio'.[72] With the revelation of Jesus – in the *Gestalt* of claim, cross and resurrection – the primitive pre-Pauline credo of the Church is in place, 'God is love'.

But what about created reality? What of non-divine Being? May we dare address all reality as love? To do so, it seems, would amount to provocation. To live is to suffer, is the basic experience of the vast majority, and even those who feel fortunate in their life circumstances realise full well that they are exceptions proving the rule. In the light of a world of famine-stricken multitudes, and of this difficult century of total war, concentration camps and Gulags, is it not outrageous to read and interpret the whole of reality as love? Much of contemporary philosophy reads reality in function of power, pleasure, knowledge, usefulness, or something else. From a phenomenological perspective, to address Being as love seems highly suspect.

To affirm that Being and Love are co-extensive would require, as a minimum, that the summit of Being should become so present and effective in the world that all finite reality would be bathed in its radiance. In particular, the painful scars of human existence – death, sin, guilt, abandonment, injustice – would have to be radically penetrated and enveloped by the presence of the trinitarian love so revealed.[73] 'The factual realisation of these conditions just specified

---

[70] *Epilog*, 31–2; 'Warum ich noch Christ bin', pp. 42–43.

[71] Joseph Ratzinger, *Principles of Catholic Theology*, San Francisco 1987, p. 22.

[72] Henry de Lubac, *La Foi Chretienne*, p. 14; see G. K. Chesterton, *The Everlasting Man*, II, C. iv.

[73] W. Löser, 'Being interpreted as Love', *Communio* 3 (1989), pp. 482–83.

cannot only be brought about by man, it cannot even be anticipated.' Is this great condition fulfilled which alone would permit the
identification of Being and Love?

The whole of Balthasar's theology is an affirmative answer to this
question. The *Gestalt* of Jesus – his mission, self-substitution for
sinners 'As it is written, the sins of others fell upon him', (*Romans*
15: 3), descent into hell and resurrection – sheds its clear light over
the whole of reality. God is now where the sinner and the atheist
thought he never could be. The eternal Son lowers himself, in the
double kenosis of incarnation and cross, so that 'death (as torment
and insult) is here the final appearance and meaning-laden, fruitful
act of love'.[74] God is not God through a triumphal display of his
power, but through a solidarity, a compassionate accompanying of
women and men, a journey God the Holy Trinity has entered upon
with absolute freedom (for God does not need his creation in order
to become God).[75] It is only this decision 'for us men and for our
salvation' as made by the Father, carried into effect 'to the end' (*John*
13: 1) by the enfleshed Son under the inspiration of the Holy Spirit,
and which reveals the glory of the descending and extending love of
God the Holy Trinity (*Philippians* 2: 6–11) that enables us to
address the whole of reality as love (*Romans* 8: 31–9).[76]

Towards a New Metaphysics

'The concretion of the Triune God' in the *Gestalt* of Christ, and the
concomitant elucidation of creation as caught up in the glory of
trinitarian love (*Romans* 8: 31–9), opens up what Balthasar calls 'the
positivity of the Other'. 'The ideal of a mere unity without the being
of the other, as the "hen" of Plotinus or the *monos theos* of the
Hebrews and of Islam, does not fit with the Christian statement,
God is Love; such a unity would keep to itself and would not be
communicable; every "being other" would represent only a falling

---

[74] *Epilog*, p. 29.
[75] W. Löser, ibid., p. 484.
[76] 'Der Zugang zur Wirklichkeit Gottes', in *Mysterium Salutis*, II, *Die
Heilsgeschichte vor Christus* (eds.), J. Feiner and M. Löhrer, Benziger, 1967, pp. 15–
43; see John O'Donnell, *Hans Urs von Balthasar*, London 1992, p. 9, 'I would argue
that the central insight of Balthasar's entire thought can be summed up in the
proposition that Being is love'.

away from it.'[77] God, in other words, can only be love if there is room in him for otherness, and this innergodly otherness justifies and grounds the positivity of the created 'Other'.

The ontology, however, that has been to the fore in Christian thought and culture is more appropriate to the Jewish, Muslim and Plotinian picture of God than it is to the revealed portrait. It is an ontology that has been monistic and individualistic. in spite of the fact that the very heart of reality is trinitarian communion, and humankind has been made, both individually and collectively, 'in the image and likeness' of this infinite archetype, our ontology owes far more to Greek philosophy than to Christian revelation. Quoting the German philosopher, Klaus Hemmerle, Balthasar shows that although traditional Christian metaphysics bears the imprint of Christian revelation, there has been 'an historical deficit of Christian ontology. The basic concern of classical metaphysics lay in the two questions, what remains? (substance in its subsisting identity), and, what changes? (the accidental and changeable). But the faith is grounded on the revealed axiom that love remains (1 *Corinthians* 13: 12; *Matthew* 25: 30). The specifically Christian, then, did not determine for once and for all the pre-understanding of Being'.[78] The crying need for today is to develop a metaphysics capable of including the other, and therefore embracing both love and communion. I am when I love, and I find my genuine self when I lose it in You and for You. Substance means transubstantiation, since I really exist only when I give myself to the other, to the You. Being, both absolute and created, is communion. With the exception of the occasional figure, such as St Bonaventure,[79] the light of the Trinity has not illuminated mainline Christian ontology. With Balthasar, though, this new ontology becomes both necessary and possible.

IV. THE WHOLE IS IN EACH PART: THE FORM AND RADIANCE OF THE CATHOLIC

In 1983 Balthasar declared that the aim of his theological labours was to portray 'the idea of the catholic'.

[77] *Epilog*, p. 29; see *Analogy*, p. 219, he learned from Rudolf Allers 'the feeling for interhuman love as the objective medium of human existence; it was in this turning from the "I" to the reality of a complete "Thou" that he found philosophical truth and his psychotherapeutic method'.

[78] *Theodramatik*, V, pp. 64–65.

[79] See *The Glory of the Lord*, II, Bonaventure, pp. 260–362; *Theodramatik*, V, p. 65.

The whole effort of his life focused on the idea of catholicity: the work of God becomes truly understandable only where all the elements of the organism are present and interact, such as the Trinity, a christology of incarnation, the cross, an ecclesiology in which the Immaculate One is the principle of internal unity, and the Petrine ministry principle of visible unity. Such fullness is open and welcomes with gratitude all fragments of truth in the world.[80]

Completeness is a notion that enters into the very idea of catholicity which in turn fits with the New Testament emphasis on fullness. Christ has the fullness of divinity (*Colossians* 2: 9) and the Church receives the fullness of Christ (*Ephesians* 1: 23), while the cosmos is caught up into Christ (*Colossians* 1: 17). The catholicity-fullness of Christ and his Church are manifest in this descending perspective.[81] However, they are also manifest in an ascending perspective, as a line from St Paul, which Balthasar loves to quote, admirably puts it, 'Paul, Apollos, Cephas, the world, life and death, the present and the future, are all your servants; but you belong to Christ and Christ belongs to God' (1 *Corinthians* 3: 22–3).

Catholicity is a quality. 'It means totality and universality, and the understanding of it presupposes a particular human attitude of mind and heart.'[82] What is most distinctive in Balthasar's understanding of the catholic is that the catholicity of the Church follows from the catholicity of the Holy Trinity as manifested and – more importantly – as communicated in the mystery of Christ. 'The unconditional, gracious, sacrificial love of Jesus Christ expresses not just the mystery of being – finite being – but the mystery of the *Source* of Being, the transcendent communion of love which we call the Trinity. Thus through the *Gestalt Christi*, the love which God *is* shines throughout the world. This is Balthasar's basic intuition.'[83] His idea of catholicity is therefore trinitarian and christological. The Church is catholic because Christ is catholic, and Christ is catholic

---

[80]   *La Realtà e la Gloria*, Milano 1988, pp. 49–50.
[81]   He writes with irony of the popular misconception of the Catholic in *In the Fullness of Faith*, p. 16.
[82]   *In the Fullness*, p. 163; see John Henry Newman, *Grammar of Assent*, Note II.
[83]   A. Nichols, *Mysterium Paschale*, Introduction, p. 5.

because it is in the mystery of the Holy Trinity that he locates the unending source of harmony between unity and plurality, exclusiveness and inclusiveness, difference and universality. Here, too, he finds the perfect antidote to two decisive and dominant polarisations of our times: the tendency towards a pluralism that ignores order, unity and harmony, on the one hand, and, on the other, the tendency to reduce everything to a fabulous fantastic original principle or dimension. The former ends in anarchy and confusion, the latter leads to ideology and totalitarianism, where the part stands for the totality. Jesus Christ is the absolutely unique and exclusive *Gestalt* who is for that very reason the all-encompassing. He is the concrete figure who is universal in significance.[84] 'Of all the names in the world given to men, this is the only one by which we can be saved' (Acts 4: 12).

UNDERSTANDING THE CATHOLIC

Balthasar explains the nature of the catholic in many places. Perhaps one of the best ways of penetrating to the core of his insight is to view it from the perspective of salvation history. In the drama of the Old Covenant the *dramatis personae* are God, man, Israel and the world. God is the creator of the heavens and the earth, and so of all things. Man, both male and female, is created in his image and likeness (*Genesis* 1: 1; 1: 27). Israel is God's beloved people (*Deuteronomy* 7: 7f.). The Scriptures of the Old Covenant articulate the resulting order of existence with increasing clarity, especially in the Prophets.

In the coming of the new and eternal covenant, these relationships are wonderfully transformed. First, the ontological abyss separating the Creator and the creature is crossed when the Word who is God and 'nearest to the Father's heart' (*John* 1: 18) becomes flesh and lets his glory as the only-begotten Son of the Father be perceived in the world (*John* 2: 11). In the evocative words of St Augustine, 'when something is said of the Lord Jesus Christ, particularly in prophecy, which would refer, as it were, to a certain lowliness unworthy of God, we must not hesitate to attribute it to

---

[84] See *Truth is Symphonic: In the Fullness of Faith*; 'Die Absolutheit des Christentums und die Katholizität der Kirche', in W. Kasper (ed.), *Absolutheit des Christentums* (= *Quaestio Disputata* 79, Freiburg 1977), pp. 131–56; *The Glory of the Lord*, I, p. 550.

him, since he did not hesitate to join himself to us'.[85] Next, the chosen people of Israel become the very Body of Christ (1 *Corinthians* 6; 12; *Colossians* 1: 23). Finally, creation itself is caught into the new creation (2 *Corinthians* 5: 17; *Galatians* 6: 15) brought about by the resurrection of Christ (*Romans* 8: 22–5).

All this happens in and through Christ who is the personal union of divinity and humanity, 'without confusion or separation'. He is the one who changes the Old Israel into the New Israel, indeed his very Body-Person. Quoting a favoured line from St Irenaeus, Balthasar affirms that 'Jesus' catholicity recapitulates the history of Adam's race.'[86] After all, did not Abraham rejoice to see Jesus' day? And did not Moses, the psalms and all the prophets concur in the principle that the Messiah would have to suffer in order to enter into his glory? (*John* 8: 28; *Luke* 24:13–35). This enables one to see the true sense of catholicity. Once God's consubstantial Son 'becomes' flesh, the whole world is involved, 'for man himself is the epitome and the recapitulation of the whole of creation'. The task of the Church catholic is to witness to and communicate these treasures which, as the Letter to the Ephesians stresses, are simply unfathomable. This catholicity 'is an inclusion: nature is included in grace, the sinner is included in forgiving love, and all plans and purposes are included in a supreme gratis – "for nothing"'.[87] As such it is more than a dialectic of reversed opposites, and it goes beyond a coincidence of opposites.

What Jesus unites and gathers (*John* 11: 51–2) in time is but the revelation of the fullness that exists beyond time. The catholicity of Jesus is not only horizontal, it is also vertical: Jesus comes not to show that the phalanx of titles forged in the Old Testament properly apply to him, but to fulfil the will of the Father.[88] This fulfilment involves 'a twofold movement: he steps forward (with divine authority) in order to make the Father visible, and simultaneously he steps back (as the Suffering Servant) in order to reveal the Father, not himself. We must not fail to discern his mode of stepping back, for he is the only way to the Father'.[89] In that way Jesus becomes the

---

[85] St Augustine, *Enarrationes in Psalm* 85:1.
[86] *In the Fullness*, p. 33.
[87] Ibid., p. 33.
[88] See *The Glory of the Lord*, VII, pp. 115–29.
[89] *In the Fullness*, p. 27.

visible self-exegesis of the Father (*John* 1: 18). The sending of the Holy Spirit is not a second exegesis, as it were, of the Father. Rather the Spirit takes what belongs to Jesus and gives it to others (*John* 16: 14–15). At the summit of the great discourse in the Fourth Gospel Jesus prays for the unity-involvement of all in the life he has brought: 'as you are in me and I am in you'. This 'as' (*kathos*) is one of the many that make the New Testament so remarkable.[90] Its import is that Jesus brings the life of the Blessed Trinity and prolongs and lodges this life of mutual love (*John* 13: 34–5; 15: 12) between the Father and the Son (1 *John* 1: 1–4) in the world and in history as the form of a new humanity. The Holy Spirit for his part has the task of drawing and coaxing humankind into this theadric communion. In that way he writes both the vertical and horizontal dimensions of catholicity. 'A Church can be catholic only because God is catholic first, and because, in Jesus Christ and ultimately in the Holy Spirit, this catholicity on God's part has opened itself to the world, simultaneously revealing and giving itself.'[91]

It may be interesting to compare Balthasar's notion of catholicity with that of John Henry Newman and Henri de Lubac. As for de Lubac, Balthasar read his *Catholicism* as his 'basic book' in theology and twice translated it into German. Balthasar admires Newman to the point where, in a key volume of *The Glory of the Lord*, he opts for the theological methodology forged by Newman: 'theological methodology ... can never be genuinely deductive (for otherwise it subjects the freedom of the form to the laws of human thought), but inductive, in the sense intended by Newman: it shows the 'convergence' of the lines and paths of discernment ... on the single focal point of surpassing brightness, where the glory flares out'.[92]

Writing to his ally of Oxford days,[93] E. B. Busey in connection with the recent definition of Mary's immaculate conception, Newman declared that the Fathers of the Church had made him a Catholic.[94] 'No Anglican had ever studied the Fathers with the intensity and passion of Newman.'[95] It was not only their writings

---

[90] See *John* 17: 22; 20: 21; 13: 34; 15: 12.
[91] *In the Fullness*, pp. 29–30.
[92] *The Glory of the Lord*, VI, p. 18.
[93] C. S. Dessain, *John Henry Newman*, London 1971, p. 134f.
[94] John Henry Newman, *Difficulties of Anglicans*, II, p. 24.
[95] S. Gilley, *Newman and his Age*, London 1990, p. 91.

but, even more significantly, their persons that influenced the leader of the Oxford Movement,[96] since 'it was in the Fathers, existing and acting coherently in history as catholic persons, that Newman felt the real force of catholic reality. They were involved with the life-giving power of God who in Christ has taken up human weakness, redeemed it and perfected it'.[97] It is legitimate to see in Newman's discovery of the Fathers his concomitant discovery of the components of catholicity. He learned that the Church of the Fathers had creeds and dogmas, anathematised heresy, celebrated sacraments, and was a visible body with a distinct structure claiming apostolic origin and authority. He also discovered a further remarkable phenomenon in the development of doctrine, and this phenomenon was in truth a 'principle' of Christianity and a characteristic of catholicity.[98] De Lubac saw in Newman a typical 'heir to the Fathers' way of thought'[99] and repeated that way of thought in the volume that enthralled the young Balthasar. There Balthasar saw how to be catholic, 'the only reality which, in order to be, does not find it necessary to be in opposition; thus anything but a closed society'.[100] The catholicity of Balthasar then, is the catholicity of the Fathers of the Church whose writings he studied so comprehensively for decades. It 'means the fundamental Christian attitude which, in complete openness, allows itself to receive from the fullness of the incarnate love of God and to be taken up by it'.[101] This catholicity is concentrated in the person of Jesus Christ, who as the concrete form of the universal fullness of the love of God the Holy Trinity 'chose incarnation and crucifixion as its means of remaining present in the world'. In this form of Christ, God's all-including love 'takes on the "special" form of the "poor (that is, all-receiving and all-dispending) love" of the incarnate and crucified One'. It is only in this *Gestalt* that this love becomes universally fruitful and therefore catholic, like the grain of wheat which drops into the soil and dies

---

[96] *Difficulties of Anglicans*, I, pp. 370–71.

[97] G. Dragas, 'John Henry Newman: a starting point for rediscovering the Catholicity of the Fathers today', *The Greek Theological Review* 3 (1980), p. 279.

[98] John Henry Newman, *Essay on the Development of Doctrine*, Second Edition, Chapter 7, 1: 4; *Apologia*, London 1910, p. 290.

[99] de Lubac, *Catholicism*, p. 150.

[100] M. Kehl and W. Löser, in *The von Balthasar Reader*, p. 7.

[101] Ibid., pp. 8, 9; see his *The Theology of Henri de Lubac*, San Francisco 1991.

only to multiply in many grains. The fruitfulness of this all-receiving and all-giving love of the 'catholic' Christ is to be seen in the Church that is catholic with the trinitarian catholicity of God and the kenotic glorious catholicity of Christ. The Church contains 'the fullness of him who fulfils all in all' (*Ephesians* 1: 23).

Such catholicity is the very antithesis of a syncretism which would gather elements from all the religions in order to make up an amicable 'world religion'. It is also the opposite of a theological liberalism which is indifferent to contradictory interpretations of the foundational revelation of the Blessed Trinity in the glory of the crucified Son, his divine forsakenness on the cross (*Mark* 15: 34; *Matthew* 27: 46) and descent into hell, and in resurrection, where non-word becomes the heart of the Word.[102] The catholic consists in the Christ who embraces the all. The Church catholic 'receives the Spirit of Christ and with it the character of the truly "catholic", that is, universal, integrating love'.[103]

SPELLING OUT CATHOLICITY

Balthasar writes with extra verve and fresh grace when he draws out the implications of catholicity. Some of those should now be considered.

First, 'the catholicity of the Catholic Church is primarily a revelation and a communication of the divine totality' and 'the acceptance of this revelation by man is primarily the work of grace'.[104] If follows that it is not discernible without faith and can be appreciated only by those who are 'changed and become like little children' (*Matthew* 18: 3). Just as the claims of Jesus to be the truth and the life (*John* 14: 6), and superior to Abraham and Moses (*John* 8: 57–9) exasperated his contemporaries, so too the claims of the Catholic Church exasperate the contemporary world. The basic scandal is, how can this man, Jesus of Nazareth, be the Alpha and the Omega? Here is the scandal at the heart of Catholicism. As for ecumenism, the issue of catholicity remains central, as it was central to both the Reformation and Counter-Reformation, and acts as an effective antidote to ecumenical counterfeit.

---

[102] See *The Glory of the Lord*, VII, pp. 77–89.
[103] *The von Balthasar Reader*, p. 9.
[104] *In the Fullness*, p. 13.

Next, there is the question of the one revelation and the many dogmas. In the one faith there is the Christ-effected *prior gift* of fullness which St Paul describes almost plerophorically in Ephesians 4: 4–6, 'One body and one Spirit, just as you were all called to the one hope that belongs to your call, *one* Lord, *one* faith, *one* baptism, *one* God and Father of us all, who is above all, and through all, and in all'. The central phenomenon of revelation is the Son interpreting the Father through the Holy Spirit as love. This revelation necessarily becomes the drama of the God of the covenant engaging human freedom in the struggle for the human heart. Here the very ground of Being smiles upon us in the face of Christ as a father or mother might smile on us.[105] Ultimately this is the only dogma that is credible, 'For he decided, together with the Father and the Holy Spirit, to show the world the glory of his omnipotence through his death and not otherwise'.[106] The fact is that 'in Christ forsaken on the cross we recognise what we have been saved from, the eternal loss of God, from which, but for the help of grace, no efforts of ours could have saved us'.[107] This one dogma, however, folds outwards (*ausfalten*) into the many dogmas, all of which must remain in closest connection with the burning source into which they infold (*einfalten*).

Each particular dogma is inhabited by the one archetypal dogma just described. It has to follow that each particular dogma participates in the maximality of God's love, trinitarian, christological and ecclesial. 'It is only in this context', claims Balthasar, 'that we can properly understand what "dogma" is, namely, a proposition that, whether it is positive (affirming things against rational negation) or negative (distinguishing itself from false positions) says that God's love extends to this maximum. Every dogma contains within itself the one, entire mystery'.[108] The whole is in each part! Here Balthasar's account of dogma resembles most closely that of Newman who writes that 'the Catholic dogmas are, after all, but symbols of a divine fact, which, far from being compassed by those very propo-

[105] See *Love Alone*, pp. 47, 58, 62.

[106] St Anselm, *Cur Deus Homo*, I, 9.

[107] *Love Alone*, p. 76; see 'Meeting God in Today's World', *Concilium* 6 (1965), pp. 14–23.

[108] *Truth is Symphonic*, pp. 67–68; see St Irenaeus, *Against the Heresies*, IV, 33, 8.

sitions, would not be exhausted, nor fathomed, by a thousand'.[109]

Balthasar gives an account of Christian origins which shows remarkable affinity to that pioneered by Newman who worked out a theology of doctrinal development that portrays the vitality of development as 'a remarkable philosophical phenomenon, giving a character to the whole course of Christian thought'.[110] Both men deal effectively with the presuppositions of an inordinate historical method which, instead of perceiving the catholic fullness-quality of the originating revelation that inevitably issues in the many dogmas, suspects creeds and dogmas, and tries to excavate down to a fabulously simple substratum of simple historical fac*. The result is a kind of theological archaeology.[111]

Thirdly, there is the question of eternity and time. Man is conscious of his temporality because he is aware at the same time of the eternal. His fragility becomes luminous in his ephemerality so that he not only asks questions but becomes a questioner under the impact of a perceived mortality. Balthasar outlines three sets of answers to this all-pervasive question. First, there is an Asiatic way out. Here the path followed issues in philosophy's perpendicular, vertical ascent. For Parmenides, Plato and Plotinus this was the only exit from the prison of the world's unreality. The Far East in her religions offers this same approach, appealing to a past and a lost origin. Second, there is the Old Testament and Jewish answer. It looks forward prophetically to a future that God will usher in, a messianic age. Marxism was basically a secularised distillation of this messianism where the eschaton is immanentised radically. Third, there is the irruption of the Blessed Trinity into time in Christ.[112] The result is that 'only Christianity has the power to affirm the present, because God has affirmed it. He became a man like ourselves. He lived in our alienation and died in our God-forsakenness. He imparted "the fullness of grace and truth"' (*John* 1: 17) to our here and now. He filled our present with His presence. But since the divine presence embraces all 'past' and all 'future' in itself, he has opened up to us all the dimensions of time.'[113] T. S. Eliot makes the

---

[109] Newman, *Oxford University Sermons*, London 1900, p. 332.

[110] Newman, *Apologia*, p. 290.

[111] See *The Office of Peter*, pp. 39–47.

[112] *Man in History*, passim.

[113] *Truth is Symphonic*, pp. 190–1.

point in an incomparable fashion:

> Men's curiosity searches past and future
> And clings to that dimension. But to apprehend
> The point of intersection of the timeless
> With time, is an occupation for the saint –
> No occupation either, but something given
> And taken, in a lifetime's death in love,
> Ardour and selflessness and self-surrender.[114]

With the gospel the seriousness of each present moment is high-lighted and its value for the kingdom of God guaranteed.

Fourthly, there is the mystery of the Church and its 'multi-layered' reality. Balthasar sees in the constellation of characters around Jesus the clues to the 'catholic density' of the Church. In correction of seriously imbalanced ecclesiologies which tended to be unconsciously reductionist, Balthasar insists that the Church is Petrine as founded in Peter and the Twelve, and Johannine as the true enfleshment in history of 'the eternal life which was with the Father' (1 *John* 1: 2), and Pauline as being the presence of the risen Lord's inexhaustible grace in conversions, charisms and missions, and Marian as having the Mary-like task of welcoming in faith and love the self-offering Christ (*Luke* 1: 26–38).[115] The conjunction 'and' is the litmus test as to whether 'catholic fullness' (Newman) is present and perceived, since the mystery of God's love poured out upon this world is fourfold.

V. THE CATHOLIC FULLNESS OF FAITH IN THE MARIAN CHURCH

Christianity is a religion of incarnation, for at its heart lies 'the wonder of the incarnation' which 'brings to the eyes of our minds a new and radiant vision of God's glory'.[116] Balthasar insists on this truth.[117] 'Something new and unheard of happens when the Word

---

[114] T. S. Elliot, *Dry Salvages*, V; see D. Schindler, 'Time in Eternity, Eternity in Time', *Communio* 1 (1991), pp. 53–68.

[115] *The Glory of the Lord*, I, pp. 351–65.

[116] *First Preface for Christmas*.

[117] *The Glory of the Lord*, I, p. 119f.

becomes flesh.' In a particular way, the incarnation highlights the assumption of humankind and so also of genealogy, history, sociology and the earth. 'Non salvatus nisi assumptus; caro cardo salutis', thundered St Jerome and Tertullian. Balthasar writes movingly of the 'axiom of St John that captures the essence of God's definitive revelation'.[118]

> Is not the synthesis of Christ as Alpha and Omega so unique that a participation in its catholicity is excluded from the outset? Yet what is Christ, what is the New Covenant? Verbum Caro! No more the old opposition, Omnis caro foenum ... Verbum autem Domini manet in aeternum (Isaiah 42: 6, 8), no more a word that only speaks at the human being, but Word and flesh. And therefore also faith-flesh. Flesh now has the Word. It is not the Spirit alone that makes that act of faith which puts God first and hopes in him, but the whole human being down to the foundations of its matter ... Whoever wishes to think about the incarnation of the Word of God must look carefully for the woman ... If the Word becomes flesh it must rise from the bottom-most foundation of life. And this bottom-most foundation must receive it not like an empty abyss, in pure passivity, but with active readiness.[119]

The enfleshing of the eternal Son presupposes the welcome, the unconditional but human welcome, of the woman. And the woman is Mary. Like the 'wild air, world-mothering air' she 'gave God's infinity dwindled to infancy welcome in womb and breast, birth, milk and all the rest'.[120] Balthasar locates the origin of the Church in Mary's open-eyed Yes to God's offer of his Son to her by the overshadowing of the Holy Spirit. 'In this foundational act in the room of Nazareth, in this alone the Church of Christ is founded as

---

[118] *The Office of Peter*, p. 10.
[119] *Das Katholische an der Kirche* (Kölner Beiträge 10; Cologne: Weinand 1972), pp. 10–11, translation in *Reader*, pp. 211–14; see Tatjana Goritschewa, 'La Madre di Dio e il Senso della Femminilità', in l'Altro Femminismo, Milano 1983; *Epilog* p. 77f.
[120] G. M. Hopkins, 'The Blessed Virgin Mary Compared to the Air We Breathe', *Poems and Prose*, London 1986, pp. 54–55; see *The Glory of the Lord*, III, pp. 353–99.

Catholic. Its catholicity is the unconditional character of the *Ecce ancilla* ('behold the handmaid') whose offer of infinite accommodation is the creaturely counterpart to the infinite self-bestowing love of God'.[121] Balthasar sees a basic error in any attempt to locate the foundation of the Church subsequently in, for example, the election of the Twelve or the bestowal of the keys on Peter (*Matthew* 16: 16–20). Mary's experience, as he stresses in the seminal first volume of the *Glory of the Lord*, 'existed prior to the apostolic experience, and it thus wholly conditions it, for Mary, as Mother of the Head, is also Mother of the Body'.[122] Balthasar stresses the Marian foundation of the Church. 'The Marian *fiat*, in its truly *unlimited* availability, is, by grace, the bridal womb, *matrix*, and *mater*, through which the Son of God becomes man, and thus it is by this *fiat* that he also forms the truly universal Church'.[123] By her cooperation Mary becomes the mould in which the Church is formed. The kenotic self-giving of the Blessed Trinity requires someone who will receive, for there can be no giving without a receiving. Mary's Yes is so perfect that it accommodates the unconditional thrust of the divine Word into human flesh and history in order to bring about the new creation (2 *Corinthians* 5: 17; *Galatians* 6: 15). Here in Mary's *fiat* the Church emerges at the very first moment of the New Covenant. Mary stands where all the lines of the Old Testament converge and pass over into the New Testament. In her the law becomes grace and truth, the synagogue becomes the Church, and 'the withered tree of history'[124] blooms again. No Mariology without Christology, and no Christology without trinitarian doctrine, this is the axiom of Balthasar. The 'Marian principle', as he frequently calls Mary's presence and action in the mystery of Christ and his Church, is simply indispensable to the proper understanding of revelation.[125]

'THE CHRISTOLOGICAL CONSTELLATION'

Balthasar develops his thinking on Christ, Mary and the Church in the light of what he imaginatively terms 'the christological constel-

---

[121] *Das Katholische an der Kirche*, pp. 10–11.
[122] *The Glory of the Lord*, I, p. 362.
[123] *The Office of Peter*, pp. 206–7.
[124] See Joseph Ratzinger, *Daughter Zion*, San Francisco 1983.
[125] 'The Marian Principle', *Elucidations*, London 1975, pp. 64–72.

lation'. Since no man is an island but stands immediately in a defining set of relationships (parents, siblings, peers, teachers, colleagues, neighbours, etc.), so the Word on becoming flesh enters into a constellation of communications with others. 'If one attempts to detach Jesus and the doctrine about him (Christology) from this constitutive group, his figure (*Gestalt*) – even when kept in a trinitarian context – becomes hopelessly abstract.'[126]

Who are the key figures in this christological constellation? Who are the stars catching and reflecting the glory he lets be seen (*John* 2: 12)? They are first and foremost his blessed Mother (*Luke* 1: 26–38) and his Apostles, pre-eminently Peter, the beloved disciple John who is 'his most profound expositor' and the virgin companion of his virgin mother. Finally, there is the one 'born out of time' (1 *Corinthians* 15: 8), Paul. Balthasar argues for their inclusion in Christology. They are also essential to ecclesiology. 'For the Lord has made them "types", "real symbols" of his Church, "mediatory figures" by which "the form of Christ" (*Galatians* 4: 19) is imprinted upon the whole People of God.'[127] He thinks out his theology of the Church in the light of each 'star' in the constellation. The result is a multi-coloured set of layers. These layers engender a totality which carries Christ through the ages.

VI. THE FACE OF CHRIST FOR TODAY: THEOLOGY IN DIALOGUE WITH CULTURE

In his early doctoral research on the problem of the end of time in German literature Balthasar effectively appropriated the rich legacy of that culture, and subsequently of the whole of European culture, Christian and pagan, ancient and modern. Like the young Augustine revelling in the text of a Cicero, or like a Jerome mastering the literary skills of the Greek and Latin masters of antiquity, he conducted an incomparable odyssey through the European anthology. 'Rarely have such intelligent and intrinsically Christian eyes scrutinised European letters, leading to an unsuspected depth of harmony between the secular and religious order.'[128] This literary

---

[126] *The Office of Peter*, p. 136.
[127] John Saward, *The Mysteries of March*, p. 77.
[128] Oliver Davies, *The Tablet* 23 February 1991, p. 244.

and philosophical attainment equipped him for an in-depth dialogue between faith and culture, between the once-for-all revelation of God's glory in the *Gestalt* of Christ on the one hand, and, on the other, the actual culture of the West. It is no surprise, then, that his theology shows on every page this dialogical character. His goal is to mediate to our times the theandric encounter of God and Man in the Lord who reveals the splendour-glory of the Trinity because Christ wants 'to be nothing but the self-revelation of the love of the Father',[129] the 'glorious reality that was beyond surmise and graciously offers itself for our participation'.[130]

His early work is a reconnaissance of the western philosophical and cultural ideal. How does he see this ideal? 'Modern thought stands under the sign of three mythological figures: that is Prometheus (at the time of German Idealism), of Ahasver (in the middle of the nineteenth century), and of Dionysius (from Nietzsche on, until well into the twentieth century)'.[131] The underlying characteristic is anthropocentrism, the commitment to the standpoint that the correct interpretative principle for the whole of reality is the subjectivity of the person. 'Being is to be perceived', seems to have achieved a curious metamorphosis. This standpoint slides easily into pantheism where 'man creates the eternal and yet is the most ephemeral', as Feuerback and Marx contended. To use the language of Eric Voegelin, the transtemporal goal of Union through the crucified-risen Christ with the invisible Father is commuted to a this-worldly goal as the supreme fulfilment of existence. The eschaton has been immanentised utterly.[132]

For the great Swiss the alternatives were clear: either the God of Jesus Christ in perfect discipleship or his substitution and elimination by man-made secondary realities. Like the Newman of the *Apologia* putting the view that 'there was no medium, in true philosophy, between atheism and catholicity, and that a perfectly consistent mind, under the circumstances in which it finds itself here below, must embrace either the one or the

---

[129] M. Kehl & W. Löser, *The von Barthasar Reader,* p. 47.

[130] *Warum ich noch ein Christ bin,* p. 30.

[131] W. Löser, 'Being interpreted as Love', *Communio* 3 (1989), p. 478.

[132] E. Voegelin, *The New Science of Politics,*Chicago 1952, passim.

other',[133] Balthasar saw the same alternatives personified in Nietzsche and Kierkegaard, respectively. He writes with poignant power, 'God is dead, I have killed him, sacrificed him: that is Nietzsche's conclusion. God is dead, he has sacrificed himself, but he has never ceased to live: that is Kierkegaard's paradox'.[134] Henri de Lubac sees here the core of Balthasar: if Hegel's synthesis consists in the gnosis of a speculative Good Friday, Balthasar's work is a contemplative Holy Saturday: 'There was a day when Nietzsche was right: God was dead, the Word was not heard in the world.'[135] The infinite consubstantial Word who is silenced by suffering and sin on the cross, and cries out in God-forsakenness, is the God for modern man and woman. 'This God is (with Hegel) identity of identity (God is all; God is eternal life) and of non-identity (God is dead) insofar as he has identified himself with godlessness. He is so full of life (so very much love) that he can afford to be dead'.[136]

Almost like the Origen in second and third century Alexandria rejoicing over the objections and difficulties posed by the pagan philosophers of the day against the Christian mysteries because these very difficulties would enable him to draw out fresh insights from the unfathomable riches of Christ, so too Balthasar: he dialogues with the difficulties and seeming cul-de-sacs of contemporary culture in such a way as to draw out something further from the mystery of faith. It is in this context that one ought to understand his theology of Holy Saturday, the event which prolongs the Saviour's cry from the cross, 'My God, my God, why have you forsaken me?' (*Mark* 15: 34; *Matthew* 27: 46). Christ thus stands forth as good news for modern humankind, post-Auschwitz humankind, post-modernist humankind. In fact, Balthasar contends that these resistances to God may be measures devised by providence to lead Christians towards a higher conception of God.[137]

[133] J. H. Newman, *Apologia Pro Vita Sua*, p. 198; see *Grammar of Assent*, Note II, appended in 1880; see my *The Theological Method of John Henry Newman*, Leiden 1977, p. 106f.

[134] *Geschichte des exchatologischen Problems*, p. 31.

[135] Henri de Lubac, 'A Witness to Christ in the Church', *Communio* 3 (1975), p. 245.

[136] 'Wer ist Jesus von Nazareth – für mich?' in H. Spaemann (ed.), *Wer ist Jesus von Nazareth – für mich?* 100 zeitgenossische Zeugnisse, Munich 1973, p. 17.

[137] *The God Question and Modern Man*, passim.

VII. IN CONCLUSION

The purpose of this chapter was to suggest the unity of Balthasar's thinking, the symphony gathering into harmony the plurality of his themes.

> In his revelation, God performs a symphony, and it is impossible to say which is richer: the seamless genius of his composition or the polyphonous orchestra of creation that he has prepared to play it. Before the Word of God became man, the world orchestra was 'fiddling' about without any plan: world views, religions, different concepts of the state, each one playing to itself. Somehow there is a feeling that this cacophonous jumble is only a 'tuning' up: the *A* can be heard through everything, like a kind or promise. 'In many and various ways God spoke of old to our fathers by the prophets' (*Hebrews* 1: 1). Then came the Son, the 'heir of all things', for whose sake the whole orchestra had been put together. As it performs God's symphony under the Son's direction, the meaning of its variety becomes clear.[138]

In this overview I have looked at key movements in God's symphony. To conclude this chapter I should like to suggest the practical originality of these movements for the theological enterprise as we prepare to enter the third millennium.

First, there is the most basic intention of the Balthasar symphony, namely, 'to show the reality of Christ as something incomparably great, the *id quo nihil maius cogitari potest*'. This is the basic discovery of the young Balthasar, an insight into the figure of Christ as the one who opens out the heart of the Father to the world (*John* 1: 18), and opens for all of humankind the way back to the Father (*John* 14: 6). His early discovery of the Fathers confirmed him in this insight, for in them he saw 'a Christendom which still carried its thoughts into the limitless space of the nations and still trusted in the

---

[138] *Truth is Symphonic*, p. 8; see *The Glory of the Lord*, I, pp. 220f., 303, 'The world is the stage which has been set up for the encounter of the whole God with the whole man – "stage" not as an empty space, but as the sphere of the collaboration of the two-sided form which unites in the encounter'.

world's salvation'. The greatness – splendour of Christ consists in the fact that he is 'the human word of God for the world, he is the most humble service of God who fulfills beyond the wildest expectation all human longing, he is the extreme love of God in the glory of his dying so that all others might have life through him'.[139] His best known book, *Love Alone*,[140] sets forth his insight and is a kind of watershed in his development. God interprets himself on the stage of world history as absolute love, a love so great that none greater can be imagined. This means that God does not come primarily as a teacher for us (the True), nor as a "redeemer" with many purposes for us (the Good), but in order to show and radiate himself, in the glory of his eternal trinitarian love, and in that absence of interest which true Love shares with true Beauty. The splendour-sovereignty of this love originates in the communion of the Trinity but radiates itself in the kenosis of incarnation and cross, and in the descent into hell of Holy Saturday. This love therefore connects the revelation of God with the centre of our existence, our being-unto-death.[141] God names himself, but names himself with the utterly unexpected syllables of suffering. 'In the New Testament this sublime glory is seen in that love of God in Christ "to the end" that led to the night of death. A love so boundless (the true eschatology), undreamed of by man or the world, can only be perceived and received as the Wholly Other.'[142]

As a corollary of this first principle Balthasar insisted upon the need to articulate Christianity in a manner both appropriate to its divinely given *Gestalt* and comprehensible to the world of today. In that way he both anticipates the Council's programme for *aggiornamento* and contributes to the implementation of this programme. He states his view in these words, 'A reflection on the specifically Christian element itself, a purification, a deepening, a centring of its idea, (which) alone renders us capable of representing it, radiating it, believably in the word'.[143] His little book, *Razing the Bastions*, published in 1952, makes the point lucidly. It is in this

---

[139] *Analogy*, p. 195.
[140] Ibid., 'This last synthesis of many earlier efforts to express the meaning and form of theology', p. 202.
[141] Ibid., pp. 213–14.
[142] *Love Alone*, p. 8.
[143] *Analogy*, p. 196.

context that Balthasar makes common cause with Karl Rahner on the issue of a subtle reduction of the core mystery of Christianity, 'Christ in us, the hope of glory' (*Colossians* 1: 27), who reveals God as Trinity and therefore as absolute love. With Rahner he speaks of the threat of 'the Islamisation of Christianity', the theological and practical demise of the sense of God as a Trinity-Communion. In articulating the Christian faith he lets the light of the Trinity shine over and into each facet.[144] Here we see a central and lasting concern in all his work. 'With such a theology both philosophy and theology become new'.[145]

Second, Balthasar forges new and strikingly original categories for thought. Who could ever have thought of speaking of the God of Jesus Christ in terms of beauty? and drama? and theological logic? Who could ever have guessed that revelation could be described as divine-human aesthetics, and Christian living as divine-human drama? Yet this is what Balthasar does in his great theological trilogy, the cornerstone of his theological edifice. These new categories, moreover, are not imposed upon revelation, rather they flow from its very heart, as we saw. For God in revealing himself, shows forth his eternal beauty-glory in his Son, dramatically pours forth his goodness, 'the sinless one becoming sin so that in him we should become the goodness of God' (2 *Corinthians* 5: 21), and, thirdly, speaks himself to humankind in the strange logic-language of incarnation, cross, pain and freely borne guilt and sin. There is here, it seems, a freshness in approaching the mystery of God which should inspire new life in all the departments of theology and provide new insight well into the third millennium. The event of Christ, then, is a divine aesthetic, a divine drama and a divine logic. This opens up extraordinary vistas in speaking, living and communicating the gospel of God 'for the life of the world' (*John* 6: 51).

Third, Balthasar's approach opens new possibilities for understanding the relationship between philosophy and theology. He is fascinated by the correspondence between the revealed biblical categories, on the one hand, and the transcendental qualities of Being, on the other. In the *Epilog*, he writes of this correspondence as a mutual illumination. 'My trilogy of aesthetics, dramatics and

---

[144] *Credo*, passim.
[145] K. Hemmerle, *Thesen*, p. 8.

logics is built upon this mutual illumination. The qualities of Being which embrace all individual beings, "the transcendentals", appear to open the most appropriate access to the mysteries studied in Christian theology".[146] Two volumes of the seven comprising the *Aesthetics* are devoted to the history of metaphysics in the ancient and in the modern world. And there is more: the revelation that Being at its summit is trinitarian love means that at the very heart of reality there is communion, the ecstasy of the exit from self. This revelation simply demands a new understanding of Being, a fresh metaphysics trinitarian in character. Unfortunately, Christian metaphysics owes more to Greek categories than to Christian revelation. The light of the Trinity has not shone on our way of thinking about person, society and history. Balthasar suggests ways of remedying this defect and asks Christians to witness to the beauty of Being by living mutual love.

In the fourth place, there is Balthasar's understanding of catholicity. From his teacher, Henri de Lubac, he learned its nature. His conception of catholicity is eminently trinitarian, christological and ecclesiological. He loves to cite Paul's reminder that 'the fullness of divinity dwells in Christ bodily' (*Colossians* 2: 9). As such Christ is the absolutely unique and original who brings the fullness (*pleróma*) of the blessed Trinity into history, and draws all of time and history into that same fullness. This is the central meaning of the 'pro nobis' of the New Testament. He writes these striking lines, 'Jesus' catholicity is not only "vertical", as it were, doing God's will on earth as it is in heaven and revealing God in the world: it is also "horizontal", recapitulating the history of Adam's race (to use Irenaeus' magnificent phrase)'.[147] His catholicity is a catholicity of the Letter to the Ephesians, Jesus being the revelation of 'the hidden plan God so kindly made in Christ from the beginning ... to bring everything together under Christ, as head, everything in heaven and everything on earth' (1: 9–10). The absolutely unique One thus incorporates all reality, and extends through the Church his presence and power in the whole universe (*Colossians* 1: 16; *John* 1: 2–3, 10). The concrete fullness of God the Holy Trinity coming in Christ grounds the catholicity of the Church. Here the catholicity

---

[146] *Epilog*, p. 37.
[147] *In the Fullness*, p. 33.

of the Godhead clearly becomes the origin of the catholicity of the Church.[148] Of this reality the cross is the centre: the Christ crucified vertically and horizontally gathers all reality into a new communion.

A corollary of this catholicity or fullness is the notion of inclusion: 'Nature is included in grace, the sinner is included in forgiving love, and all plans as purposes are included in a supreme gratis – 'for nothing'.[149] The Church catholic reflects always this inclusion, this fullness. Balthasar underlines the Church's multi-layered constitution. He lists these layers as the Marian, and the Johannine, and the Pauline, and the Petrine. Whoever fails to perceive the completeness and proportion of these layers cannot understand the Church.

Finally, as the heir of the fathers of the Church and in particular of their theology of the Word, Balthasar carried on a dialogue between the inspired Word and the word of culture, literary and artistic, all his life. In the incarnation the Word took on flesh, and so a human face. The glory of God-Love radiated from that face all the dazzling weight, power and light, the *kabod*, the *doxa-gloria* of God revealing himself in Christ in death and resurrection. That face shines most in his crucifixion (*Isaiah* 53: 5) and descent into hell. 'The face in revelation is not the limit of an infinite without face; it manifests an infinitely determined face'.[150] There have been many faces of Christ over the ages according to the correlation appropriate to the age. Thus in the early centuries there was a Christus Pantocrator, the Christ in glory above all creation. In the centuries after St Francis, there was the face of the Christus Pauper, underlining the all-receiving and all-giving love of the Son of God. And for today? Balthasar would suggest the face of Jesus crucified and forsaken, since he radiates the most wonderful love of God to a humanity often God-forsaken through atheism, agnosticism and suffering. Here is the portrait that speaks best today, since it a portrait of One who accompanies human beings 'to the end', even to the terrible end they freely and responsibly bring upon themselves by choosing against God. It is this face of the God-Man, who is God-forsaken with those God-forsaken, which is the Face of God for today. Whoever understands, lives, and announces this truth in his or her daily living shows the true face of God and manifests to his brothers and sisters a living gospel for our times.

---

[148] Ibid., p. 42.
[149] Ibid., p. 33; see *Analogy*, p. 228f.
[150] *Paradox and Mystery*, p. 119.

APPENDIX

DO WE GET BEYOND PLATO?
A CRITICAL APPRECIATION OF THE
THEOLOGICAL AESTHETICS
Noel Dermot O'Donoghue

The Man and the Work

I come to speak about the 'theological aesthetics' of Hans Urs von Balthasar not as what might be called a Balthasar scholar or expert, who has read all that this man wrote in the original German and has, as it were, lived with him; nor do I come as a *follower* of Balthasar, as a man in whose wake I would be content to sail the seas of theology, its open seas and its various straits and headlands. I am not a scholar or expert in face of the laden shelves of books *by* the man and *about* him, nor yet a follower; but I find myself happily at home with the man's mind and spirit. I am neither a scholar nor a follower in the world of what may be called the Balthasar adventure, and I hope that those who belong to either category will be gracious in their listening and will accept the existence of a third category of relationship with an author of substance and power, the category of what may be called mind-friendship, a relationship at once heart-warming and inspirational. It is true that when I look at that well-chosen photograph which comes on the back flyleaf of all seven volumes of the English translation of *Herrlichkeit* – surely one of the great achievements in theological translation of our century – I am somewhat '*taken* aback' and chastened by that firm inquisitorial mouth. But, at least to my fancy, the eyes tell of immeasurably large horizons and pastures always new – also of a childlike quality of wonder and humility which alone makes mind-friendship akin to that soul-friendship that held together the men – and also near and with them the women – of Monasterboice, Iona and Sgeilig

Michael. I was not surprised to hear some time ago that a certain old English Carmelite nun, whom I know not, received from this indefatigable writer of what Thérèse of Lisieux called 'heavy tomes' regular personal letters, and that she loved him dearly and thought him a saint of God.

Moreover, there is one advantage which I have even over my friend John Riches and his constellation of translators *quorum memoria in benedictione est*, and it is this. I was born in 1920 and am old enough to have shared that training in what I take the liberty of calling the Great Tradition which has been for two thousand years (almost) the confluence of Hellenism and Christianity in the West: knowing Homer and Vergil as deeply as Isaiah and Paul, knowing Augustine and Thomas, knowing Plato and Aristotle in their ancient dress, knowing the great Plotinus, lover of beauty and glory; coming into the fields of theology not only with minds fortified by the *sic et non* of the *philosophia perennis*, as it was called, but with the voices and images of poets and masters of the written and spoken word still sounding in memory and assuring us that life was bigger than the theological manuals and that Horace was not doomed to his own *nox perpetua dormienda*. In other words, Balthasar the theologian received his basic theological training or mindset in terms of that Christian Humanism defended by Maritain and his contemporaries and which only becomes problematical with Karl Rahner in his later years, though he too shared this training and only thus could reach so brilliantly beyond it.

Now against the background of this early training, but greatly enriched by his encounters with Henri de Lubac and Karl Barth, we can see how Balthasar's mighty work – which, with Olympian humility, he calls a sketch – emerged both in its thematic and in its treatment. The theme comes directly and naturally from the deepening of his humanistic studies in various directions, classical and modern, against the background of the philosophical vision of the Great Tradition. As he looked at theology and its presentations he saw that it was centred on the *truth* about God and the *goodness* of God, that is to say under the light of two of the *transcendentalia*, or universal attributes of being, of traditional philosophy, to the complete exclusion of the third transcendental: beauty, which of course overlights the whole enterprise of Christian humanism. Why should it not overlight the whole enterprise of theology? And why should that enterprise not take into itself some of what has been nobly said by poets, ancient and modern, and by masters of the written word as well as theologians *de métier*. So we have not only these marvellous portraits of twelve 'clerical' and 'lay' 'theologies and world pictures of the highest rank', (II 13) ranging from Irenaeus and Augustine to Péguy and Hopkins, but also, in the fourth volume, that amazing tour de force in which not only the Greek philosophers are called in but also Homer and Vergil and the Greek tragedians – under that last heading one finds some of our author's most genial writing.

All this, as I have said, is based on the traditional philosophical thesis or *locus* of the *transcendentalia*, and this I want to go on to examine, coming to it mainly from the viewpoint of that training and mindset which I feel that I share with this mind-friend from the country of the high mountains and lofty ideas.

THE TRANSCENDENTALS

In the North Strand near the eastern end of the North Circular Road in Dublin there is a streetlamp at the top of which there is a kind of cluster of five separate lamps, which together give a strong illumination to the whole surround. There are five lamps which casts each its own light, yet these lights add up to a single source or centre of light as they support each other and permeate each other. This five-in-one and one-in-five may be taken as an image or similitude of the traditional scholastic doctrine of the transcendentals as it is foundationally present in Balthasar's *Herrlichkeit*. The transcendentals are a set of ideas that belong to all reality, transcending all differences of class and category, breaking through even the polarity of finite and infinite, temporal and eternal. As they appear in *Herrlichkeit* they are: being, unity, truth, goodness and beauty (*ens, unum, verum, bonum, pulchrum*). But let us listen to Balthasar himself as he speaks in that powerful 'Introduction' to Volume 4 of his great work:

> The 'transcendental' qualities of being are so called because each of them holds sway over the totality of being. They cannot, therefore, be marked off from one another but indwell each other and make their voices heard in each other. The man of Antiquity would never for a moment have thought

of marking a boundary between the transcendentally beautiful and the transcendentally true and good for between these there is a *circumincessio*, so that that which is beautiful and whole never lacks that which is morally sound or the radiance of truth in its work of reconciliation and healing by grace. It is true that there can be various stages of the integration of these qualities: the stage of integration which is found in the poets from Homer to the tragedians appeared to Plato to be imperfect, when compared to the integration at which he aimed, and so it is that the 'aesthetic' myth must give place to the more serious, more existential philosophy – for Socrates dies for the truth. For the old Plato the cosmos is *kalos* because the creator of the universe is *agathos*. In Vergil and Plotinus the mutual indwelling of the *transcendentalia* has become complete. The mediaeval period held fast in principle to this indwelling and was able to make it clear in a subtle metaphysics which simultaneously encompassed the indwelling of the beautiful in the good and in the true and its separateness from these two as something with its own sphere of interest. The Renaissance and the Baroque at their best live off the capital of this metaphysics of Antiquity and the Middle Ages and important aspects of it come to light once again in Heidegger (IV, 21).

Before going on to speak of the transcendentally beautiful which is the main concern of Balthasar's theological aesthetics I want to look more closely at the general presentation of the transcendentals in this passage, one of those rare passages in *Herrlichkeit* where the author stands still long enough to tell us what he is about.

The passage is not so much about the transcendentals, though it begins with a clear description or definition of them as each holding sway over the totality of being, as about the mutual indwelling or *circumincessio* of the transcendentals, especially of truth (*verum*), goodness (*bonum*) and beauty (*pulchrum*). Yet we are firmly assured that each of the transcendentals, including beauty, has its own sphere of interest. The philosopher of the old school, or whose training was in the old school of the now rejected scholastic manuals, is not at all surprised by this, nor by the statement that in Plotinus, Augustine's mentor, 'the mutual indwelling of the *transcendentalia* has become complete'. If he has gone beyond the manuals he will recall those passages in Book 7 of the *Confessions* where Augustine recounts his mind-blowing discovery of the transcendentals, in Plotinus, as the 'light above the mind', and how at last Augustine could see his way through the problem of evil left over from his time with the Manichees.

Our philosopher of the 'manuals' who has hopefully gone a bit beyond the manuals will be interested rather than disconcerted by the reference to Vergil, for he has long known that the presence of the transcendentals is one of the keys to Shakespeare for example and to the balance and universality of his greatness. But his eyes will begin to open wide as he reads on. For he knows that so far were the great medievals from a cosy unanimity on the topic of the transcendentals that there were deep differences even within the one 'school' or tradition as for instance between Albertus Magnus and his brightest pupil Thomas D'Aquino, and he knows, moreover, that there was no unanimity at all as to whether or not beauty had a real and equal place among the transcendentals.[1]

Balthasar is, of course, entitled to take his own line in his concept of the transcendentals and in his option for the inclusion of beauty

---

[1]See, for example, the article by J. B. Lotz on 'Transcendentals' in volume 6 of *Sacramentum Mundi* (London: Burns and Oates, 1970); De Raeymaeker, *The Philosophy of Being* (London: Herder 1954) Chapters 2 to 5; E. Coreth, *Metaphysics* (ed by Joseph Donceel: Herder and Herder, 1968) Chapter 5. According to the tradition of the *philosophia perennis* a certain formula can be applied to *unum, verum* and *bonum* as well as to *ens,* that is, *omne ens est* etc. But while we commonly and consistently find *omne ens est bonum* we meet a kind of hesitation as regards the use of the formula *omne ens est pulchrum,* as also in the use of the companion formula, *ens et pulchrum convertuntur.* 'Being and beauty are convertible terms' sounds daring and paradoxical.

This matter is important in the understanding of Balthasar. For as *The Glory of the Lord* proceeds we find the notion or 'note' of beauty giving place to glory, for 'the "glorious" corresponds on the theological plane to what the transcendental 'beautiful' is on the philosophical plane' (*Analogy of Beauty,* ed Riches p. 213). But 'glory' is not for Balthasar a transcendental but a divine attribute, which God does not share with his creatures. If the formula 'all being is beautiful' had been emphasised it would have been extremely difficult for Balthasar to claim any real correspondence between universal beauty and the kind of glory that is not shared by way of any kind of true analogy with the natural world (see, however IV pp. 1–14). It seems a pity that Balthasar did not take up more centrally the medieval concept of *subjective* glory (of which heaven and earth are 'full') as *clara cum laude notitia*: clear knowledge with praise. *Herrlichkeit* radiates and resonates with the glory of *God* but does not seem to realise at all that this glory is as much in the great chorus of poets, philosophers and theologians who reflect it as in that from which it issues forth. It is like the *eros* of man when it does not find its home in the heart of the feminine: static and unfruitful.

as one of these 'lamps of the mind'. What is somewhat distressing, however, is his cavalier and superficial attitude to what the traditional philosophy has to say of itself and for itself, and I tend to locate this attitude in what may be called 'the de Lubac revolution' of the fifties according to which the traditional distinction of levels between natural man and supernaturally graced man was broken down, so that theologians began to feel free to take heed of, use and develop the Great Tradition in their own way. Thus a new Catholic theological arrogance was ready and ripe to make common cause with the Protestant theological arrogance of Karl Barth. The drama that is played out in the background of *Herrlichkeit* is that of the rights of philosophical man over against the word from on high of theological-revelation man. Much could be said about this.[2] For now, however, it is necessary to see what Balthasar does with his concept of transcendental beauty which he has taken with such scant courtesy from philosophy.

TRANSCENDENTAL BEAUTY

What sharply distinguished Balthasar's theology of beauty from both the apologetical aesthetics of Chateaubriand and the genuinely

---

[2]What could be said especially is that Balthasar in the wake of his mentor, Henri de Lubac, rejects the traditional concept of 'pure nature' and therefore was left without any clear and confident concept of the *humanum*, of natural man and natural law. It seems at first sight reasonable that the Christian, for whom all men and women are called, in God's original design, to grace and glory, as their only and proper finality, should find the concept of 'pure nature' and that natural ethics which Aquinas inherited from Aristotle, a kind of irrelevance; yet this attitude has been disastrous. In the first place it made any real dialogue between the Christian and his millions of non-Christian fellows, men and women, impossible and, even more important, it blocked off man's relationship within himself between his natural self and his Christian self. Nobody has spoken more clearly on the need for (natural?) philosophy than Balthasar himself when he writes, towards the end of the second edition of his celebrated book of Karl Barth: 'If there is no philosophy, then the whole hierarchy of values and scholarly disciplines collapses. If there is no philosophy, then there are no absolute truths and values anymore' (*The Theology of Karl Barth*, Tr Drury, Holt, Rinehart and Winston: New York, 1971, p. 297). It cannot be said, however, that this clear statement could have been regarded by its author as a motto for his great work on *The Glory of the Lord*. There is a deep ambiguity here which is only tolerable because of the triumph of *Herrlichkeit* as a work of orchestral imagination.

theological aesthetics of Scheeben, both of whom are presented by our author with his usual expository brilliance in the introduction to the first volume of *Herrlichkeit*, is simply his grounding and rooting of the concept or idea of beauty firmly in the transcendentals. Beauty, *to kalon, pulchritudo* is not simply an optional adventitious, strictly accidental attribute of Being, natural or supernatural, finite or infinite. 'Psychologically, the effect of beautiful forms on the soul may be described in a great variety of ways. But a true grasp of this effect will not be attained unless one brings to bear logical and ethical concepts, concepts of truth and value: in a word concepts drawn from a comprehensive doctrine of Being. The form as it appears to us is beautiful only because the delight it arouses in us is founded upon the fact that in it the truth and goodness in the depths of reality itself are manifested and bestowed, and this manifestation and bestowal reveal themselves to us as being something infinitely and inexhaustibly valuable and fascinating. The appearance of the form, as revelation of the depths, is an indissoluble union of two things. It is a real presence of the depths, of the whole of reality, *and* it is a real pointing beyond itself to these depths' (I, 118).

'The appearance of the form as revelation of the depths': *Die Erscheinung als Offenbarung der Tiefe:* the core of Balthasar's aesthetics is here. Beauty is a revelation of the depths of Being and brings the depths along with it, as do truth and goodness. This connexion with the depths, that is to say, with Being as Being, is essential and unbreakable both ways. He is, if I understand him, saying that all beauty has its source in Being, in the depths, and that beauty is moreover a special revelation *of* the Source, *of* the depths of Being itself, and this in the same way that truth and goodness are each a revelation of Being itself, and in this sense a universal attribute of being: *omne ens est bonum, verum et pulchrum.*

Anybody even slightly versed in the *philosophia perennis* of the great Western tradition and realising that Balthasar was given his early training in this tradition expects the next step in this analysis of transcendental beauty to proceed by way of the division within Being between finite and infinite and the opening of finite being to the possibility and the *convenientia* or fittingness of revelation on the part of infinite Being as infinite goodness, infinite truth and infinite beauty. And the *vox Dei* might sound, as it did for Augustine and for Aquinas after him, by way of what Etienne Gilson named the 'metaphysics of Exodus' by way of the *I am who am* spoken to Moses and heard as *ego sum qui sum* by the Great Tradition. Here there opens up the exciting possibility of drawing on the Augustine of the *Confessions* and on his discovery by way of the *Platonici* of the *pulchritudo tam antiqua et tam nova*, the 'beauty ever ancient and ever new': the vision indeed of a theological aesthetics that has never yet been worked into a theological systematics and for which Balthasar was so well fitted by genius and erudition to undertake.

But Balthasar went another way, at least he went another way as he set up his great enterprise in the first volume of *Herrlichkeit*. He is convinced that 'we can never approach Christian *eros* and Christian beauty from a merely Platonic tradition and expect to interpret them adequately' (I, 123). It is only 'grace that allows us to see' (I, 126). It must be noted that Plato and the Platonic tradition stands here not simply for the particular philosophy of Plato and the tradition that passes through Plotinus and Augustine but for philosophy in general or the natural man in general. What the natural man is being told is not simply that when he enters the precincts of theology he must take off his sandals, as Moses was told to do, but must do something else which Moses was not asked to do: he must close his eyes in the hope that he will be issued with a pair of supernatural spectacles in which everything appears upside-down, as in Kierkegaard's Absolute Paradox, by which alone he can rid himself of Plato and Socrates. But the natural man (or woman) may well say, 'Please give me back my own eyes by which I saw Mary's Magnificat and the Crucifixion of her Son as indeed turning all worldly values and ideas upside-down, but also saw right side up the Transfiguration and Resurrection. With these faith-paradox spectacles I see *everything* upside-down which only means that *nothing* is upside-down, not even the event of Calvary. Do please give me back my natural eyes, for it is only by way of them that I can see the beauty and glory of the Christian revelation and what you call the supernatural.'

I have mentioned Kierkegaard and his famous Absolute Paradox according to which all philosophical light is negated – it is set forth in chapter 3 of *Philosophical Fragments*. Balthasar himself tells us that his encounter with Kierkegaard as a relatively young man was crucial. We find this stated as the end of a heavily ironic critique of Karl Rahner and the ecumenical-style theology and theologians of the post-Vatican II era. After an extended ironical passage worthy of Pascal's *Letters Provinciales* in which we are told how 'nice' it all was and is, so much so that anonymous Christianity could even renounce 'the troublesome formality of the name', Balthasar goes on: 'To my misfortune, however, I had read Kierkegaard in my youth (Guardini had expounded him to us in Berlin), and there I learned that the Apostle of Christ is one who lets himself be killed for Christ.'[3] At first reading this seems a strange discovery since it is one of the constants of Christian asceticism and is all over those *Spiritual Exercises* in which Balthasar had been formed. If one reads on, however, and notes the reference to Matthew 19.12, one begins to see that there is question of the death of all reasonableness and even of all reason, that kind of suicide of reason which the acceptance of Kierkegaard's Absolute Paradox involves. As it came about Balthasar did not have to sacrifice his mind but he had to sacrifice that part of it which he had in common with Karl Rahner.

In the meantime, or at the same time, Balthasar was reading Karl Barth and with it beginning to see that the world of theological exploration and elucidation can, as it were, be fired from above like the tramcars of his day and that one could go a long way in theology provided one stayed on the rails of revelation *as one understood it* and preached this message to others loud and clear and above all discussion.

What is, however, more important even than the intellectual influence of Barth is the fact that Balthasar the writer stayed all his life close to the part of himself that could be called imagination and kept closely in touch with the great masters of the imagination, ancient and modern. It was because of this particularly that his theological aesthetics is poised above history and the centuries like Hopkins' Windhover poised above the earth.

ABSENCES AND LIMITATIONS

'The revelation of the form as manifestation of the depths' – to repeat Balthasar's own formula occurs at two levels: 'Along with the seen surface of the manifestation there is perceived the non-manifested depths: and it is only this that lends to the phenomenon of the beautiful its enrapturing and overwhelming character, just

---

[3]John Riches, *The Analogy of Beauty*, 20.

as it is only this that ensures the truth and goodness of the existent' (I, 442). The non-manifested depths, *die nicht erscheinende Tiefe*, have become wonderfully, though never fully, manifested over the Christian centuries, and Balthasar has devoted directly and indirectly a large part, more than half indeed, of his theological aesthetics to these different ways of seeing. 'This display of this plenitude of perspectives will prepare us not to overlook anything essential in the dogmatics of glory and to formulate out of the wide-ranging induction of the Church's theological tradition the leading themes of this theological discipline which is today so neglected as scarcely to exist' (II, 14). And so he launches forth on his truly marvellous set of studies of what he calls 'theological styles', which includes not only a selection of well-known theologians such as Augustine and Anselm (not Aquinas, however) but, as well, poets and 'men of letters' such as Dante, Pascal, Hopkins and Péguy.

Nobody will grudge Balthasar his preference here, nor the use of his rich treasury of past scholarship, yet, allowing for this, there are, it seems to me, two things to be said by way of reservation about this 'wide-ranging induction of the Church's theological tradition'. In the first place since the central theme is that of the beauty of the divine humanity in Jesus Christ it seems incredible that Teresa of Avila should not have been included, and not simply as a token woman. In this respect Balthasar is a man of his time and in a special and deeply significant sense he is influenced by the theology of Adrienne von Speyr, so one could hardly expect him to consider Edith Stein or that lover of Christ and Plato who stood so brilliantly on the threshold of the Church, Simone Weil. It is true that Hildegard and Mechtild are included in a list of those who would have been 'worthy of presentation' (II, 20). But, all in all, Balthasar's heralds of divine beauty radiating through Jesus Christ do not include the seeing of the feminine eye, nor the seeing of the feminine heart as represented by Margaret Mary Alacoque and a whole marvellous constellation of women mystics up to our own day. It is especially through them that a *practical* theological aesthetic has leavened the Christian consciousness, evangelical and Catholic, and has given a vital glow to the thinking of a Teilhard or a Rahner, indeed to that of Balthasar himself. Of course, von Balthasar is immensely impressed by the theology of outstanding women over the centuries as is evident from his studies of Thérèse of Lisieux,

Elizabeth of Dijon, Madeleine Delbrêl and many others.

Let us look again at that list of 'examples' of those 'worthy of presentation' as expressing in an original and profound way 'the glory of divine revelation' (II, 14: already by Volume II Balthasar is beginning to switch from the natural and Platonic word 'beauty' to the more biblical and theological word 'glory'). It includes poets and mystics as well as theologians, but no more than the roster of the twelve thinkers actually treated, does it contain any philosopher. One does not expect to find Kant or Hegel, because the list in both cases is confined to Catholics but what of Descartes and Malebranche? What of Maritain? What of Mercier? The philosopher *as* philosopher has nothing original and profound to say even when he belongs to that 'third discipline' distinct from pure philosophy and from pure theology in which truths of reason are illumined by the light of revelation (I, 159 n. 9).

It is not simply that there are omissions in Balthasar's canon of writers on Christian and Catholic aesthetics, for within its own limits there is an unbelievable richness of exposition and erudition in the seven large volumes of *The Glory of the Lord.* It is rather that the omission of women, on the one hand, and philosophers, on the other, gives a certain slant or definition to the whole enterprise. What is missing is not styles of thinking or intellectual seeing but rather styles of imagining within a very great work of imagination, great both in what the author sees and says in his seven volumes, and great in those whom he had chosen as companions along the way. Yet our sense of what is missing must open up our own imagination to what is so triumphantly there.

ORCHESTRAL IMAGINATION

If Balthasar had set out to present an intellectual treatise on theological aesthetics understood as the analysis and synthesis of a theme or idea in the manner of Newman's presentation of the idea of a university or Bergson's presentation of the idea of creative evolution then one would expect the work to stay within the dimensions of a single volume. Why then does the work go on and on to the dimensions of seven large volumes – surely a question that the brave band of translators must have asked themselves now and then? After all we are not being given a *history* of theological aesthetics in whole or in part. I have puzzled about this and about the fact that the reading of the work as it came to me has been an exhilarating adventure once I took it at its own pace and rhythm, and I think I picked up a clue indirectly from a musical friend who asked me why Balthasar could include some of the poets without including even one of the great musicians, such as Palestrina or Mozart. I leave this question to my readers, but the clue that came with the question and the topic was this: that Balthasar is basically a conductor endowed to an almost unexampled degree with what may be called orchestral imagination, the kind of conductor who writes his own score and chooses his instruments and players under the heavenly guidance of his own genius. This I see as that highest kind of imagination in which the conductor identifies, in turn and together, with each of the players and binds them into one by graceful, sweeping gestures.[4]

[4]By way of intelligence there arises conceptual discovery and clarity, or at least the search for it. Intellectual knowledge, like sense knowledge, is bound by the object, whether that object be seen as within the mind, or outside it, or beyond it; in all cases the mind is bound and held by the object and is under the sign of the true, of that transcendental truth which is a universal attribute of Being as it connects with knowing and being known. This is pure thinking and there is much of this in *The Glory of the Lord*. But there is also thinking about thinking, not about one's own thinking (which is still a fixed object, in a sense) but about the thinking of others, and this involves a kind of detachment, a kind of distance between the thinking and the object, a kind of obliquity or slant which allows several approaches to the one subject, which is thus strangely provided with a most delicate and beautiful veil of mystery. For a writer thus to orchestrate the light of other writers, of 'the mighty minds of old', is not simply a work of sympathetic imagination, the kind of imagination allied to memory that is the servant of conceptualisation in the Aristotelian or Kantian sense but is rather the master of conceptualisation in its concrete colourful variety, and leads it beyond the realm of truth, and the light of truth, to the light of beauty and the realm of glory. Here is the Platonic link of memory-imagination and anamnesis as clarified by Plotinus and exploited by St Augustine in those chapters of Book 10 of the *Confessions* which lead up to the *Sero te Amavi* passage, Chapter 27 (38). Here, in Balthasar, as in Augustine before him, philosophy, theology and poetry meet in the service of eternal beauty and glory.

Of course what I have named the veil of mystery, may to a certain kind of mind seem rather a fog of confusion and the seven volumes of *The Glory of the Lord* a kind of 'much ado about nothing' or a confusion even more confounded. But this kind of reader has entirely missed that excitement and enthusiasm with which Balthasar's imagination invests his narrative as he orchestrates and conducts his mighty array of men of genius so variously achieving a great harmony *Ad majorem Dei gloriam* – to recall that Jesuit motto which Balthasar never relinquished.

Here is an example, taken more or less at random, of the power and sweep of our author's orchestral imagination, all the more powerful by the fact that a section of the great orchestra is being muted into silence. I quote:

But for the meanwhile there is something else to be done which is no less difficult. It has to be shown how the ancient theological aesthetic (with its mythical *a priori* regarding revelation) was transformed through the mediation of Christianity into the modern, supposedly 'purely philosophical' aesthetic. That all ancient theory and practice (of the art) of beauty ascribed itself to the revelation of the divine, so that all canonical Western art is of a theological lineage, can be seen to be the result of what has already been expounded. For the men of Antiquity all worldly beauty is the *epiphany* of divine glory. But while the Christian world prepared to give to this theological *a priori* its all-focusing centre and crown and for many centuries indeed gave itself out as the synthesis (not ever thoroughly thought out) of natural and biblical theology, it provoked counter claims from the history of human thought. The Renaissance and the Reformation destroyed this unreflected configuration from opposing directions: the former, with its enthusiasm for Antiquity, dissolved the Christian glory into an all-embracing cosmic revelation (which was then perfected in the Enlightenment), while the latter so stressed the distinctiveness of the biblical glory that by comparison all cosmic beauty faded and was submerged. All that resulted from this crisis – speculative aesthetics from Kant, through Schiller, Goethe and Hölderlin to Schelling, to Romanticism and to Hegel and the variety of post-Hegelian hangers-on – necessarily stands under a double judgment of the tradition: can such philosophical aesthetics be justified in the face of the theological *a priori* of Antiquity to which it still for the most part appeals (in part against Christianity)? Further: can this aesthetics recover the fundamental presupposition, common to Antiquity and Christianity, that reality as such, being itself, is *kalon*, radiant goodness, glory endlessly to be affirmed? And if it no longer has the power, what can such an aesthetics have to say? If the transcendental *kalon* is to be removed from being, why then is being any better than non-being? If we have come to a period which no longer has any answer to this question, then the beauty that we meet with within the world will sooner or later be stripped of its radiance and worth; and even where it is still perceived it will simply be classified pleasant, as a mere quality of nature, to which one has no sooner succumbed, than in that very moment one has seen through it. Aesthetics then becomes an epiphenomenon of psychology and relinquishes any claim to being a philosophical discipline (IV, 323–24).

It is clear that the metaphysics of the transcendentals holds this passage together with the dominant theme of the aesthetics as a whole, but it is clear also that a great symphony is being orchestrated by a conductor of enormous range and subtlety in whom the 'eternal verities' shine and shimmer with a kind of beauty that is itself a testament to that eternal beauty which is the imperial theme of the whole work. Perhaps I should not go any further lest my musical metaphors get out of hand: suffice it to say that here is a high work of imagination of a kind that can legitimately be termed orchestral imagination, a work therefore that cannot properly be judged either in terms of *thesis probatur* nor yet of historical completeness. The criticisms I have been making: the sustained opposition to Karl Rahner, or, more precisely, to his transcendental method, the marginalising of philosophy *as* philosophy, the perhaps inadequate attention to the aesthetic contribution of women to the great diapason of Christian consciousness, and finally (what has been scarcely mentioned) the increasing ecumenical deafness of our author – all this in the end adds up to no more than a fulfilment of the wisdom of the Gaelic proverb: *ní bhíonn saoi gan locht* – every wise man has a flaw. Flawed wisdom is the most we humans can expect from one another. The question is whether the light that shines through and beyond the flaws is good and true, and beautiful. I have no doubt whatever as to the answer to this question.

A BALTHASAR READING LIST

The following books by Hans Urs von Balthasar are currently available in English translation on both sides of the Atlantic. For a complete list of current titles, please apply to the publishers.

An exhaustive German bibliography under the title *Hans Urs von Balthasar: Bibliographie 1925–1990* is available from Johannes Verlag Einsiedeln (Lindernmattenstrasse 29, D–7800 Freiburg, Germany).

The Christian State of Life, San Francisco: Ignatius Press, 1983.

Convergences: To the Source of Christian Mystery, San Francisco: Ignatius Press, 1983.

Creator Spirit, Vol. III of 'Explorations in Theology', San Francisco: Ignatius Press, 1993.

Credo: Mediations on the Apostles' Creed, New York: Crossroad/Continuum, 1990 and Edinburgh: T&T Clark, 1990.

Dare We Hope 'That All Men Be Saved'? With a Short Discourse on Hell, San Francisco: Ignatius Press, 1988.

Does Jesus Know Us? Do We Know Him? San Francisco: Ignatius Press, 1983.

First Glance at Adrienne von Speyr, San Francisco: Ignatius Press, 1981.

The Glory of the Lord: A Theological Aesthetics, edited by Joseph Fessio S.J. and John Riches, Edinburgh: T&T Clark, and San Francisco: Ignatius Press.

I: *Seeing the Form* (1965).

II: *Studies in Theological Style: Clerical Styles* (1984).

III: *Studies in Theological Style: Lay Styles* (1986).

IV: *The Realm of Metaphysics in Antiquity* (1989).

V: *The Realm of Metaphysics in the Modern Age* (1991).

VI: *Theology: The Old Covenant* (1991).

VII: *Theology: The New Covenant* (1989).

Love Alone: The Way of Revelation, London: Sheed & Ward, 1968.

Mysterium Pasquale: The Mystery of Easter, Edinburgh: T&T Clark, 1990, 1994, Grand Rapids: William B. Eerdmans, 1994.

The Office of Peter and the Structure of the Church, San Francisco: Ignatius Press, 1989.

Prayer, San Francisco: Ignatius Press, 1986.

Razing the Bastions: On the Church in This Age, San Francisco: Ignatius Press, Communio Books, 1993.

Spouse of the Word, Vol. II of 'Explorations in Theology', San Francisco: Ignatius Press, 1991.

Theo-Drama: Theological Dramatic Theory, San Francisco: Ignatius Press.

I: *Prolegomena* (1988).

II: *Dramatis Personae: Man in God* (1990).

III: *Dramatis Personae: Persons in Christ* (1992).

IV: *The Action* (forthcoming).

V: *The Last Act* (forthcoming).

The Theology of Karl Barth: Exposition and Interpretation, San Francisco: Ignatius Press, Communio Books, 1992.

Truth is Symphonic: Aspects of Christian Pluralism, San Francisco: Ignatius Press, 1987.

The Word Made Flesh, Vol. I of 'Explorations in Theology', San Francisco: Ignatius Press, 1989.

Students of Hans Urs von Balthasar may also be interested in the following:

Hans Urs von Balthasar: His Life and Work, edited by David L. Schindler, San Francisco: Ignatius Press, Communio Books, 1991.

The Analogy of Beauty: The Theology of Hans Urs von Balthasar, edited by John Riches, Edinburgh: T&T Clark, 1986.

The von Balthasar Reader, edited by Medard Kehl S.J. and Werner Löser S.J., New York: Crossroad, 1982.

The Mysteries of March: Hans Urs von Balthasar on the Incarnation and Easter, by John Saward, London, Collins, 1990, and Washington DC: Catholic University of America Press, 1990.

Hans Urs von Balthasar, by John O'Donnell, 'Outstanding Christian Thinkers', London: Geoffrey Chapman, 1991.

Communio: International Catholic Review, published quarterly, available in the UK and Ireland from T&T Clark, Edinburgh, or in N. America from PO Box 4557, Washington DC, 20017.

INDEX OF PROPER NAMES

SUBJECT INDEX